FOUR
KITCHENS

FOUR KITCHENS

MY LIFE
BEHIND THE BURNER
IN NEW YORK, HANOI,
TEL AVIV, AND PARIS

A MEMOIR

LAUREN SHOCKEY

GRAND CENTRAL
PUBLISHING

NEW YORK   BOSTON

Grand Central Publishing
Hachette Book Group
237 Park Avenue
New York, NY 10017

www.HachetteBookGroup.com

Printed in the United States of America
First Edition: July 2011
10 9 8 7 6 5 4 3 2 1

Grand Central Publishing is a division of Hachette Book Group, Inc.
The Grand Central Publishing name and logo is a trademark of Hachette Book Group, Inc.

Library of Congress Cataloging-in-Publication Data

Shockey, Lauren.
    Four kitchens : my life behind the burner in New York, Hanoi, Tel Aviv, and Paris / by Lauren Shockey.—1st ed.
        p. cm.
    ISBN 978-0-446-55987-4
    1. Shockey, Lauren.   2. Cooks—United States—Biography.
3. Cooking.   4. Cookbooks.   I. Title.
    TX649.S284A3 2011
    641.5092—dc22
    [B]   2010041891

To Cathy and George

Acknowledgments

Writing a book of this scope was not a simple task and could not have been done without the help of many, many people.

Most important, to Wylie Dufresne and the staff of wd~50, Didier Corlou and the staff of La Verticale, Daniel Zach and the staff of Carmella Bistro, and Alain Senderens and Jérôme Banctel and the staff of Senderens—thank you all for the enormous privilege of working beside you in the kitchen and for teaching me how to cook. Because of all of you, I truly know what it means to be a chef, and I have the utmost respect for people who make their living behind the stove.

Emily Griffin, my wonderful editor at Grand Central Publishing, helped shape this book with her insightful comments and unwavering support.

I am deeply grateful to Jenni Ferrari-Adler who took a chance on me and on my idea. Thanks for being an outstanding editor who just happens to also be my outstanding agent.

I would like to thank everyone at Grand Central Publishing for helping to produce and champion this book, especially Jen Musico, Tareth Mitch, and Diane Luger. Thank you also to Sona Vogel for being an amazing copy editor and to Deborah Feingold for taking the cover photo.

My narrative became infinitely better thanks to Ellen Gordon

Reeves who read the entire manuscript despite barely knowing me. Krishnendu Ray also provided me with considerable academic assistance, editorial advice, and personal mentorship. And I'd like to thank the people who reviewed my book proposal long before there was ever a deal in sight—Irene Sax, Laura Shapiro, and especially Amanda Hesser, who graciously responded to my fan letter six years ago and has been a friend ever since. A big thumbs up also goes to Stephanie Bourgeois, who tested what seemed like all of the Vietnamese recipes in one sitting, and Alainna Lynch for taking my author photo.

Undertaking a project like this was not an inexpensive endeavor yet I was fortunate enough to receive grant money from New York University and from the Culinary Trust/the Julia Child Foundation to help fund my travel expenses.

I met so many amazing people outside of the professional kitchen during my travels, and I am lucky to now count the following among my friends: Sami El-Sawi and Beatrice Wandelmer, Rebecca Palkovics, Andrew Burman, Belinda O'Dea, Sally Gardner, Suchi Bansal, Hung Ba, Coreen Kopper, Kate Rosenshine, Asher Gelman, Mati Bar, Alex Fred, Sharon Labaton, Natan Gesher, Carole and Andrea Rogerson, Max Shrem, Tom Samiljan, Paule Caillat, Steve Zylbersztejn, John Gabriel, Joe Navin, and Nell McBride. Other people who were instrumental in the logistics and planning of this project include: Caitlin Aherne, Eric Murnighan, Marc Bauer, Rebecca Vitale, Daniel Vo, Hannah Janal, Rupa Bhattacharya, and Christine Muhlke.

And to Cathy and George Shockey: I couldn't have asked for—or found anywhere—more devoted line editors, recipe testers, personal assistants, cheerleaders, and, most important, loving parents. Thank you for giving me the opportunity to pursue my dreams and for believing in this book before I had written a single word on the page.

If you can't take the heat, get out of the kitchen.

—*Attributed to Harry S. Truman*

An qua nho ke trong cay.
(*When eating a fruit,
think of the person who planted the tree.*)

—*Vietnamese proverb*

מי שאוכל לבד מת לבד
(*He who eats alone dies alone.*)

—*Hebrew proverb*

Un bon repas doit commencer par la faim.
(*A good meal must begin with hunger.*)

—*French proverb*

Introduction

HERE'S A $40,000 SECRET. For all of its glamour and mystique, I learned only three things in culinary school: how to salt food properly, not to fear cooking over high heat, and to knock back beers like a pro. Nearly every chef who attended culinary school will tell you that your real education begins once you're working in a restaurant. And that it's a hell of a lot harder than any class.

Culinary school wasn't an obvious choice for me after I graduated from the University of Chicago in 2006. When I returned home to New York City, my parents expected me to pursue a "real" (read: office) job befitting my almost two decades of rigorous schooling, but I saw things differently.

"I want to cook," I announced to them one evening at the dinner table.

"You can cook any night you want. Think of it as earning your room and board here at home until you find a job," my mom joked.

"No," I said. "I want to really cook. In a restaurant."

"Lauren, don't be silly. Think about the money we've spent on your education. What was the point of all that hard work?"

"Maybe I shouldn't have gone to college," I said, pushing her buttons.

"Don't be ridiculous," she said.

"So if you become a cook, will the Bank of George Shockey be supplementing your nine-dollar-an-hour income?" said my father, finally mustering the energy to take part in our debate.

"Money doesn't always bring happiness, you know," I said.

"Maybe not, but it does pay the bills," said my father. Maybe he was right. There might be a reason that chef jobs weren't advertised on the University of Chicago's career counseling website.

Yet despite the repetitive and sometimes menial aspects, I saw cooking as an intellectual process. It's been argued that cooking—that is, applying fire to food—is what spurned our evolutionary development and made us human. Even though techniques and ingredients differ across oceans and lands, cooking is performed multiple times a day in every single culture in the world. It nourishes our bodies and propels our existence.

We can trace the rise and fall of modern civilizations by examining the transport and consumption of specific foods like salt, sugar, peppercorns, apples, or potatoes. We can learn more about a specific culture by analyzing the foods it cultivates or by discovering its culinary taboos; a book of recipes from a particular era is a diary of cultural tastes and mores. I love reading cookbooks and recipes for the stories they tell—whether they are about a famous chef, a home-cooking guru, a celebrated restaurant, a cuisine, or a culture—as much as for their recipes.

But cooking has always attracted me for other, more personal reasons. I wanted to cook because of the calmness that washes over me when I peel the ruddy outer layer of a carrot. As the blade emits soft grating sounds and thin strips of nearly translucent flesh fall into the garbage can, I contemplate the range of possibilities at hand. I can shred the carrot and transform it into a salad; I can chop it in chunks and boil it in salted water; I can leave it whole, rubbed in Moroccan spices, and grill it until caramelized; I can cut it in pieces, dip it in tempura batter, and fry it until golden brown; I can dice it and sauté it in a wok with sesame oil; or I can eat it plain and simple. I can follow any number of carrot recipes, or I can invent my own recipe on the spot. With cooking, the opportunities for creativity are boundless.

I had learned the culinary basics from my father (and, to a lesser extent, my mother), and growing up, I took pride in being a good amateur cook, though I still relied on cookbooks to guide me through the kitchen. When I was twelve years old, I cooked an elaborate dish of braised lamb shanks for my parents' anniversary. To their annoyance, I used every pot in the kitchen and made a complete mess, but they didn't leave a single bite on their plates. In my teens, I began throwing dinner parties for my friends, following recipes from cookbooks and savoring the praise that came at the end of the meal. To me, cooking for others was an easy means of finding approval and was a way that I, a somewhat shy person, could open up to others. But I wanted to become a bona fide chef so I could create my own recipes and cook for people with more discerning palates than those of my friends and family.

Unfortunately, my parents didn't see this in my future, and I was eager to please them, so we compromised. I moved out of their place and into a small apartment in the Lower East Side, and I joined a public relations agency that represented major food companies. If my job couldn't be making food, I could at least talk about it on a daily basis. Or so I thought. Instead, under the stark glare of fluorescent lighting, the photocopying machine became my primary companion. Shipping packages to clients became the highlight of my day, since that required leaving my gray-walled cubicle, stretching my legs, and giving my eyes a welcome break from the computer screen. The corporate environment just wasn't for me; with each hour I spent at the photocopier armed with a mountain of press clippings, I vowed to escape.

"This job sucks," I complained to my mother over the telephone after a particularly fruitless day.

"Lauren, all entry-level jobs are like this. Stick it out," she said.

So I did, but I still felt that I was shriveling in that office. As the months of perdition in my cubicle crept by, my craving for the warmth and pleasures of the kitchen increased. I began cooking more frequently in the little apartment that I shared with Alainna, a college friend. We baked pies and made homemade ice cream, scattering flour and sugar all over the twelve inches of counter space, and I strolled through nearby Chinatown to procure bok choy and lemongrass for one-pot dishes, since we lacked a dishwasher and our rack dryer perched precariously against the sink's faucet. After a year, in a big leap of faith, I quit my job and enrolled at the French Culinary Institute in SoHo, in downtown New York.

Culinary school was a revelation. No photocopying! No cubicles! No pantsuits! Where before I had been on the fast track to carpal tunnel syndrome from typing in a desk chair, I now used my hands to chop carrots into perfect little squares and to break down a chicken into eight pieces in less than two minutes. I whisked oil and egg yolks into mayonnaise and crimped uniform edges on an apple tart. Culinary school was physically tiring, even in the required orthopedic-style shoes, but it wasn't that difficult. Sure, we had practical and written exams, but they were a far cry from my college statistics exams and twenty-page papers on seventeenth-century French literature.

Or maybe culinary school was hard, but I was just too excited to realize it. At my office job, the most human interaction I had consisted of small talk over coffee from the communal machine. But in culinary school, my new friends and I chatted a mile a minute as we cut potatoes and turnips into jardinière-sized pieces—an exact five millimeter by five millimeter square, four centimeters long—and played juvenile pranks like sticking our hands up chicken carcasses to make them dance or mooing while holding cow tongues up to our mouths. With each new day came a new kitchen skill to learn and a task to master, so different from the monotony of low-level corporate life. My new classmates shared my obsession with good food and drink, and we spent our afternoons over cold beers at nearby Toad Hall or martinis at Onieal's. After cocktail hour, which began at three on the dot and ended around seven, we headed out for long dinners at lively restaurants like La Esquina, Momofuku Ssäm Bar, and Dos Caminos, where we ordered for the table and critiqued the chef's offerings. "Needs more seasoning! *Oui, oui!* More seeeeeesoning!" we joked in mock French accents, mimicking our instructors.

When culinary school ended, my practical education was far from complete. I had more to learn and more to see, so I sought out a *stage*. A *stage*, which—like most culinary terms— is French (and is pronounced "stazj" in English), is culinary-speak for an apprenticeship offering hands-on experience and familiarity with new techniques and cuisines. I decided to go to France to learn traditional techniques, and with the help of the school's job coordinator, I found work at a tiny restaurant in Toulouse called Au Gré du Vin, owned and run by Sami El-Sawi, an American chef of Egyptian descent, and Beatrice Wandelmer, his French wife. I was fortunate enough to secure grant money to fund my kitchen adventures, and I hopped on a plane to spend the summer of 2008 learning French cuisine as a *stagiaire* (pronounced "STAH-zjee-air"), or kitchen apprentice.

Toulouse is known as "La Ville Rose" for the red-and-pink brick buildings that line its narrow streets. Although it is France's fifth largest city, it feels like a small town, divided by canals and the Garonne River and dotted everywhere with sidewalk cafés. At Au Gré du Vin, I was hired to work five days a week, from ten a.m. through the lunch service. After an afternoon break, I would return at seven to work the dinner service and finish around midnight.

"Hello! Welcome, welcome. We're informal here," Sami said in English at the restaurant on my first day of work which began with that night's evening shift. He led me through the brick-walled dining room and into the minuscule kitchen.

"I guess I don't need to wear my neckerchief," I said nervously. In culinary school, all of the chefs wore white jackets, but Sami wore blue jeans, a black chef's jacket, and an apron tied around his waist. He resembled a late-forty-something James Dean: rugged and rebellious, with a pack of Camels always within arm's reach.

"Do whatever you're comfortable with," he said. He escorted me to the restroom, located in the adjacent courtyard, where I could change into my culinary school uniform of a white chef's jacket, black-and-white houndstooth pants, apron, baker's cap, and black leather clogs.

When I returned to the kitchen, Beatrice had arrived and was ironing a pile of white cotton napkins and folding them into neat little squares. She was petite, reaching only to Sami's shoulder, and she trotted back and forth between the kitchen and dining room, setting out napkins and lighting votive candles. In black slacks and a short-sleeved blouse, she looked effortlessly chic, even without makeup.

"You do everything for the front-of-house?" I asked, wondering how Beatrice managed all the restaurant duties that weren't specifically kitchen related.

"Yes. I greet the customers, take orders, pour wine, and I also do the ironing and serving and I take the dishes away. Since it's only me and Sami here, I'm like an actor, always taking on a new role," she said.

"How do you manage it all?" I said. Even with only a handful of tables, I couldn't envision running a restaurant without at least one waiter or dishwasher to help out.

"It's been slow recently. We don't have any reservations tonight. I hope you won't be bored," said Beatrice.

"Oh. Um, okay," I said, trying to conceal my disappointment.

I began by following Sami's instruction to snap off the woody ends of a heap of asparagus, my first official task. Asparagus can be tough and will break naturally at the base when snapped, letting you know exactly where the woody end stops. It was a basic task, but I was happy to do it, since it was virtually impossible to screw up. Even though I had excelled in culinary school, being in a real restaurant—even one as small and homey as Au Gré du Vin—made me anxious.

"Here, you can clean these, too, when you're done with the asparagus. We picked them ourselves in the woods by our country house," said Sami, materializing from his cigarette break and retrieving a large crate of chanterelle mushrooms from the refrigerator.

I faced nearly five pounds of firm chanterelles, the golden-hued mushrooms that look like miniature tree trunks. I hunched over my workstation and set about precisely scraping the stems with a paring knife and removing excess dirt with a small wooden brush.

"Some people wash mushrooms under water or soak them in a bowl of water filled with a couple drops of lemon juice to remove the grit and sand, but they can get waterlogged that way," Beatrice explained. "Instead, you can just use a brush to wipe off the dirt and then a paper towel to lift off what remains."

As I worked, I listened to the sounds of silence punctuated only by the repetitive tick-tock of the wall clock. Why weren't there any reservations tonight? Or walk-ins? Why didn't Beatrice or Sami appear concerned as they multitasked their way through the interminable silence?

"Perhaps when we're done with this, I can show you around the neighborhood," Beatrice said an hour later. Clearly no one was dining at Au Gré du Vin tonight. I wondered if Sami had prepped food earlier in the day and if it would go to waste. Since the only menu options were prix fixe four- or five-course meals, though, I figured their food costs were probably lower than those of restaurants offering six or seven different entrées. Or maybe the prepared food would be served to customers tomorrow. If there were customers tomorrow.

"That would be great," I said, noticing that Sami had tied up his apron and left without bidding either of us farewell. This was an odd situation, but I appreciated Beatrice's thoughtfulness. I didn't know a soul in Toulouse, after all; I was renting a cramped, un-air-conditioned room overlooking a stairwell in an apartment occupied by a woman and her two teenage sons, and I already felt like an intruder in their home.

We placed the cleaned mushrooms back in the crate and covered them with a damp paper towel, which Beatrice explained would keep them from drying out overnight. I changed back into my street clothes, sat at one of the seven empty dining room tables, and waited while she locked up. The snug dining room, with its chalkboard wine list and dried flower arrangements, was certainly welcoming, but as a mournful aria played on the restaurant's radio, I wondered whether I might be entering my own culinary tragedy.

A cool evening breeze accompanied us as we meandered through the cobbled streets, observing the bustle of the city's nightlife. Suddenly Beatrice halted in front of a generic-looking pizzeria. She said in a voice tinged with resignation, "This restaurant is always packed."

She wasn't kidding: Every table was occupied, and frenzied waiters hopscotched among them.

"But it has no soul," she added, and we continued walking.

As I left her, I couldn't help but think that even though that pizza restaurant might lack a soul, it had paying customers. Which was more than I could say for Au Gré du Vin.

Over the summer, tension lingered in the kitchen air like mildew on a damp wall, festering anew with each customer-less day. Sami and Beatrice's situation illustrated the difficulty of becoming a chef and owning a restaurant, a topic rarely discussed at my culinary school (unless, of course, you took the separate restaurant management classes, which came with an additional $9,000 price tag). Sami had forged his own path, but at a high price. At Au Gré du Vin, Sami and Beatrice were literally chief, cook, and bottle washer. As much as I wanted to learn to cook, my savings were limited, and I didn't want to end up like Sami and Beatrice, always worrying about paying the bills. I also didn't want to ask my parents for financial assistance. Was it time to unpack my business-casual attire and rejoin the corporate world?

But when I remembered the photocopying machines, computer screens, and gray cubicles, I couldn't give up. In the kitchen I felt at ease and at home, but I fantasized about a different kitchen life—one in the spotlight, with lots of cooks and a full dining room. So I contacted Wylie Dufresne, chef at the acclaimed molecular gastronomy restaurant wd~50 in New York City, to see if I could be a *stagiaire* there. Molecular gastronomy, which is based upon rules of food science, is a new school of cooking that focuses on manipulating the flavors and textures of food using high-tech equipment. While the movement has been popular in Europe for about fifteen years, it hasn't yet gained the same traction in the United States, where only a few restaurants specialize in it. Some restaurants in New York City may use specific techniques like *sous-vide*, in which you cook foods in vacuum-sealed bags at low temperatures for extended periods of time, but wd~50 is the only restaurant in New York City that serves molecular cuisine exclusively, and it had the reputation of a place that intellectualized food without taking it too seriously.

I heard nothing for weeks and figured it was a lost cause, but then I received a voice mail message from wd~50's manager. She said there were no openings for *stagiaires* until February 2009, but I would be welcome to undertake a *stage* then. *A six-month waiting list for free labor? Wow.* This made me even more determined. I could learn to cook traditional French food anywhere in France (and probably in New York as well), but I could learn molecular gastronomy in only a dozen or so restaurants worldwide. Yes, Wylie Dufresne was worth waiting for. I was eager to replace my whisks and wooden spoons for immersion circulators and culinary syringes and check out a larder stocked not with basics like butter and flour, but with unpronounceable ingredients like methylcellulose, hydrocolloids, and alginates. And in the interim, I could keep busy by continuing classes at New York University for a master's degree in food studies, a program I had begun the year before while still enrolled in culinary school.

Then it occurred to me: If I really wanted to immerse myself and learn the best techniques possible, why limit myself to one restaurant in one city—and in my hometown, no less? At twenty-four, I wasn't ready to settle down into something predictable. And although there wasn't a big gender divide in my culinary school class, I wanted to discover what it meant to be a female chef in different countries around the world. Graduate school had also cultivated my interest in knowing more about the ways of the kitchen; I realized that if I wanted to analyze this from an ethnographic standpoint, then I'd literally have to get my hands dirty. So I started to plan my year-long world tour of kitchens.

Financially, it would be challenging. Apprenticing around the world rather than taking a paying chef job would mean working for free, since I didn't want to be unfair to the chefs and restaurants by applying for and taking a paid position only to leave a short three months later. But I had some savings, and I reasoned (or rationalized) that it would actually be cheaper to live anywhere but in New York City.

I thought about the best places to cook and eat. I wanted to go to Vietnam because I knew almost nothing about Vietnam's food culture except that I wanted to know everything. I had fallen in love with Vietnamese food in New York, but I knew that couldn't be the real deal. I wanted the authentic experience, filled with bowls of steaming pho and plates piled high with grassy herbs and slippery rice noodles.

I wanted to go to Tel Aviv because I figured it might nourish me, professionally and spiritually. I am Jewish, though actually more like Jew-ish, and I wanted to explore my ancestral home. And I knew that Israeli cuisine, long thought of only as cucumber salads and hummus, was finally coming into its own.

Finally, I would go to Paris because I needed to give France another shot.

So, armed with a set of chef's knives and determination, off I went.

wd~50

50 CLINTON STREET

NEW YORK, NEW YORK

Chapter 1

SPRAWLED ON THE FLOOR was not how I'd envisioned myself during my first week of work at wd~50. But there I was, in my crumpled white chef's coat, houndstooth pants, and egg yolk-stained apron, while everyone's eyes shifted their focus to me. I tried to ignore the tingling sensation in my left forearm, which I had slammed against the oven after slipping on a small puddle of oil. My cheeks blushed bell-pepper red, and my arm matched. Miraculously, though, the paper-thin Canadian bacon I had just fried was still on the metal sizzle platter I was holding and not on the floor. At least no one could yell at me for ruining the food.

"Are you okay?" asked Brian, the restaurant's sous-chef, from a few feet behind me.

"I'm fine," I mumbled, and jumped up to deliver the bacon to the *garde manger* station, where all of the appetizers were prepared and plated for service. Spencer, one of the *garde manger* cooks, strode by me and said, "Ohhhhh, you don't have non-skid shoes, do you?"

Guilty as charged. My black slip-on clogs, which I'd worn throughout culinary school without any problems, were no match for this kitchen. "It's hard to find them in my size," I said in a tremulous voice. A plain old "No" sounded too lame. And I *did* wear a size five shoe. Spencer raised a skeptical eyebrow and returned to his station.

Lesson #1: Before working in a professional kitchen, make sure you own *nonskid* black leather shoes.

~

"YOU'RE THE ONLY PERSON I would do this for, Shock," said Chase a few days before the bacon incident. He stood in my apartment's tiny kitchen, gently pouring water over a small brown whetstone and trying not to spill it all over my cracked granite countertop, my landlord's one concession to "gracious living." He continued, "Do you have any paper towels I can use to put under this?"

"No, sorry. How's toilet paper?"

He rolled his eyes at me and then smiled, his brown hair flopping over his forehead as he lined up my knives in a row. I had met Chase in graduate school, where we were both hoping our eventual master's degrees would complement and make our culinary school backgrounds more marketable.

Although we knew each other socially, our friendship had accelerated when we enrolled in "Theoretical Perspectives in Food Studies." The course was much more about theoretical perspectives than food studies, and as a result, we spent most of the time sitting in the back of the classroom writing notes to each other, as if we were in middle school. Chase quickly became my go-to person for any food- or restaurant-related question, because in addition to attending culinary school, he had worked in several restaurants, for a catering company, and as a private chef. He had recently completed a two-month *stage* at the celebrated restaurant Momofuku Ko, run by chef and media darling David Chang, who was also a good friend of

Wylie's. So when I complained to Chase that the kitchen staff at wd~50 would think I was inept if my knives weren't sharp, he generously volunteered to sharpen them before my first day. I didn't refuse, especially since he was cute.

I sat on my purple love seat watching him as he carefully rubbed the knives back and forth on the whetstone. He explained that he first needed to create a burr, the technical term for the flat line on the bottom of a knife etched into the metal.

"Here, let me show you," he said as I got up and stood behind him, peering over his shoulder at the knife, which was now covered in dark brown residue from the stone. Placing his hands on my shoulders, he stepped behind me and instructed me to hold the knife. He positioned his palms atop my hands and guided them gently up the stone. "Just press your fingers on the blade and push at a twenty-degree angle," he said. Like every chef I had met so far, Chase was convinced that whetstones were the only way to sharpen knives, since they actually rub off part of the blade to create a sharp edge rather than just smoothing out the existing blade the way a steel rod will.

"Why don't you just finish it? You're much better than I am," I said, sure I was doing it all wrong.

"You're doing fine. Just press hard with your two index fingers against the knife and rub up and down. Pretend you're using the knife to smooth down the crease of a folded piece of paper. Just go up and down the stone about fifteen times, then move your knife over and repeat the same motions on the next part of the blade until you've done the whole knife. And then do the same thing on the softer side of the whetstone to smooth everything out."

"I'm so nervous! What if they yell at me at wd~50?"

He patted my shoulder. "You'll do great. Just keep quiet and work hard, but be yourself. They'll love you."

ᙠ

DESPITE ITS CUTTING-EDGE reputation among foodies in New York City and beyond, wd~50 is marked only by a blink-and-you'll-miss-it sign in red and blue neon lights in its window. Formerly the location of a dilapidated deli, wd~50 helped pioneer the transformation of the once gritty Lower East Side into a playground for hipsters (and opportunistic real estate agents).

Wylie Dufresne, its chef and owner, graduated from Colby College in 1992 with a degree in philosophy and the dream of, but not the physique for, a career in baseball. Like me, he enrolled in the French Culinary Institute soon after graduation. Afterward he worked at JoJo, celebrity chef Jean-Georges Vongerichten's place to be seen in the 1990s—and still a safe bet to take a visiting great-aunt afraid to leave the safe and sterile confines of the Upper East Side. Wylie continued as Vongerichten's shining star, this time at his eponymous restaurant Jean Georges. However, Wylie struck gold when he ventured out on his own (with the financial backing of both Vongerichten and Dewey Dufresne, his dad) at 71 Clinton Fresh Food, where he became a key player in making the then up-and-coming Lower East Side a culinary destination. My mouth still waters when I think about the seared scallops over lentils that I ate there on my eighteenth birthday. Even then, I could tell that Wylie was special.

In 2003, with the help of his business partners, Wylie opened wd~50, a small restaurant whose name is an amalgam of his initials and the spot's address, 50 Clinton Street. The name is also a riff on WD-40, the household water displacement spray indispensable in any technological setting. Fitting indeed.

As I walked the short distance from my apartment on Essex Street to the restaurant, I reread the confirmation letter I had received: "You will be expected to arrive at work promptly at

1:00 p.m. on each day of your *stage*, and to work until the end of service, which may be as late as 2:00 a.m. You are expected to bring a baker's hat, a set of knives . . . and a pair of shoes suitable for kitchen work." Although the letter stated the restaurant would provide me with a full set of uniforms, I packed my own just in case.

"Hi, I'm here for a *stage*," I said to the receptionist once I arrived. Because the restaurant served only dinner, the dining room was empty except for a uniformed janitor mopping the floor beneath a row of small square tables.

"Okay, go back to the kitchen. Someone there will help you," she said, motioning behind her.

I looked around, thinking this was not the sort of place that looked like it sold $30 entrées. There were no tablecloths or chandeliers or fancy artwork, except for a large marble slab spanning nearly the entire length of one wall. A communal red leather banquette divided the room in two, separating the three private booths used for larger parties from the main part of the dining room. Each wall was painted in a different shade of red, blue, and green, illuminated by whimsical, multicolored hanging glass light fixtures. The fireplace in the corner and the exposed ceiling beams added a touch of faux rustic, and I thought that the decor would be right at home in a place like Santa Fe. Not that I've ever been to Santa Fe.

I walked into the modestly sized rectangular kitchen, which was partially open to the dining room, and stood next to a large, custom-built stove engraved with the wd~50 logo. A tall, broad-shouldered chef with a full mop of curly hair and an elaborate tattoo creeping out from under his jacket sleeve introduced himself as Drew. "I'll give you a tour," he said.

As he showed me around, he explained that Wylie and Claire, the only female cook who didn't work in the pastry kitchen, ran the fish station on the left side of the stove, while he and Brian worked the meat station on the right. Each side had a dedicated space on top of the stove for cooking. To the left of the fish station was an aisle where the servers deposited dirty dishes for dishwashing in the back corner without getting in the way of the cooks. And along this aisle was the pièce de résistance: the "spice shelves"—rows of white plastic containers with screwoff lids were stacked on top of one another, displaying labels demarcating chemical formulas and names like hexophosphate, N-Zorbit, sodium alginate, gellan low, and methylcellulose. Though I spotted regular kitchen staples like steel-cut oatmeal, dried pasta, cornstarch, and kosher salt, this part of the kitchen resembled a college chemistry lab more than a restaurant.

Of course, this was what made wd~50 unique and why I'd wanted so much to be here. These bizarre ingredients allowed the cooks to transform mayonnaise into a fried food and yuzu juice into a thick gel and to glue skirt steaks together into a single filet. I admired Wylie's mastery of these powders, but I was also personally apprehensive. Science was never my strong suit; how on earth was I ever going to remember the difference between Ultra-Sperse 3 and Ultra-Tex 3?

After showing me around upstairs, Drew led me down a staircase at the back of the room to another kitchen, this one enclosing a small pastry kitchen in the middle.

"This is Lauren. She's going to be *stag*ing with us," Drew said as we approached another chef, tall, tanned, and lanky like a California surfer.

"Hi. I'm Brian, the sous-chef. You'll be with us for five days?" he said.

"No, three months," I said, surprised that wd~50 would take on an apprentice for such a short *stage.* From what I was told in culinary school, the average *stage* is about one to three months, but I figured that maybe a one-week *stage* would cater to seasoned chefs wanting to learn a few of Wylie's tricks to add to their own repertoires.

"Great. Well, Wylie's out of town this week, but you'll meet him when he gets back. This here is the prep kitchen, where you'll be spending most of your time," he said. Then he led me into a narrow walk-in refrigerator housing the restaurant's produce, meats, and perishable foods.

"*Mise en place* for meat, *garde manger.* Fruits and vegetables in these bins. In the Lexans here, we have fish, and in the bus tubs, meat," he said, pointing to the large ice-filled white containers and then the smaller black plastic ones. Closer to us were pint and quart containers filled with sauces, sliced vegetables, cut herbs, and liquids in a chaotic parade of color.

Every plastic container in the walk-in was labeled with green painter's tape, denoting its contents and the date it was packed. Above the meat shelf was the family meal shelf, denoted by the small label "Familia," where the components of the quick dinner made by the cooks and eaten by the whole staff before the evening service were stored. Brian explained that the staff also kept leftovers from family meals here so that they could sneak a snack when they were hungry. As he talked, I made mental notes of what went where, but I knew I'd forget it all by tomorrow.

Next Brian walked me to the dry storage closet, which held the real spices. Plastic containers bulging with coriander and yellow mustard seeds stood beside smaller quart containers of curry powders, cinnamon, and poppy seeds and rarer flavorings like house-made lime powder and shichimi togarashi, which was a Japanese spice blend the restaurant used to season octopus before it was made into a terrine appetizer. The air in the closet smelled earthy and complex, like the pages of an old and well-worn recipe book. Nuts and grains were grouped in smaller clear plastic containers called Cambros, along with ingredients like tomato powder, deviled egg powder, amaranth, pale green bamboo rice, dried white figs, and chicory. But I noted with a smile that alongside the argan oil and dried buttermilk powder sat Heinz ketchup, Tabasco sauce, and Lea & Perrins Worcestershire sauce. And as I learned early on, no matter what, the refrigerator always held Wylie's favorite food: blocks of sliced processed American cheese.

After the tour, Brian steered me back into the prep kitchen and introduced me to a pubescent-looking cook whose wiry brown curls peeped out from underneath his white cap. "This is Jared, the man who runs the show down here. You'll be spending a lot of time together," he said.

"So you're in school?" asked Jared, sizing me up

"I'm at NYU, getting a master's in food studies," I said.

He frowned. "No, are you in culinary school?"

Oh, right. Obviously. "I graduated from FCI last year."

"Chef went there, too, you know."

I nodded, unsure if I was supposed to ask him about his life and background. Chase had told me to keep quiet, after all.

"Let's get started, then. Take out your chef's knife and a paring knife, but leave the rest of the stuff in your knife roll. You can put it on the shelf above the meat slicer," he said, pointing to a heap of three knife bags. I did as he said and took a deep breath. I was ready to cook.

＊

OF COURSE, I didn't start out actually cooking; my first task at wd~50 was separating eggs. Jared told me to get five flats of eggs from the walk-in refrigerator, which I knew meant that I'd be separating 150 eggs. As instructed, I placed a layer of plas-

tic wrap on my work surface and set out three metal bowls—
one for whites, one for yolks, and one as the separator bowl so
that if a yolk broke while I was separating it, it wouldn't taint
the whites. Because plastic covered the counter, cleanup was
easy: Just lift up the plastic wrap and throw it all away. Genius!
I made a mental note to do this when I made messy cake batters
that required lots of bowls at home.

"You can either crack the eggs individually into your hands,
or you can crack ten whole eggs into a bowl, and then just scoop
out the yolks with your hands and put them into the other
bowl. I like doing it this way, since it saves you time if you're
doing a lot of eggs," said Jared, deftly plucking out the yellow
orbs. After he'd returned to his station, I mimicked his motions
but ended up breaking several of my yolks and decided it would
be safer for me to separate eggs individually.

"Oh, and you want to be wearing gloves for this," Jared added
from across the room.

Right. I spotted a cardboard box of gloves on a shelf and
grabbed a pair. As I put them on, they bunched up instead of
squeezing against my skin. Unlike Jared's hands, mine were
not made for size "large" gloves.

Tom, who ran the *garde manger* station along with Spencer,
was standing next to me, filling metal molds with foie gras.

"Are there any smaller gloves?" I asked him.

He looked at me and then down at my hands and answered
brusquely, "No. Why don't you just get bigger hands?"

"Oh, okay," I said, unsure how to read his tone as I tried my
best to juggle the yolk in my palm.

After I had spent thirty minutes meticulously transferring
the yolks into one bowl and the whites into another, Jared
glanced over my shoulder and into the bowl. "Don't worry about
the whites. They just get thrown out," he said nonchalantly.

"All of them?"

"You can save a quart or so for pastry, but just throw the rest of them out down the drains in the storage room where we pour out the used oil," he said.

Oh. Now you tell me. "You really don't need the whites?"

"Nah, just the yolks. We go through hundreds of egg yolks each week for the tasting menus, since we use them for the carbonara and the eggs Benedict, which is one of Chef's signature dishes. We season the yolks with salt and a dash of cayenne pepper, and place them in a machine called a Cryovac to remove any air bubbles, and then transfer them to either long narrow bags or large square bags and re-Cryovac them to vacuum-seal them shut." He then explained that the egg-filled bags were cooked *sous-vide*—meaning for a long time at a low, controlled temperature using a thermal circulator in a pot of water—until they turned thick and custardlike. The yolks in the long bags were then unwrapped and cut into cylinders using a knife, forming the "egg" component of the eggs Benedict. The yolks in the square bags, meanwhile, were transferred to a pastry bag and piped directly onto the plate, forming the "pasta" in the pasta carbonara, a play on the traditional pasta dish in which the egg yolks are used to create a creamy sauce to coat the pasta. *How clever,* I thought, wondering what the end result would taste like.

The next day, while we were rolling out Parmesan dough into little balls that would be baked and used as a garnish for the carbonara dish, Tom examined my hands, again submerged in baggy latex, as I struggled to shape the dough into uniform spheres. "Didn't I tell you to get bigger hands?" he said without a smile, and walked away before I could reply. *Ouch!*

The wd~50 kitchen was certainly not built for anyone with a small frame. On a daily basis, I had to stretch to see what was cooking in the salamander, the overhead broiler located on a

metal shelf a few feet above the stove. I jumped up to reach
the quart containers located on the mounted shelf above the
garde manger station. I needed Jared to help me carry the plastic
Lexan containers of meat because I lacked the strength to do it
alone, and I nearly threw out my back carrying a fifty-pound
container of thawed octopuses. Jared had to unscrew parts of
the meat grinder for me because I was too weak to pull them
apart on my own. When I had to transfer a boiling hot brining solution from the stove to the sink to pour it into a plastic
container, I couldn't hold the heavy pot's long handle with both
hands and instead held one hand on the handle and another on
the rim. As soon as I started walking, the salty liquid splashed
up like a tidal wave up against the side of the pot and onto my
wrist, scalding it puffy and bright red.

The only time I relaxed was during family meal, a precious
thirty minutes in the grueling twelve-hour workday when
we ate a cross between lunch and dinner. It was a collective
effort: Brian prepared the meats; Drew did the vegetable and
starch dishes; the *garde manger* boys put together a salad; and
Celia, the pastry sous-chef, who worked under Ed, the pastry
chef, made desserts, which were usually sheet cakes or cook-
ies. While some restaurants serve their staff whatever is on its
last legs, family meal at wd~50 was generally delicious. Over
the next three months, Brian whipped up juicy lamb meatballs
with tabouleh, spaghetti with tomato sauce and garlic bread,
beef Bourguignon over parsleyed noodles, franks 'n beans, fish
and chips, and beef tacos with all the fixings and two kinds of
salsa. Sure, we also ate lots of stews and curries, which were
quick and easy to throw together. But because duck breast was
often on the menu, we also devoured duck confit in one form
or another each week: duck confit Thai curry over rice, duck
confit hash with pancakes and creamed spinach, duck confit

barbecue sandwiches with coleslaw, and garlicky duck confit over polenta. Best of all, though, was smoked-chicken salad day, which was greeted with particular exuberance by the staff. "Of all the dishes I created on the menu here, it'll be the chicken salad family meal I'll be remembered for," Brian joked. It was true; there were never leftovers for post-shift snacking on days he served it for family meal. The wd~50 signature ingredients and techniques—crumbles, tuiles (thin, crunchy shards), sprigs of microherbs, or pieces of "glued" meat—were nowhere in sight. And the other ingredients you'd be hard-pressed to find at a wd~50 family meal were raw tomatoes, dill, anything overtly spicy, and onions. Why? Because Wylie didn't like them. And what the boss wants, the boss gets.

During family meal, I joined two pastry *stages*, Mathias and Min, and the entire front-of-house staff: the hostesses, managers, waiters, and bar staff. We sat in the wd~50 dining room and savored every bite, regaining energy for the next eight hours we'd spend on our feet. The pastry kitchen was kept pretty separate from the regular kitchen, so I didn't interact much with Mathias and Min outside of family meal, but they were good (if quiet) company. While the *stagiaires* and front-of-house staff chilled out, the cooks, who never had time to sit down at the table to eat, hastily dumped their food into plastic quart containers and ate it standing at their workstations, usually in no more than four bites, while simultaneously finishing whatever needed to be done before service. For the cooks, it was the beginning of the storm. Occasionally, Wylie stole a minute to sit in the dining room at one of the restaurant's private booths, but usually he, too, was busy putting the finishing touches on his latest experimental dish.

My first few days were a blur of chopping and picking, and I had never been so exhausted. When I was in my office job, I

twirled in my ergonomic swivel chair, thinking about how boring it was sitting in front of a computer screen all day. But after
standing on my feet for twelve hours a day, I understood just
how hard kitchen work was. I had to take an aspirin each morning to relieve the constant pain in my back from standing and in
my forearms and shoulders from lifting heavy crates of meat and
trash bins filled with ice. When I received an e-mail from Chase
asking me how my first few days were going, I had time only to
dash out a hasty, "Good. Exhausted. Gotta go to work now."

⌐⌐⌐○

TOWARD THE END of my first week, Jared gave me a bag of
confit lemon quarters to cut into a *brunoise*, meaning tiny, tiny,
tiny (no more than a millimeter wide) identical little cubes. I
first filleted off the pulpy flesh from the lemon quarters to
reveal the sweet-salty rind. Then I gripped my knife and began
slicing, the sliminess of the confit residue making a clean cut
difficult, if not impossible.

"Let me see how you're holding the knife," said Jared, his
kitchen antenna on alert.

I clasped the handle and sliced into the lemon.

"Yeah, you're holding your knife wrong. You should be holding it so that your knuckle rests against the blade," he said.

I looked at my hand wrapped around the handle of the knife.
I moved it farther up the knife, grasping it so that the side of my
index finger was flush with the blade. I instantly gained a new
sense of control over the knife.

"Like this?" I said, astounded that my culinary school cur-
riculum had skipped this lesson. Or, if it had been covered, that
none of my instructors had noticed the error of my ways.

"And you want to rock back on your knife. It doesn't matter

for something like this as much, but when you're dealing with herbs, you'll bruise them if you don't," said Jared.

He demonstrated this a few days later while I was cutting chives. I had been attacking them with a downward slicing motion. He held up one of my chives, then sliced another and offered it in comparison. I squinted at the two, not sure I could identify the difference, but I nodded because I didn't want to appear stupid. But then, after practicing for an hour, I saw what he meant. The chives cut with a forward-backward motion were darker where they had been sliced, whereas those cut using a rocking motion were uniformly green. Yet another thing I hadn't learned in school.

Jared was a good teacher, and even though he was two years younger than me, I began to solicit his advice. He was reserved, a hard worker who knew a lot more about food and culinary technique than you would think upon first glance. His long, disheveled hair curled out like corkscrews under his white baker's cap, and he always appeared lost in thought. He was like the kid who sat in the back of algebra class looking stoned, then surprised everyone by graduating at the top of his class.

Jared and Tom were best friends in the kitchen, but while Jared patiently explained and demonstrated things to me, Tom took the opposite approach, shaking his head or glaring at me to signal a mistake or that I was too slow. It didn't matter that he, too, was once a wd~50 *stagiaire*, who had worked his way up to *garde manger* after two years.

Two weeks after my initial slip and tumble, I was shelving some quart containers filled with bagel-flavored ice cream base when I skidded along the painted red floor of the prep kitchen. As my arms flew out in front of me, Tom demanded, "When are you going to get some proper shoes?"

"I know," I said with a meek smile.

"Don't smile. You're going to slip and break your fucking face. I had those shoes for a day and I threw them out. They were a piece of crap." He walked away, shaking his head in disgust.

When I got home that night at a quarter past one in the morning, I immediately ordered a new pair of shoes online, even paying extra for express shipping. I wasn't going to spend the remaining ten weeks of my *stage* tiptoeing around pools of water and oil and hiding my feet from Tom. My new shoes prevented any further literal slipups in front of Tom, but he continued to comment on my other mistakes.

"Cryovac these," he said a few days later after the dinner service had ended and I was cleaning the prep kitchen. He handed me three quart containers filled with foie gras that had been melted down but had now cooled and solidified. The Cryovac machine was one of the crown jewels of wd~50, since it vacuum-sealed pouches of food, a requirement for *sous-vide* cooking. The *sous-vide* technique enables consistency and a tender, full-flavored product, unlike cooking foods in boiling water or in a hot skillet.

Vegetables, too, were cooked *sous-vide*, though often with the addition of other flavorings, since the vacuum-sealing of the bag guaranteed that any flavoring would be pressure-forced into the vegetable. Turnips were vacuum-sealed with turnip seed oil, imbuing each turnip with extra turnip oomph. Lentils were cooked in a bag with orange juice instead of water, so the lentils took on a pronounced citrus flavor instead of being earthy and bland. The machine was also used to help meats last longer in the refrigerator by avoiding exposure to air.

Since I figured that the foie gras would be melted down again, I began scooping it out of the container with a large metal spoon, until Tom suddenly barked, "What are you doing?"

"I'm putting the foie gras in the bag. Isn't that right?" I said.

"If you don't know how to do something, ask," he said, and stomped away in a huff.

Well, I thought, *maybe if you had told me how to do it at the beginning, we wouldn't be in this situation.*

"Jared," I said, "how am I supposed to Cryovac this?"

Jared grabbed a quart container and placed it under hot running water, turning it around frequently until the cylindrical block of foie gras slipped out in one neat piece into a new bag. I took another quart container and mimicked his actions, pressing the container to jiggle it free, but the foie gras didn't budge. I held it under the water longer, still to no avail.

Tom marched back into the kitchen and seized the quart container from my hand. "Stop! See, it's breaking down now that it's been under for too long. And make sure you use a spatula to get out all of the remaining foie from that first container. This is an expensive product, you know," he growled.

"Yes, Chef," I mumbled. I slunk over to the Cryovac machine, head hanging in shame. I'd been an A student in college and had so far maintained a perfect GPA in grad school, yet I was unable to fill up a plastic bag properly.

The prep kitchen was deserted when I returned, and I leaned against the counter, playing with my cell phone, waiting alone in silence. We weren't allowed to leave until Brian confirmed that the kitchen was spanking clean, with everything in its proper place. Only once Brian gave the okay would the keg of beer—which I learned was a permanent fixture of the walk-in refrigerator—be tapped into a six-quart plastic jug to be distributed to us kitchen serfs. No cups, though; we drank the beer from individual quart containers—yes, the same ones we used to store food in the walk-in.

This was a major staff perk. Anyone who has ever worked long hours on her feet knows there's nothing like a cold beer at the end of the day. It didn't matter that the beer was always flat and frequently tasted like dishwater. We relished the reward, the acknowledgment of a hard day's work. Sometimes we talked if the evening's service had gone well, but if it hadn't, we drank in numbing silence. While we peons nursed our beers, Brian slowly sipped his yuzu cocktail from a martini glass while Ed and Celia clinked gin and tonics in the pastry kitchen. At wd~50, the executive chefs and sous-chefs drank whatever cocktails tickled their fancy after the dinner service ended.

The restaurant's kitchen hierarchy was as rigid as that of any blue-chip investment bank, white-shoe law firm, or crack military unit. Wylie, the executive chef, was followed first by Ed, the pastry chef; then Brian, the sous-chef; and then Celia, the pastry sous-chef. Next in line was Claire, who ran the fish station with Wylie; followed by Drew, the *entremetier*, responsible for the accompaniments to the meat dishes. Then came Tom and Spencer, who ran the *garde manger* station; trailed by Jared, who headed the prep kitchen; and then Hector, a prep cook. Then us *stagiaires*. Our number varied from week to week, but there were usually four or five at any given time. Pastry *stagiaires* and culinary *stagiaires* were equally low on the totem pole, but I frequently stole glimpses into the pastry kitchen, where Mathias and Min were often making an ice cream or brioche batter or pouring steamy liquid nitrogen into a container. Pastry *stagiaires* executed far more dishes from start to finish, while culinary *stagiaires* almost exclusively did prep work for other members of the kitchen staff.

However, I quickly grasped that while on an economic level we represented free labor, Wylie took *staging* at wd~50 seriously. A high percentage of his cooks started as *stagiaires*, and Wylie favored those with little experience so that he could mold them and teach them properly, cultivating them with the wd~50 culinary sensibility. Even though Wylie had attended FCI, he didn't require or even seem to prefer to hire people with culinary school degrees. Brian was self-taught and had honed his craft at well-known restaurants like New York City's Aquavit. Jared and Tom were both culinary school dropouts who had started as *stagiaires* at wd~50. Even Drew, who was an accomplished cook before he began working at wd~50, *stag*ed for a short period of time there before coming on board full-time, and Claire had worked her way up from *stagiaire* to fish cook.

But hierarchy reigned in more ways than one, and notably in our choice of headwear. While I didn't always see Wylie, Ed, and Brian wearing cotton baker's caps, I was required to wear one at all times, and the one day I forgot mine, I was forced to don a disposable paper one that made me look like a waitress at the Duluth Dairy Queen.

Wylie was also never called "Wylie." He was always "Chef." "Yes, Chef!" or, "Right away, Chef!" we responded whenever he asked us to do something. Celia and Ed were also called Chef. In some professional kitchens, everyone calls everyone else "Chef," no matter their rank, but when I called Spencer "Chef" one night during service, he laughed and told me never to call him that again. During my first week of work, I even avoided conversations with Jared, my direct supervisor, because I wasn't sure if I should call him "Chef" or "Jared." Until I realized that no one else called him "Chef," I began every conversation with "Um" or "Hey" to avoid another faux pas. Of course, no one called *me* Chef, except a facetious Tom when he explained the proper way to do something I had screwed up ("See, Chef, *this* is how you do it"). Usually, I was just *"Stage!"*—a term everyone used for both the person and the position.

As the minutes ticked by, I remained perched on the countertop at the end of the evening, waiting for the okay to go home.

Finally, Brian came into the prep kitchen, cocktail in hand. He sat on the countertop opposite me and said, "So, how are your first few weeks here going? Are you liking it?"

"Good. I mean, I know I'm not very good at things...," I said.

At this, his brow furled. "What do you mean?"

"I know I'm slow at doing things and I don't have any experience," I said, keenly aware of how defensive I sounded.

Smiling, he said, "The only way you'll get experience is by getting experience. And you know, Claire said the Brussels sprouts have been the best they've ever been."

"Really?"

He nodded and patted me on the shoulder.

After Brian left, I reflected on his words. I had done something right in the kitchen. In order to obtain two quarts' worth of Brussels sprout leaves to last throughout the dinner service, I had sliced about six pounds of Brussels sprouts in half, removed the central cores, and plucked off all the leaves before rounding them into perfect circles, just so they could be a garnish for the tasting menu's dish of lobster legs with banana kimchi. It took me two hours, which was a long time, I knew. But after hearing Brian's words, I grinned. Okay, I was slow, but my Brussels sprouts were the best they'd *ever* been. *Ever.*

Recipes Inspired by wd~50's Family Meals

I love making these meals at home, because even though I'm unable to reproduce most of the "creative" dishes served at wd~50, these are what I think of when I recall my time there.

Our dinners were good, flavorful, filling food—just what you need to keep you going.

LAMB MEATBALLS WITH CUCUMBER-YOGURT SAUCE

We ate lamb meatballs with cucumber-yogurt sauce, but they are also great with spicy tomato sauce over pasta, or you can mold the raw mixture into a meat loaf and bake it. Panko are Japanese bread crumbs, but you can use regular bread crumbs if unavailable. And to save time and energy, mince the onion and garlic in a mini–food processor. I regularly do. Just don't tell Wylie.

SERVES 4 TO 6

FOR THE MEATBALLS:
1½ pounds ground lamb
4 tablespoons unsalted butter, softened to room temperature
¾ cup panko
2 egg yolks
3 cloves garlic, minced as small as possible
1 small to medium-sized onion, minced as small as possible
1 tablespoon minced fresh rosemary
2 teaspoons minced fresh thyme
¼ teaspoon freshly ground black pepper
2 teaspoons kosher salt
2 tablespoons olive oil

FOR THE SAUCE:
1 cup Greek-style yogurt
1 cup roughly chopped cucumber (preferably an English cucumber)

¼ *teaspoon minced garlic*
¼ *teaspoon kosher salt*

Preheat the oven to 350 degrees F. Prepare the meatballs: Combine all ingredients except for the olive oil in a large mixing bowl. Using your hands, mix until thoroughly combined. Shape into balls about 2 inches in diameter. Using some force and throwing the balls from hand to hand will help release any air pockets and maintain the shape of the meatballs. You should end up with about 15 to 20 balls.

Heat the olive oil in an ovenproof skillet over high heat. When the oil begins to smoke, add half the meatballs and cook until browned. Turn and cook the other sides. Remove from the pan and add the remaining meatballs, cooking until browned on all sides. Return the other meatballs to the skillet and bake in the oven for about 10 to 12 minutes, or until fully cooked on the inside.

While the meatballs are cooking, make the sauce. Combine all ingredients in a food processor and pulse until the cucumber is in small chunks. Serve the meatballs with the sauce.

KIMCHI STEW

Kimchi stew was a popular dish on the days when Wylie wasn't in the kitchen, because it is spicy and often studded with tomatoes. Kimchi, a pungent combo of pickled cabbage and chiles, can be found at most Asian grocery stores. If the kimchi is made of very large leaves, you'll want to cut them into smaller pieces. This recipe is pretty basic; to jazz it up, feel free to add cubes of tofu after you uncover the pot or add bite-sized pieces of raw chicken breast when you add the garlic, ginger, and onion and then continue with the recipe as directed.

SERVES 4

> 2 tablespoons vegetable oil or olive oil
> 4 garlic cloves, sliced
> 1 tablespoon chopped ginger
> 1 medium onion, halved, then cut into thin slices
> 1 tablespoon tomato paste
> ¼ teaspoon cornstarch
> 3 Roma tomatoes, cored and cut into chunks
> 1 bunch scallions, cut into 2-inch pieces
> 1 pound kimchi (about 2 cups' worth)
> 1 cup water
> Kosher salt as desired (about ½ to ¾ teaspoon)

In a large pot, heat the oil over medium-high heat. Add the garlic, ginger, and onion, and sauté until the onion has softened somewhat, about 3 minutes. Combine the tomato paste and cornstarch until smooth. Add to the pot, along with the tomatoes and scallions, and sauté until combined. Add the kimchi and water, and bring to a boil.

Lower the heat to a simmer and cover. Cook for 5 minutes, then cook uncovered for an additional 10 minutes, then season with the salt. The stew should be thick but with some liquid remaining. Serve in bowls or accompanied by white rice.

CHILI DOGS

Hot dogs are easy to prepare, so we often ate them for family meal. But a hot dog family meal wasn't merely franks on a bun. No, the cooks went all out, making spicy chili, gooey beans, coleslaw, and pickled jalapeños (and, of course, American cheese) to add to the franks. It's great for feeding a crowd of forty, but when I'm cooking at home, I like to keep things a bit simpler, so I make a quick chili. For hot dogs, I personally like Hebrew National brand. I broil them in the oven since I live in New York and am sadly grill-less, but use whatever you've got available.

SERVES 4

> *2 cloves garlic*
> *1 small to medium-sized onion*
> *1 jalapeño pepper*
> *1 tablespoon olive oil*
> *1 teaspoon cayenne pepper*
> *½ teaspoon cumin*
> *½ teaspoon chile powder*
> *¼ teaspoon ground coriander*
> *½ pound ground chuck*
> *2 tablespoons tomato paste*
> *1 tablespoon molasses*
> *½ teaspoon cornstarch*
> *½ teaspoon kosher salt*
> *½ cup beef stock*
> *Kosher salt*
> *4 hot dogs*
> *4 hot dog buns*

Finely chop the garlic, onion, and jalapeño. Heat the olive oil in a small pot over medium-high heat. Add the garlic, onion, and jalapeño, and sauté until softened, about 4 minutes. Add the cayenne, cumin, chile powder, coriander, and chuck, and sauté for a minute or two until the beef is no longer raw. Add the tomato paste, molasses, cornstarch, and salt, and stir until combined. Add the beef stock and raise the heat. When the mixture reaches a boil, lower the heat to a lazy simmer and cook for 15 minutes or until thick. Season to taste with salt, if needed.

Meanwhile, preheat a grill or broiler to high. Cook hot dogs until they begin to wrinkle and the edges brown slightly, about 5 minutes. Lightly toast your hot dog buns, if desired.

To serve, place hot dog inside of bun and top with lots of chili.

Chapter 2

AFTER A LITTLE MORE than two weeks in the prep kitchen, I was finally deemed competent enough to go upstairs and assist Spencer and Tom with plating and preparing all the appetizers during the dinner service. Per Brian's advice, I spent my first evening upstairs observing, trying to memorize the placement of the garnishes on each dish while marveling at the men's speed; but I gradually got the hang of things and began getting my hands dirty, so to speak. In addition to the eight appetizers on the à la carte menu, the *garde manger* team was responsible for the first four dishes on the ten-course tasting menu after the introductory *amuse* (sometimes called *amuse bouche*), the small morsel of food designed to whet the appetite and set the tone for the rest of the meal. On a busy night (meaning one where we served about 110 diners), the men easily churned out over three hundred plates of food. Even though I was getting the hang of things, I still worried about messing up an order in front of Wylie, who occasionally glanced over from his post at the fish station.

At many restaurants the executive chef is there primarily to oversee the kitchen's operations and will maybe work an occasional night on the meat station. Wylie, however, was a fish guy and cooked on the line every night he was in the kitchen, which averaged about three weeks a month; the rest of his time was devoted to culinary events, television show tapings, and food festivals.

One night about three weeks into my *stage*, I was helping Spencer and Tom work their station when they ran out of sliced endive and asked me to cut some from a new head. I ran downstairs to the walk-in, grabbed an endive, and proceeded upstairs to remove the leaves, cut off the yellow tops, and stack them in groups of three to maximize efficiency. Using the new back-and-forth rocking motion Jared had shown me, I sliced a small mound of endive until I felt a looming presence behind my back. I thought it was Tom, as he had demonstrated a predilection for hovering, but it was Wylie. Chef himself.

My initial encounter with Wylie was a, "Hi, I'm Wylie. Welcome," when he had returned from his travels, but other than that we hadn't exchanged any words, and my shoulders automatically tensed whenever he came into the room. Wylie was far from physically intimidating; his round face hid behind massive sideburns that almost reached the crest of his smile, and his sandy brown hair swung back and forth just above his shoulders. But when he walked through the kitchen, he did so with authority, and behind those wire-rimmed glasses was a gaze of concentration and intellect.

"Honey, if you're going to be in this kitchen, you're going to have to slice properly. See the motion you're doing? You're bruising them, and I can't serve my customers bruised endive," Wylie said calmly but firmly. He took the knife from my hand and sliced the endive in clean, even strokes. "And save those scraps," he added, pointing to the yellow leaves I had discarded into the trash bin.

"Sorry, Chef," I said, mortified, but also puzzled because I'd thought I was cutting the endive perfectly, and Jared had told me to discard the yellow part. But "honey" was certainly not a term of endearment. I began cutting the endive again, this time slowly, trying to reproduce Wylie's motion, but Tom, exasperated that I was taking too long, took over and finished chopping the endive in mere seconds while I looked on in shame.

The next day was worse. I was upstairs helping Spencer plate the scallop dish for the tasting menu, a fairly involved procedure that required eight different components. Fortunately, it was a Wednesday night and service was slow. Spencer swooshed parsley sauce out of a small plastic squeeze bottle, forming a single circle across a plate with an artistic curved line jutting out of it. He turned to me and asked, "Do you want to try?"

I took the bottle and imitated his movement, flicking my wrist from side to side. While his design looked clean and precise, mine looked as though someone had vomited pureed parsley everywhere.

Spencer tried to stifle a laugh, but his pitying look instantly shamed me. "What *was* that?" he said.

"Let's just hide it," I said, trying to grab the plate from the counter.

Brian overheard us laughing and came over. "What's going on here? Lemme see that," he said.

"No, no, you can't," I said, quickly trying to dump the tainted plate in the plastic dish bin. But Spencer grabbed it out of my hands, and seeing the commotion, Wylie came over and glanced at the plate before turning to me. My face reddened as the three men encircled me as if I were a sacrificial lamb before the slaughter.

"I know! I'm really bad! I'm practicing," I said. Their pity was evident—they were wondering how I had made it past level one of culinary school, no doubt. I wanted to tell them that culinary school hadn't taught me smearing and swooshing and dotting and dragging. I'd learned impractical skills like cocotting—turning carrots or potatoes into uniform football shapes—and quenelling—transforming ice cream into smooth spheres—that is, making shapes of food last seen aboard a cruise ship in the 1980s. But I accepted my shortcomings and kept silent.

Wylie walked back to his station, then turned around and said, "Go home tonight and practice with a squeeze bottle of ketchup."

"Yes, Chef," I said. From then on, I stocked my refrigerator with multiple ketchup and mustard bottles. I practiced far more than I like to admit, but I never managed to achieve a perfect swoosh like Spencer's. Sometimes practice just doesn't make perfect.

〰

A FEW DAYS LATER, I had my third run-in with Wylie when he walked into the prep kitchen as I was scooping diced shrimp into a Cryovac bag to be frozen.

"My dear, raw fish and bare hands are not good," he said, his voice quiet but his eyes full of disapproval.

I froze. "I'm so sorry, I didn't know," I said. I really didn't; we plated all of the dishes with our bare hands, so I assumed that I could touch shrimp that would later be cooked. All of the shrimp were already in the bag, so I went to the Cryovac machine to seal it up. Jared was using it, though, so I walked back into the prep kitchen, where Wylie was having a tête-à-tête with Tom, who glared at me. Although I couldn't hear them, I was sure they were discussing my screwup.

After I finished putting away the shrimp and went back into the prep kitchen, Brian approached me and said, "Don't worry,

Wylie's just wound up right now. But whenever you're work-ing with raw meat or fish, be sure to use gloves. I saw that you got your own gloves, too. I was down here the other day and I thought maintenance had gotten the wrong size, but then Jared was like, 'Oh, Lauren brought her own because the others were too big.' And that's awesome of you to do that."

I nodded as my eyes began to well with tears. *Lauren, don't cry! This is just shrimp! This isn't brain surgery,* I told myself. It was almost harder that he was trying to be nice about the whole situation, as though he thought I couldn't handle yelling.

"Okay. I'm really sorry," I said. I lost count of how many times in a twelve-hour shift I said those words. Out of the misty corner of my eye, I saw Tom and Jared in deep discussion.

"Wylie yelled at you for what she did?" Spencer called out to Tom from across the room.

"I'm so sorry," I interjected, now composed.

"He got mad that I wasn't watching her," said Tom, casting an evil eye in my direction.

Spencer said to me, "Don't worry, Wylie likes to yell at Tom. There's an order to the way things run around here. You'll get used to it."

~

INDEED, as the days went on, I acclimated more and more to restaurant life. I no longer took aspirin in the morning or asked Jared a second time on what shelf I was supposed to deposit the long beans I had finished slicing. In the process of performing repetitive tasks day after day, I was learning the fastest way to accomplish them.

This epitomizes the initial professional kitchen experience.

Diving into the deep end is neither glamorous nor creative. An average day for me at wd~50 went something like this: I sliced endive for an hour; trimmed Brussels sprout leaves for an hour; separated six flats of eggs, seasoned the yolks, sucked the air out of them in the Cryovac machine, and poured them into plastic bags before tying them closed, all over the course of an hour and a half; and sliced chives for half an hour before breaking for a thirty-minute family meal. Next, I would spend an hour deep-frying squares of bacon, dehydrated cooked orzo, and dehydrated beef tendons and packaging them up in pint containers for service. Then, if I were deemed worthy enough, I would go upstairs for the dinner shift and assist the *garde manger* station in plating the cold appetizers. That part was fun, because that's where the energy and rush were, but the first six hours were an exercise in repetitive chopping motions. If I weren't one of the *stagiaires* lucky enough to get to assist upstairs that night, I returned to the prep kitchen and rolled Parmesan balls for an hour; made brines for the pork and duck breasts for an hour; defrosted and beheaded fifty pounds of octopus by grabbing them by the head and slicing right under their eyes until their heads fell off; and processed a case of mustard greens while hoping they wouldn't clog the juicer. If there was any time left, I might trim the fat off some beef before spending half an hour straining and icing down poultry and rabbit stocks. Then I'd store the bags of cooked meats that were cooling in ice baths in the walk-in; pack up the Worcestershire spaetzle and red onion confit that the meat station had made earlier in the day into quart containers; sweep and mop the walk-in; and scrub, squeegee, and towel-dry the entire kitchen and toss my food-stained apron into the laundry basket. That was an average twelve-hour day in the life of a *stagiaire* (or prep cook, too) at wd~50.

⌁

MY FRIEND REBECCA was celebrating her birthday on a Friday night a few weeks after I started working. I missed the dinner portion of the party because of work, obviously, but I was looking forward to the drinks later on. I invited Chase, hoping that clinking beer bottles together might lead to other, more romantic things. A first kiss, at least. Work ended at about twelve thirty a.m., early for a Friday night, and I took a taxi to the bar where she'd told people to meet. I texted Chase that I'd arrived and then found Rebecca and her friends polishing off a bottle of wine.

"The lounge is kind of small, so we're going to go somewhere else," Rebecca said after she greeted me with a hug.

"Sure, no problem. I invited Chase as well. I hope that's cool," I said.

"Of course! How *is* your fake boyfriend?" she asked. That's how she'd begun to refer to him, since he and I had been spending so much time together but nothing romantic had happened yet.

"Still fake. I don't know if he likes me or what. What kind of a guy spends that much time with a girl he wasn't even friends with beforehand and doesn't make a move by now? But who knows, maybe tonight's the night. So where are we going? I need to call and let him know."

"Home Sweet Home," she said, naming a basement-level hipster bar with dim lighting and strong drinks.

I stepped outside to call Chase. "Hey, sorry for the change of plans, but we're actually going to Home Sweet Home on Chrystie."

"Shocks, our first date and you have me running all over town!"

"Sorry. It'll be fun, though, I promise," I said.

"Sure thing. See ya soon."

Back inside, I raced to Rebecca's table. "He said 'date,'" I said, brimming with excitement.

"That's promising."

Chase arrived at the bar wearing his uniform of a bright green T-shirt, cargo pants, and black clogs. These seemed to be the only clothes he ever wore, except for his interview outfit of a blue dress shirt and slacks. His hair was unkempt, as though he had just rolled out of bed. "Hey," he said, kissing me on the cheek.

"Hi. Get a drink," I said, sipping my whiskey.

"Nah, I'm good," he said.

I frowned. Why didn't he want a drink? Was he not planning on staying?

"So, wd~50? It's going well? What's Wylie like? Tell me all the stuff they've taught you," he said, glancing over my shoulder and waving to a willowy girl.

"Good, but tiring." I was slightly annoyed that he seemed more interested in the restaurant than in me.

"Oh, hey," Chase called out to the girl, who had walked over.

"Hey. What are you doing here?" she said.

"This is Lauren," he said, pointing at me. "We're here for her friend's birthday." He turned to me and explained, "We used to work at Momofuku together. She was one of the hostesses."

Chase left to make a phone call, and I made small talk with the girl, asking her about life in David Chang's kitchen.

"So, are you guys dating?" she asked.

"I'm not really sure," I said, and she nodded. How do you know exactly when you're dating someone? I was spending more time with Chase than anyone else in my life (save my co-workers, of course), but I couldn't tell if he was only a friend who gave me culinary advice and sharpened my knives.

When Chase returned, his friend went back to her group, and he and I worked our way across the bar to chat with Rebecca and her friend Amy.

"How do you guys know each other?" Amy said.

"We're at NYU together," I said.

"Our relationship is blossoming," said Chase.

Blossoming? What was that supposed to mean? "Chase's been explaining kitchen life to me," I said, trying to keep the conversation light.

At two a.m., Chase abruptly announced, "I'm going to go home now."

"I'll walk you to the train," I said, hoping for a moment alone together.

"Nah, I'm fine." He hugged me good-bye. "Talk to you soon. Have a good week at work! Cook something exciting." And with that he was gone, and our "first date" was over.

⟡⟿

SINCE WD~50 WAS CLOSED on Mondays and Tuesdays, Sunday was the staff's big night out. Usually we congregated at a local bar, which shuttered its doors shortly after midnight so the denizens inside could smoke (illegally), but any cheap bar within a three-block radius worked. The kitchen staff went out together, with Jared, Tom, Claire, Spencer, and Celia forming the core group of drinkers. The bosses, Wylie and Ed, never came out with the group, but we *stagiaires* were always invited. Even Brian came on occasion to buy tequila shots for his hard-working crew. The explicit hierarchy and professionalism of the kitchen disappeared at the bar, and I enjoyed these times together. This Sunday evening, we took our usual places at the Whiskey Ward. Tom propped himself up on a bar stool next to Claire and bought rounds of whiskey shots for us (even me!), only to be outdone a few minutes later by Jared, who bought yet another round.

"How's pastry?" I asked Mathias as he approached the bar to order a beer.

He narrowed his eyes. "Ed is intense," he said.

"He does seem scary. And he's really young, right? To be the pastry chef at a top restaurant and not even thirty years old is a big deal," I said. "At least you get to do a lot in the pastry kitchen. A lot of what I do is chopping."

"Yeah, it doesn't look that fun."

"Just wait until you're there doing it. Only two months away!" Mathias was doing a six-month *stage*, which seemed like an eternity to me.

I plopped down next to Claire once Tom got up to talk to Jared in the corner. "Hey. How are you doing? Are you enjoying things and learning a lot?" she asked me.

"Sure. I can tell that there's definite improvement from when I started. My knife skills are much better," I said. *Was I enjoying it?* Yes, in a masochistic sort of way. I was perpetually exhausted, and I rarely saw old friends, but at least I didn't need the gym. I now had bulging arm muscles from all the manual labor.

"Even just knowing how things work in the kitchen is important," she said.

"Totally." And I was still learning. It had taken me a month to realize that "one up on table twenty-one" meant that one of the customers had left table 21 for the bathroom or a cigarette break, so we shouldn't send out that table's appetizers. And the day before, when Brian asked me to hand him a *passoir*, I had to ask him what it was. He patiently explained that it was only a fancy word for a small strainer.

"I was like you once. Back when I *stage*d," said Claire.

"Did you go to culinary school beforehand?" I asked.

"No. I worked in children's book publishing for three years after college before I came here. I even remember my first task in the prep kitchen. Do you know what water spinach looks like?"

"Not really."

"The leaves are on a large stalk, and I had to do a bus tub's worth of leaves every day. I went so slowly at first, picking each leaf." She imitated a dainty plucking motion with her index finger and thumb. "Until one day the prep cook, Wayne, told me, 'Girl, they're just going to wilt it down in a pan. You gotta go like this and pull off all the leaves in one fell swoop.'"

"Yeah, it took me a while to realize that not every parsley leaf had to be perfect and entirely stemless, since *garde manger* was just going to puree them all into a sauce." But like Claire, I was absorbing kitchen wisdom by osmosis and simply by being in an environment driven by innovation and creativity. And I was learning through practice, practice, practice.

While we talked, Claire explained her progression up the culinary ladder to prep cook and then to *garde manger*, to meat, and now to fish alongside Wylie. Having spent the last three years at wd~50—a lifetime by restaurant standards—she was a cook second only to Wylie in tenure and widely considered to be one of the best cooks and Wylie's favorite.

While Claire's words reassured me that even the best cooks started at the bottom, it was taking a lot of trial and error (really, more error and less trial) to get my footing in the kitchen.

"HOW DOES CHEF COME UP with the recipes for the restaurant?" I asked Jared one evening while I chopped a square of
doctored and gelatinized buttermilk that would be mixed with
a whey-based fluid gel until it resembled ricotta cheese. Buttermilk ricotta, Wylie called it.

"Basically it's just by playing around and seeing what
works. Scientists will send him samples of their stuff. They
don't get credit or anything on the menu, but Wylie will invite
them to eat and will comp their dinner. These guys are science
geeks, so they're excited just to see their products being used in
this way."

"Oh," I said. It sounded so much more mundane than the
images I had in my mind of Wylie conducting "mad scientist"
experiments.

"And you know, Brian's also put a ton of things on the menu,
and so has Claire. I remember she figured out this technique to
take the silver skin off some beef she had and transform it to a
crispy chip. It was so cool because it worked the first time she
did it," he said.

"That's nice that it's a collective process," I said.

"Yeah," said Jared, and we returned to our chopping. I wondered if Jared was biding his time in the prep kitchen until he,
too, would be able to invent something to add to the wd~50
menu.

A few weeks later, while I manned the deep fryer before the
dinner shift began, Brian, who worked at the station next to it,
asked me, "You have any burns yet?"

"Yep," I said, and showed him the patches of pink spotting
my hands and wrists. I hadn't yet sliced any of my fingers, but I
was burning myself at least once a week, either when the fryer

splattered me with hot oil or when I accidentally dripped sizzling oil onto my hands in the process of transferring puffed orzo from the *chinois* (the fancy name for a big mesh strainer) onto a paper towel to dry.

"Good, it's the mark of a chef. Look at mine." He rolled up the sleeves of his jacket to show me the kaleidoscope of rose and white scars covering his arms.

"Damn, that's a lot," I said.

"Yup. If you didn't have any, I was gonna have to throw your hand in the fryer or something," he said with a wink.

We both laughed. "It could be the wd~50 branding initiation—you know, to make a man out of me."

I was the girliest girl in the kitchen by far. Making a man out of me would require a lot more than hot oil.

I watched the bacon squares bubbling up from the fryer baskets as they turned dark brown and crispy. I was still thinking about what Jared had told me. "Hey, Brian, how long does it take for a dish to go from conception to being on the menu?" I asked.

"It depends. A month or two. We joked about the cold fried chicken at New Year's. And one day I made it and it was fucking awesome," he said, referring to a dish that consisted of breaded fried pieces of a chicken terrine (made by gluing together chicken thighs using a transglutaminase, also known as meat glue), served with a Tabasco gel and the buttermilk ricotta and topped with caviar. It was an expensive play on the traditional cold fried chicken.

"David used to do research and development for us before he ran the bar here. And a lot of the dishes that appear on the menu come out of *amuses*. You know, we catalog every *amuse*. That's how the lamb belly dish got on the menu. We started off with a feta and date flavor pairing, and we had made fried ricotta balls before, and so I thought we should try it with feta. And I had been wanting to do a baba ganoush purée forever, so then it all came together. You know, once you get the bug for creating something, that's what's great about being a chef here. I don't know of any other kitchen where you can do that. Which is sad, and which is also why it's hard for people to leave this place."

I now understood what he meant. I was learning that molecular gastronomy wasn't just a series of crazy and nonsensical kitchen experiments; it was more like a puzzle, unlocking the secrets of new culinary techniques and flavor combinations. Spencer, for example, was on a quest to make lily bulb noodles, and he had spent his brief moments of free time after he'd finished his prep work trying to figure it out, first pureeing fresh lily bulbs and then combining them with rice flour to form noodles. When that didn't work, he dehydrated the lily bulbs and ground them into a powder, which he combined with flour and milk powders and water. I don't think Spencer ever ended up with a successful version, and lily bulb noodles didn't make it onto the menu while I was working at wd~50, but I witnessed the thought and reasoning behind molecular food. Anyone can create food pairings based on flavors—say, beets and goat cheese or asparagus and morels—but it takes someone with an in-depth understanding of chemistry and food to make noodles out of lily bulbs and to make molecular gastronomy actually work flawlessly and not seem gimmicky. I wasn't there yet, but with each passing day in the wd~50 kitchen, I was inching closer.

Recipes That Will Help You Gain Knife Skills—Or Just Wear Out Your Hands

Here are some recipes that will give you an idea of the daily tasks I performed at wd~50: cutting long beans, cleaning lily bulbs, trimming Brussels sprouts, and slicing endive. You'll gain a whole new appreciation for your vegetables!

COLD LONG BEAN AND LILY BULB SALAD

Cutting long beans and cleaning lily bulbs were two tasks that I performed at least every other day at wd~50. This salad uses both techniques but reworks the flavors into a simple Asian-inspired salad. Lily bulbs (and long beans to a lesser extent) can be hard to find outside of Asian markets, so feel free to substitute green beans.

SERVES 4 AS A SIDE DISH

¾ pound long beans
4 lily bulbs
1 tablespoon sesame seeds, toasted until pale golden brown
2 tablespoons sesame oil
½ teaspoon kosher salt
½ teaspoon sugar
½ teaspoon rice vinegar

Trim the ends off the long beans. Lining up four beans at a time horizontally in front of you, hold your knife at a 20-degree angle and slice the beans on the bias, then cut into 3-inch pieces.

Slice off the top and bottom of the lily bulbs, about half an inch on each side. Place the petals in a bowl of cold water and swirl around to remove any dirt or grit. Drain and repeat until the water is clear. Drain, then discard any petals that are brown or blemished.

Bring a medium-sized pot of water to a boil. Add the long beans and cook until crisp-tender, about 2 to 3 minutes. Remove with a slotted spoon and place in a bath of ice water to halt the cooking process. Add the lily bulb petals to the boiling water and cook for 30 seconds. Drain, then add to the ice water. When the beans are cold, drain the water and let dry on paper towels.

In a mixing bowl, combine all remaining ingredients. Add the long beans and lily bulbs and mix well.

BRUSSELS SPROUT LEAVES WITH BACON AND ORANGE ZEST

At wd~50, I was queen of the Brussels sprout leaves, since I meticulously trimmed each leaf into a perfect circle. It was a time-consuming task, since the outer leaves of the sprouts were generally too blemished to be used and the leaves closest to the core were too curly, so each sprout yielded only about six usable leaves—the number required for each individual dish of lobster legs with Brussels sprout leaves. Needless to say, I plowed through a lot of Brussels sprouts. At home, though, I won't trim the leaves, and I'll even use the curly leaves. Unless I'm *really* trying to impress my dining companions.

SERVES 4 AS A SIDE DISH

   2 ounces bacon (about 2 to 3 slices)
   1 pound Brussels sprouts

2 tablespoons water
½ teaspoon orange zest
Scant ¼ teaspoon kosher salt
Pinch of freshly ground black pepper
1 teaspoon olive oil

Place the bacon slices in the freezer. Slice the bottoms off the Brussels sprouts and discard any damaged outer leaves. Cut the Brussels sprouts in half, then remove the leaves until just the core remains. Using a paring knife, trim the edges of the leaves so that each leaf is a perfect circle. After 5 minutes, realize this is overly tedious and stop trimming the leaves.

Remove the bacon from the freezer and slice into strips as thin as possible. Heat a skillet over medium-high heat and add the bacon. Cook until the bacon is crisp, about 3 to 5 minutes. Remove the bacon with a slotted spoon and let dry on a paper towel, leaving the bacon fat in the skillet.

Turn the heat up to high. When the bacon fat begins to smoke, add the Brussels sprout leaves. Stir occasionally, then add the water when the bottom leaves just begin to brown. Continue cooking for another minute or two. When done, the leaves should be somewhat crunchy but tender. Add the orange zest, salt, pepper, and olive oil, and stir well. Serve immediately.

ENDIVE SALAD AND BLUE CHEESE TERRINE

Slicing endives and chives isn't as time-consuming as trimming Brussels sprout leaves, but it does require a careful eye and a sharp knife. A ring mold makes this presentation look clean and elegant, but if you don't have one, just cup your hands around the endive to make a small mound.

SERVES 4 AS AN APPETIZER

> ½ cup hazelnuts
> 1 pound endive
> 2 teaspoons minced chives (about 15 to 20 chives);
>   see procedure below
> 1 tablespoon olive oil
> ¼ teaspoon kosher salt
> Pinch of freshly ground black pepper
> 2 teaspoons lemon juice
> 2 ounces blue cheese (like Roquefort)

Preheat the oven to 350 degrees F. Spread the hazelnuts out on a baking sheet and bake for about 10 minutes or until golden brown. Remove and set aside to cool, then chop as finely as possible. (Alternatively, you can blitz them in a food processor, saving you lots of time and energy.) Set aside.

Cut the base off the endive stems and separate the leaves from the base, cutting off more of the base if necessary. Place the leaves in a bowl of cold water. Stacking three endive leaves together and beginning at the base, slice as thinly as possible, making sure to slice through the endive and not down on it. When you reach the yellow tips of the leaves, discard what remains. (Alternatively, if this process sounds too tedious, you can cut off the base and then slice the whole endive as thinly as possible.) Place in a bowl.

Slice the chives as thinly as possible, making sure to rock back on your knife so as not to bruise the chives (though it's doubtful your guests will notice whether or not a chive is bruised!). Add to the endive along with the olive oil, salt, pepper, and lemon juice. Mix well.

Arrange half the endive onto four plates, placing a small,

flat mound in the center of each plate in a ring mold. Scatter the minced hazelnuts on top of the endive, then crumble the blue cheese on top of the hazelnuts. Fill the ring molds with the remaining endive, then press down to create a compact mound. Remove the ring mold. Serve immediately.

Chapter 3

IT TOOK A MONTH and a half after starting at wd~50 before I grasped with relief that I wasn't actually the world's worst *stagiaire*. Because that was when I *met* the world's worst *stagiaire*.

Anthony joined the kitchen brigade in early March as part of his externship from culinary school. Although my school hadn't required this, many schools have a mandatory externship so that their students enter the field with some notion of cooking in the real world. Anthony had a boyish face, with a porcelain complexion and innocent, cornflower blue eyes. His chef's coat, evidently too wide for his beanpole thin body, flapped around his waist, and he exuded the general awkwardness that came with being well over six feet tall.

Now, several unspoken rules govern a kitchen staff, especially for those on the bottom rung. Chase had nicely forewarned me about these, but as soon as I stepped foot into wd~50 it was clear that *stagiaires* were expected to be quiet, keep our heads down, and work quickly. Anthony broke all of these. *Within the first hour.*

Stagiaires at wd~50 are initially given menial tasks to assess how well they can function in the kitchen and to determine their knife skills. *Brunoising* lemon confit assesses the latter, since cutting sticky salted lemon rind into perfect one millimeter cubes is no easy feat. Of course, you're not cutting each cube individually, since you first cut the lemon into thin strips and then slice a large pile of the strips into cubes; nevertheless, it takes several hours to fill up a pint. Picking parsley is another beginners' task, since it's pretty much impossible to do it incorrectly. All you do is pluck the leaves off the stem and place them in a bowl, while reserving the stems to later flavor stock. The leaves would then be pureed by Spencer or Tom and made into a bright green parsley sauce to garnish the scallops on the tasting menu.

The general kitchen rule is to work as quickly as possible, but at wd~50 it was better to take the time to do a task well than do a bad job fast. As Brian said, referring to the endive salad's garnish, "I don't care how fucking long it takes to cut parsley stems if they look perfect in the end." This was why they tolerated how long it took me to do Brussels sprouts. As Claire had noted, mine looked beautiful. But Anthony set a world record in kitchen incompetence (at least at wd~50) by taking four hours to pick a pound's worth of parsley leaves, earning him the unshakable nickname "Four-Hour Parsley."

News of his ineptness traveled upstairs fast. While I was frying some chicken-skin chips, Brian, who was slicing logs of beef that had been shaped into individual portions using transglutaminase (aka meat glue), said, "So that new guy's a fucking idiot, huh?"

"I guess you could say that. It seems like he's never been in a kitchen before. It's going to be a long five months for sure," I said.

"A five-month *stage*...," Brian said, shaking his head.

After the parsley fiasco, Anthony was demoted to mincing quarts of shallots that were used in the butternut-squash-and-shallot relish that garnished the squab dish on the tasting menu.

Picking parsley was humdrum, but mincing shallots was easily the most mind-numbing job in the whole restaurant, not to mention a strain on the neck and hands. Unlike at home, where I blitzed shallots in my mini–food processor, at wd~50 shallots first had to be crosshatched. This meant making a series of horizontal slices through the shallot but leaving the root in place so the bulb would keep its shape. Then I made a series of vertical slices through the shallot before slicing along its width, so that each piece was nearly the same size. Chopping by crosshatching ensures precision, and it's a worthwhile step for dishes like risotto, where you want uniformity. But these shallots ultimately needed to be minced, so after I crosshatched them perfectly, I had to go over them continually with my knife until they were just shy of a puree. Yes, putting them in a food processor would create uneven pieces and would invariably puree the mix if you pulsed the machine too long, but this method of mincing seemed a bit over the top, particularly since these shallots would eventually be turned into a sauce! It was a job I deemed worse than cleaning huge tubs of ramps, peeling fifty heads of garlic, deveining pounds of shrimp, or peeling soft-boiled quail eggs (which have a tendency to break precisely when you've removed almost all of the shell), all of which I had spent many hours doing at one time or another.

"Keep going," said Jared when Anthony had finished one quart's worth.

"Sure, I don't mind mincing shallots. I could do this all day," Anthony replied in a singsong voice tinged with facetiousness. So Anthony minced until Jared decided he could stop—three whole hours later. His demeanor wasn't so blasé then.

A few days later, I was peeling bulbs of sticky black fermented garlic for Claire to puree with chicken stock for a sauce garnishing a chicken-and-rabbit sausage when I saw Jared glancing at his watch and rolling his knuckles on the counter.

"Where's Anthony?" I asked, peering up at the clock, which read a quarter after one—fifteen minutes after we *stagiaires* were to report for duty.

"I have no fucking clue, but it's not good."

"New *stage* is going down," I said.

"Fuck, yeah."

Anthony waltzed into the kitchen an hour later. "Hi," he said nonchalantly.

"Why are you late?" asked Jared, adopting a drill sergeant tone.

"I was on the train from New Jersey, since I'm staying at my friend's parents' house there and commuting in, and I even left early, but there was train trouble..."

"So why didn't you call?"

Anthony giggled. "I don't have a cell phone. I'm so broke right now, and cell phone plans are so expensive, and I thought the train would be working. I left the house at nine this morning, which is over three hours before I needed to be here," he said, then launched into a long-winded treatise about his endless commute.

Jared shook his head. "Whatever. Go talk to Brian." Jared was sick of Anthony's never-ending comments about things with no direct relation to the restaurant, and this incident wasn't helping.

Anthony returned to the kitchen, presumably having been scolded, but not fired, by Brian, and Jared handed him a bus tub of parsley to pick. Anthony got to work but continued to blab on and on to me about his commute.

"You have to ignore him. When he starts talking to you, just look away and pretend you're doing something else," Jared said to me when Anthony brought his parsley upstairs.

"I can't completely ignore someone who is working right

next to me. I don't want to be mean," I said, although I too found Anthony's complaints tiresome. There were four main workstations in the prep kitchen: one next to the meat slicer that prep cook Hector usually took; one overlooking the pastry kitchen that was Jared's home base; and two (or three if need be) for *stagiaires* on either side of the sink across from Jared. I worked the closest to Anthony, and I was a *stagiaire*, too, so he figured we should talk. Usually I nodded or mumbled an acknowledgment while he droned on, although I wanted to say, "Look, you chose this job and this restaurant, and if it's too hard for you, get a different job. But don't complain about it to me."

Perhaps Jared pitied Anthony, because a few days later he was allowed to clean lily bulbs instead of mincing shallots. To clean lily bulbs, you need to cut off the tops and bottoms and place the snow white petals in a solution of water mixed with a drop of sodium bisulfate so that they don't discolor. This water removes much of the dirt, but because this was wd~50, not just any petal fit the bill; only the perfectly white ones would do. A minuscule speck of brown *anywhere* on a petal, and it was tossed out. Then the perfect petals were transferred to a new tub of water and cleaned again. It was a task that took patience and good eyesight, and I actually excelled at it. Experience taught me that the bruised petals were generally only on the outer layers, so if I left the trimmed bulbs whole to soak, I could discard those outer petals and then quickly go through the inner ones. Anthony, meanwhile, hunched over his work space. I thought about sharing my trick with Anthony but refrained when I caught Jared rolling his eyes at me. Even though I felt bad for Anthony because everyone hated him, I was secretly relieved and a little smug. Not only were my kitchen skills evidently better, but Jared was making fun of Anthony *to me*. I was now in the inner circle!

Just then, Spencer sauntered into the prep kitchen, holding a tray of circular molds he filled daily with foie gras and frozen passion fruit puree. It was one of the tasting menu's signature dishes, an elegant cylinder of foie gras that oozed bright yellow over curled strands of Asian celery when broken into with a fork. "If you keep standing that way, I'm going to drop-kick you," he said to Anthony, pretending to kick his stomach.

"But it's hard because my arms are so long," said Anthony, who had been leaning on top of his work space. I braced myself for another ridiculously long explanation of how his parents were tall and how he'd always been tall for his age and how at the last restaurant he'd worked the work spaces were higher up. But Spencer interrupted him.

"Just put the bowl on top of a bunch of sheet trays, but don't keep standing like that," he said.

Across the room, I smiled to myself as I continued slicing endive. Another strike against Anthony was one more point for me as far as I was concerned. In the kitchen, it's survival of the fittest.

⟡

SINCE CHASE WASN'T WORKING full-time, he was one of the few people who had Tuesday afternoons free like me. Ever since I had started working, we had spent every Tuesday together exploring the hidden treasures of the New York culinary scene, and today we decided to spend it eating Thai food in Queens.

"We need to get the crispy pork with basil, and the drunken noodles. Do we need the chicken, too? And what would you rather have as an appetizer—tom kha soup or the papaya salad?"

"Let's get them both," I said.

"Shocks, that's what I love about you," said Chase, and he reeled off our order to the waitress.

And eat we did: There wasn't a morsel of food left.

"So good," said Chase, reclining in the plastic chair.

"Totally. The salad and soup rocked. The pork could have been a bit better, but the other stuff made up for it. I'm not sure it was as good as the first time I came here, but still worth the trip. And we did need all that food."

"Yeah, I was impressed with you."

"I told you so. We should cook together sometime," I said.

"Yeah, maybe. I don't really like cooking for others, though. I only cook for people I'm in a relationship with."

"Oh," I said, annoyed and wondering if he was trying to tell me that I would never attain that status. And what kind of cook didn't like making food for other people? That was what I loved *most* about cooking. All I wanted was to show Chase my affection by making a hearty beef stew, butter-laden mashed potatoes, and homemade ice cream. But the more time we spent together, the more I wondered if that would ever happen.

⌒

"SO YOU DON'T THINK he likes me?" I asked Jared and Nick, one of the newer *stagiaires* who had come to wd~50.

We were collectively ignoring Anthony, who was peeling red pearl onions in the corner. Pearl onions are notoriously hard to peel since their skins are thin, so soaking them first in warm water helps the process go faster. But, naturally, Jared hadn't told Anthony that trick, and neither Nick nor I volunteered it, either.

Most of the kitchen staff had considered Nick to be a joke after he picked parsley leaves by holding the bunch by the stems and slashing in a downward, machete-worthy motion. However, everyone tolerated him because he was entertaining and friendly, calling everyone "bro." He was at wd~50 for a six-week *stage* because he had been laid off at his last kitchen job and was biding his time until the next one came along. Nick knew that Wylie would never hire him because he didn't have the passion for or interest in working long-term at wd~50. So he made a lot of fun of himself and became the prep kitchen's unofficial morale booster.

Jared turned to me and said, "No."

"But he came over and sharpened all of my knives before I started work. And we spend every Tuesday together, eating our way through New York City."

"Well—no," he said. Jared's reasoning was that if a guy liked a girl, then he'd make it happen. If over a month had gone by and there hadn't been a kiss, then there was about a 100 percent chance there never would be one. As much as I could see the truth in what he was saying, it wasn't what I wanted to hear.

"I dated this girl at Brown University once...," began Anthony, but we all turned our heads away to avoid hearing the saga of his love life.

"So, Jared, how should I meet someone? These restaurant hours don't leave much time for dating."

"In this business you can't maintain a relationship," he said.

"How often do you see your lady?" Nick asked Jared. Jared had a long-term girlfriend ten years his senior, and like so many cooks, he had met her at his old restaurant.

"Once a week," he said flatly, making it difficult for me to tell how he felt about that.

Great. If chefs who were already in relationships saw each other only once a week, what were chefs looking for relationships supposed to do? Maybe I could start an online dating website for chefs that could facilitate dates after midnight on weekdays!

At least I was now rocking the kitchen, or at least sort of. I helped work *garde manger* more frequently, and I was starting to master the timing of things so that all of the dishes arrived concurrently in the central area of the kitchen known as "the pass," where they would be presented to the waiters. By now, Drew had quit and moved back to California, so now Spencer ran the *garde manger* station along with a new hire named Patrick, and Tom had been promoted to Drew's old position. Needless to say, not having Tom constantly breathing down my neck probably helped, too. But unlike the first few times I had worked the dinner service, when I waited until Spencer told me to start setting up a plate with various garnishes, I now knew to begin molding the salmon furikake on small circular plates as soon as an order for the tasting menu came in. When I pressed the foie gras cylinders out of their molds and onto the plates, they were no longer embossed with my fingerprints or nicks from the mold's rim, since I had finally grasped Spencer's technique, which involved placing the mold directly on the plate after warming it with my hands and gently pressing out the foie gras.

"Service, please! We're going to twenty-one; octo one, foie two, benny three," I called out to the waiter, which was our way of telling him that the dishes I had just plated were destined for table 21 and that the diner at the position closest to the waiter when he took the table's order was awaiting the octopus terrine with saffron cake; the diner at the second position was getting the aerated foie gras with pickled beets; and the third diner expected the deconstructed eggs Benedict dish.

"*Stage*, you still need to make the plates look nicer. Your swoosh looks rushed. Make it look more fluid," Tom said to me as he walked over to our station to grab a few slices of the corned duck that went into the "deconstructed pastrami sand-wich" appetizer. He squeezed purple mustard over the meat and shoved the whole thing in his mouth.

"That's gross," said Spencer.

"You want to see gross? How do you like this?" asked Tom, and began licking the inside of Spencer's ear.

"Fuck off, man," said Spencer, kneeing Tom in the groin while I watched like a hapless babysitter in charge of two-year-old twins. Although cooking in the wd~50 kitchen was very serious, the atmosphere often slipped into brief moments of juvenile male behavior. You needed something to calm those stressful moments, after all.

"Oh, you like that? Gonna try and rape me, huh?" said Tom. "Oh, you know who I really want to rape is that new *stagiaire*. Get him up here and get him in the weeds so we can yell at him. Mmmm."

"Yeah, we can totally rape him. But don't worry, Lauren, we're not going after you," said Spencer.

"Gee, thanks," I replied. As a woman, I was excluded from these antics. The guys could take it to another level with one another, but they knew that once you started talking about raping girls, you crossed the fine line between joking and offensive harassment.

When I returned to the prep kitchen after service ended, I encountered Nick and Jared discussing Anthony. "I don't know how he's going to last five months without someone killing him," said Nick.

"What happened? What did I miss tonight while I was upstairs?" I asked, joining the conversation.

"Anthony fell asleep standing up while peeling garlic," said Jared.

"How do you fall asleep standing up?" I said.

"No fucking clue. So anyway, I sat him down in the wine room like Wylie did to me—"

"Wylie used to sit you down?" interrupted Nick.

"Yeah, all the time. So I told Anthony that I know he wants to be here because he's asking questions and showing interest, but sometimes actions speak louder than words, and he needs to shape up. You know, I was probably the worst *stagiaire* ever at first, but I kept my head down and worked my ass off and convinced Wylie to hire me."

"You were really the world's worst *stagiaire*?" asked Nick. Jared was so confident and in charge of things, it was hard to imagine him ever being the world's worst *stagiaire*.

"Yeah. But I worked hard to ultimately become the best," Jared said. "You know, I had a really hard time after my first week as a paid employee, so Dewey, Wylie's dad, came up to me and told me that when Wylie started at Gotham Bar and Grill, Alfred Portale told him he'd never make it as a chef."

"But back to Anthony, do you think he'll improve? Five months is a long time to be working here if he doesn't," I said. Even with that much training, I couldn't picture Anthony as the next Wylie Dufresne.

"I don't know how he'll make it. He better shape up. Lauren, if you see him doing something wrong, tell him. You've earned that privilege," said Jared.

"Really? Thanks," I said, although I wasn't sure I should be instructing Anthony on knife skills.

As it turned out, I never had the chance, for one week later was Anthony's last day, four months and two weeks ahead of schedule. He received an urgent phone call on the restaurant's line one night during service and vanished for twenty minutes. He looked agitated when he came back, and Jared asked if he needed to leave. He nodded and left, mumbling about a problem at home. We never saw him again. He looked shaken up when he left, but sometimes I wonder if maybe he had a friend call the restaurant and invent an emergency just to give him a proper excuse to quit the hazing and misery.

⟿

"WHEN YOU'RE DONE with that," Tom said to me a few days later, pointing to the pile of sliced endive on my cutting board, "can you *mise* something out for me?"

*Mise*ing (from the French *mise en place*, or "put in place") is basically doing all of someone else's prep work so he can do the fun part. It's the main function of the prep kitchen, and Jared, Hector, and I were responsible for ensuring that the upstairs stations had all the necessary ingredients to last through the dinner service. Each morning, the chefs wrote on our whiteboard what they wanted, so we filled pint and quart containers with sliced long beans and chives, peanut-butter "noodles," cauliflower chips, and Brussels sprout leaves, which they then cooked to order upstairs. When you *"mise* out" a specific recipe, you measure out all the ingredients exactly and place them in separate containers on a tray so that the chef doesn't have to waste his time. Assembling one's entire *mise en place* is probably the most important aspect of running a kitchen—both a professional kitchen and a home kitchen—since it ensures that you have everything you need before starting any cooking so you don't accidentally leave out essential ingredients needed halfway through the cooking process. It was a lesson I'd taken to heart, and now I always organize all my ingredients before I start anything. It may seem time-consuming, but it's often much quicker in the end.

"Sure," I said as Tom handed me the recipe for the jerk

consommé, part of the pork ribs entrée. Consommés using gelatin clarification are a staple of wd~50 and turn ingredients like black sesame, Chinese sausage, Swiss cheese, or spice bread into a crystal-clear liquid. Traditionally a consommé is made using a raft, which is a mixture of egg whites, vegetables, and ground meat, to trap any particles and create a clear broth. Gelatin clarification does the same thing but doesn't leave traces of any additional flavors or particulate matter. It takes time and effort, however, because you have to add in .5 percent of the consommé's weight in gelatin, freeze the consommé, wrap it in cheesecloth, and let it melt in the refrigerator over a perforated pan to trap the gunk in the cheesecloth while the consommé drips out. The jerk consommé combines a bevy of spices like allspice, cinnamon, cayenne, garlic, thyme, and black pepper as well as orange and lime juices and vinegar for acidity. Using gelatin to make a consommé was a technique from wd~50 that I was looking forward to experimenting with at home, since it didn't require any fancy equipment or specialty products—just gelatin, cheesecloth, a freezer, and whatever ingredient you wanted to make into a consommé. I thought about all the variations I could try: popcorn consommé, teriyaki consommé, tandoori consommé, pimento cheese consommé...the possibilities were endless.

"Chef, that's not 960 grams of vinegar. Did you measure that?" Tom said brusquely as he stalked back into the kitchen to inspect my work. Even without looking at him, I felt his sharp, narrow eyes cutting through me like a climber's ice pick on an Everest ascent.

"Yes, it is," I said, turning around, confident that I had measured it correctly. Then suddenly paranoia hit. Had I measured in ounces instead of grams? Had I accidentally forgotten to set the scale back to zero grams?

"Wanna bet?" Clearly Tom wasn't backing down. He placed a new quart container on the scale and poured my quart of vinegar into it. The scale's small screen read 960 grams.

I smiled, and Tom walked off without a word.

"Was it 960?" asked Jared from across the room.

"Of course it was," I replied, vindicated for once.

From then on, Tom entrusted more of his prep work to me, even telling Jared to assign mincing shallots to me instead of the other *stagiaires* because he thought I did a better job. It was a double-edged sword, since I ended up with a lot of tedious work, but it signaled that he was starting to trust me in the kitchen.

⸙

IN MID-APRIL, my parents came to the restaurant to celebrate my father's sixty-second birthday. Time was flying in the kitchen; by now Nick had left for another kitchen job, and a slew of other *stagiaires* had come and gone as well. First came Pedro, a Peruvian who ended up slacking off in the kitchen, but his father was friends with Wylie so we couldn't complain about him. Hung Huynh, the winner of season three of *Top Chef*, also did a week-long *stage* in the kitchen, but he was upstairs most of the time and never had to pick parsley, though he did peel shrimp next to me in the prep kitchen. Then it was only Jared, Hector, and me—the three amigos of the prep kitchen.

While my parents have had their fair share of gourmet meals, I wouldn't call them adventurous eaters. I planned on steering them away from the more challenging $140 tasting menu and toward some of the less "inventive" dishes, like the seared duck breast with Worcestershire spaetzle and parsley root for my mother and the lamb loin with apples and celery and green "tomatertots" for my father.

I was excited to have my parents come to dinner and see what I was doing with my life. Since I had started at the restaurant, I rarely saw them, even though I lived only a short subway ride away. I had hoped to be in the main kitchen helping *garde manger* that night, but someone was trailing—kitchen-speak for auditioning for a cooking job. At wd~50, and throughout the restaurant industry, prospective candidates spend a night or two in the kitchen working alongside the cooks and are evaluated on speed, organization, knife skills, attitude, and general kitchen competence. So I kept quiet and called home during family meal to tell my mom I'd be spending service in the prep kitchen but that maybe I'd be allowed to come upstairs to say hello when they visited the kitchen at the end of their meal.

After family meal, as I held my knife nearly parallel to the cutting board, slicing long beans along the bias so they would appear longer and more elegant, Brian popped in and said, "I saw on the reservation list that your parents are coming in tonight."

"I know. It's my dad's birthday and they want to see where I work."

About half an hour later, Wylie summoned me upstairs and steered me by the shoulders toward the dining room. "Do you see your parents anywhere?" he asked.

I looked around and glanced at my watch. "No, I think they're coming at seven thirty. You can't miss them, though; my mother's, like, yea tall," I said, raising my hand to my shoulders. And they were always punctual.

"We want to be sure we know when they're here," Wylie said.

"No problem," I said, and promptly went back downstairs.

"I think it's ramp time," Jared said when I returned to the prep kitchen.

Ramps, also known as baby wild leeks, are highly rare and seasonal, growing for only a few short weeks in early spring. Chefs love ramps for their delicate flavor, and our walk-in was filled with bunches upon bunches that would be pickled and vacuum-sealed to last through to the following year. The pickling part is easy, but cleaning the ramps to get to that stage is a bummer: After you chop off the base of each ramp, you need to individually wipe and pull off the outside layer with a damp paper towel, which latches on to the slimy skin. Multiple bus tubs of ramps awaited me in the walk-in, and the astringent, onionlike scent wafted through the cold air.

"Actually, make a stock first. There are two cases of bones in the walk-in," Jared said.

Every few days we made chicken stock (and occasionally rabbit or pork stock), primarily to make a base for the various sauces on the menu. We used the leftover bones from the squab and duck breast items on the menu and from the chicken bones when chicken was served for family meal. While we had a lot of chicken for family meals, it was considered a bit too commonplace for the wd~50 menu, so it was seen only in Claire's rabbit-and-chicken sausage.

I was gathering the garlic, onions, celery, and thyme for the stock when Brian reappeared, placed his hand on my back, and said, "Get dressed. We want you to go have dinner with your parents tonight."

I was stunned. "You don't have to do that," I said, not wanting any special treatment that might alienate me from my co-workers.

"I know, but we want to—unless you don't get along with them or something."

"No, nothing like that. Dinner would be great. Thank you so much. That's so nice of you guys."

"It's only because we like you," he said, winking.

I changed out of my uniform into the gray T-shirt, black jeans, and gold flip-flops I'd worn to work. Although wd~50 claims its dress code for diners is casual, I felt out of place in my street clothes, with a greasy ponytail and a sweaty complexion. I walked up the employee staircase to the dining room, my shoes clacking at every step, and hoped that my feet didn't smell from standing in my chef clogs all day.

I immediately spotted my parents at one of the larger tables in the main section of the dining room—it was one of the best tables, as it had a prime view of the kitchen.

"Hi," I said, approaching them.

"Oh, hello. Why aren't you downstairs?" said my father.

"They wanted me to eat with you guys tonight," I said.

My mother beamed. "Why, isn't that nice of them!"

My father turned his head toward the kitchen and nodded toward Wylie the way men do to acknowledge each other's presence. Anna, our waitress, came over with three glasses and filled them with rosé champagne. "Compliments of Chef Wylie," she said, smiling warmly at me even though we had barely spoken before.

Unfortunately, I had already gorged myself that afternoon at family meal—succulent braised pork with creamy polenta and broccoli in cheese sauce—so I ordered only two appetizers. The chestnut-horseradish soup intrigued me, as I had tasted it only cold and without the verjuice gel, diced pear, chestnut chips, and powdered mackerel that accompanied the finished dish. I also wanted the lamb belly because I am a sucker for anything vaguely resembling bacon, and its Mediterranean flavors of cucumber relish, eggplant puree, and smoked feta were some of my favorites. Following my suggestions, my mom ordered the soup and duck and my dad the foie gras and lamb.

I wondered how my parents would react to the meal. Molecular gastronomy frequently disarms guests' preconceptions and imbues them with wonder and intrigue, yet these emotions are often coupled with disorientation, confusion, trepidation, anxiety, or embarrassment: *What is that ingredient, and how do I pronounce it? Why doesn't the menu have descriptions and only lists ingredients? How do I eat this dish?* While this doesn't occur as much at wd~50 as it does at, say, Alinea in Chicago or elBulli in Spain, two other temples of molecular gastronomy, the average diner will be ill at ease for at least part of the meal. The molecular gastronomy restaurant becomes a site of performance, and the diner, confronted with new foods and methods of eating, is both spectator and participant. Wylie, though, liked to add touches of whimsy and fun with items like the "everything bagel," which was the first dish that Scott, the manager, brought over after taking our order.

"Also from Chef Wylie," he said, then explained to my parents that the bagel was actually everything bagel–flavored ice cream dotted with poppy and sesame seeds, resting on a curved mound of smoked salmon "threads." Next to the bagel was a tiny mound of pickled red pearl onions and a whisper of crispy cream cheese paper, and the plate was garnished with three miniature sorrel leaves. It's a tiny dish—you can eat it in three quick bites—that is served at the beginning of the tasting menu, helping set the tone for the wd~50 dining experience.

"How cute!" exclaimed my mother.

"I like to say it's the smallest bagel in New York," Scott said.

"Sometimes I make the salmon for this dish," I told my parents, pleased that we were being served something I'd had a significant part in creating. "It's actually a pretty tedious job, which is why they give it to me. Basically you stand over the stove, stirring a shallow pot of salmon for about an hour until there's no moisture left at all and it's just dry, tiny threads of protein. It's a traditional Japanese technique. Then I cold-smoke the salmon threads twice for added flavor. You can do it with almost any fish, I'd imagine, but it works well with this dish because the creaminess of the ice cream offsets the fish's dry texture."

I noticed that I was speaking with confidence, as though it were my own creation, and I relished my parents' pleasure in the meal, although I saw—and inwardly cringed the way any chef does when food returns to the kitchen uneaten—that my father had not touched his concentric tangle of ruby red onions. I wondered if they would take note of that in the kitchen. When plates returned to the kitchen only partially eaten, which occurred maybe once every week or two, Wylie offered the customer a new dish instead, but I often wondered if he secretly looked down on the diner for lacking a distinguished palate.

"I prepared those beets, and I also cut those cilantro stems, which is slightly less exciting, but it's probably the first time you've seen cilantro stems as a garnish, no?" I said after Anna brought over our appetizers. I pointed to the four slivers of green that garnished the craggy rocks of my father's aerated foie gras. Using a combination of chemicals and the Cryovac machine, Tom and Wylie had recently mastered how to pump air into foie gras so that it resembled a huge sponge with nooks and crannies. My mother murmured in appreciation as the frozen mackerel powder melted in her mouth, and my father, a man who has eaten foie gras in virtually every possible iteration, remarked, "Well done."

As a diner, I couldn't resist stealing glances into the kitchen. I saw Spencer plating a dish in the pass and Claire looking flustered as she sautéed several pieces of bass on the stove's flattop. Yet the dining room was calm, the sounds of laughter and clinking glasses replacing those of sizzling food on the stove and the constant, harried dialogue between cooks and servers.

The food at my father's birthday meal also tasted much better than I expected. Not because I thought the food at wd~50 was going to be bad (although the restaurant has its fair share of dissatisfied reviewers on online food sites), but because I had become jaded by it. Cutting cilantro stems into tiny pieces that probably go unnoticed by the diner makes you think the whole thing is a little silly. Sadly, being a chef in the kitchen and working with food all day can make you appreciate it a little less. When it's your job, you don't have time to sit back and enjoy sharing your meal with others. Instead, you're praying you can plate the cold fried chicken for the table of six who ordered the tasting menu while you fire off a smoked eel and simultaneously set up four more everything bagels for two new tickets.

But it's doubtful that even the most curious diner wants to know *everything* that goes into making a dish. Take, for example, the scallop dish on wd~50's tasting menu: First, the plate is garnished with the oh-so-difficult-to-perfect Nike-esque swoosh of parsley sauce (a pound of parsley is picked—hopefully in under four hours—and is then quickly blanched and added to a stock infused with garlic, leek, and white grape juice and pureed until thick). Then scallops are placed at the edge of the swoosh. These scallops have been cooked *sous-vide* and cut into pieces before being tossed with hazelnut oil and lemon confit. Atop the scallops rests a slice of beef tendon that has been cooked confit, then pressed into a terrine, then chilled and sliced. The tendon is charred with a blowtorch so that it melts into the mound of scallop. Next to the scallop/tendon heap is a small pile of endive, dressed with olive oil and salt. Atop the endive are a few cut parsley stems. On the other side of the scallops lies a spoonful of yeast crumble (first, a yeast batter has to be made, then frozen, grated, and baked). Atop the scallops lies another slice of beef tendon, this time a slice of dehydrated beef tendon terrine that's been deep-fried and looks nearly identical to a fried pork rind. Finally, the dish is topped with Meyer lemon zest.

When you're in the kitchen looking at the dish, that's all you see—components working together—all the while stressing out about how quickly you need to send it out. If you spend every day pulling out the bloodlines of foie gras before melting it down and piping it into little molds, you're probably going to like foie gras a little less than you did before, no matter how tasty it is. Yet when the diner looks at the foie gras, he or she sees it first as food and then maybe as art, but rarely in the light of the product of hours' worth of hard work (and so often the handiwork of someone other than the chef!).

After our appetizers were cleared, three small, tasting-sized portions of the eggs Benedict appetizer from the regular menu were sent our way. One of Wylie's other famously playful dishes, this one uses the traditional components of eggs Benedict (eggs, Canadian bacon, hollandaise, and English muffins), but they are transformed: The egg yolks are cooked *sous-vide*, then smeared on the plate and garnished with paper-thin slices of bacon, a crisscrossing of chives, and a touch of black salt. The "hollan-daise" cubes are made by mixing a hollandaise-flavored base with several chemicals to harden it before it is breaded in English muffin crumbs and deep-fried (so that when the diner bites into it, warm, oozing hollandaise comes running out of the crisp exterior). Wylie's ingenuity impressed my parents, and though I'd eaten my fair share of the hollandaise previously (we always cooked one more than we needed, in case one popped open unexpectedly in the fryer), it tasted much better in the company of the custardlike eggs and crisp, meaty bacon. Of course, the fact that I was seated at a table with a glass of champagne, as opposed to standing over a kitchen counter, helped too.

We then tackled our entrées. Because the meat was cooked *sous-vide*, my mother's duck and father's lamb were perfectly medium rare throughout, and I finally tasted the soup in all its glory. The flavor combination was spot-on: sweet from the chestnut, tart from the verjuice and pear, earthy from the mackerel, and with a hint of fire from the horseradish. Once those dishes were cleared, we were served vanilla ice cream filled with a balsamic vinegar center and dusted with bright red raspberry streusel made from dehydrated raspberries, "compliments of Chef Ed."

"There wasn't any need to order dessert," Mom said, but I disagreed. I was incredibly curious about how the wd~50 philosophy would carry over into the pastry kitchen. Our waitress set a hazelnut-and-coconut-ganache tart garnished with chicory foam before me. My mother's caramelized brioche was filled with apricots and served with a lemon-thyme sorbet—a perfect expression of springtime. My father, true to form, ordered marc, a French brandy made from the stems of grape plants, which packs a wallop like jet fuel. But as the birthday boy, he also received a birthday "candle," which was a thin curved wafer surrounding a candle stuck into a meringue filled with root beer gel. The desserts were impressive and refined, but with a little less of the playfulness found in the savory items.

"No more!" my mother cried to our server when the mignardises—chocolate bonbons and "cocoa packets" given to VIP tables—arrived with the bill. "Can I take them home with me?"

"There's milk ice cream inside, so no," I told her.

"Well, I guess I'll have to eat it," she said, and we popped them into our mouths.

"That was certainly interesting," said my father after we'd

polished them all off. "Better than I expected," he added, leaning back in his chair. Coming from George " 'Stoic' is my middle name" Shockey, that meant he had thoroughly enjoyed the meal.

Anna returned to clear away the last of our plates. "Also, Chef has taken care of Lauren's food."

Wylie, true to form, had exceeded my expectations.

After my parents paid the bill (and left a tip generous enough to cover my food, as one should always do when food is comped), I gave my parents a tour of the kitchen, pointing out the different stations and introducing everyone. Wylie greeted them the way he greeted so many diners each night who wanted to see the open kitchen. Some guests who visited the kitchen were culinary school students who had saved up for a big night, and others were curious about its inner workings. And many were fans of the television show *Top Chef*, on which Wylie occasionally appeared as a guest judge, who posed with him for pictures to put on the refrigerator back home.

"Thanks so much. The food was great," my mom said, shaking Wylie's outstretched hand. "It seems so calm in here, too. I expected restaurant kitchens to be filled with shouting and chaos."

"Well, we try," said Wylie, laughing. He returned to his fish, and I escorted my parents to the downstairs kitchen and introduced them to Jared before sending them off.

"You're back?" Jared said when I returned to the kitchen, once again dressed in my full chef's outfit.

"Yeah, well, they didn't tell me I could leave, so...," I replied.

"What did you eat?"

"Just the lamb belly and the soup. And I had the hazelnut tart for dessert."

"The soup rocks, doesn't it? And the desserts are really the best part of wd~50." He paused, and then kitchen life returned to normal. "Okay, well, can you make a duck brine?"

All of the poultry on the menu was brined, meaning it sat for a certain amount of time in water that's been flavored with salt and sugar and maybe an extra spice or herb, which ultimately creates a much more flavorful product—essential when you're cooking something relatively bland like chicken or rabbit. I was astounded by the difference between brined and unbrined chicken and had taken to brining meats at home on the rare occasions I actually had an opportunity to cook dinner.

I had begun to assemble the thyme and garlic for the brine when Brian came downstairs and said, "What are you doing here?"

"You didn't say I could leave, so I thought I had to come back to work," I said.

Brian looked at me, shaking his head. "Well, kid, your stock just got raised with me," he said, and headed into the downstairs office.

A few minutes later, Wylie came downstairs and said in a bemused tone, "Lauren, what are you doing here?"

"I didn't know I could leave," I said for the third time, now embarrassed.

"You should have gone out for a celebratory drink with your parents," he said.

"Nah, Chef. I know where I'm *really* needed—right here in the prep kitchen," I joked, now comfortable enough with Wylie to let down my guard.

He laughed, then turned to address the whole kitchen. "Well, gang, it's our sixth-year anniversary tonight. In ten minutes we're having a toast upstairs."

Once Jared and I finished scrubbing down and putting away all of the *mise en place* for the following day, we went upstairs and were greeted with glasses of rosé champagne for everyone on staff. All of the diners had left, and jazz music was playing softly. With the chefs on one side and the waitstaff on the other, we formed a semicircle and Wylie raised his glass, saying, "I just wanted to thank you all for the past six years." He then toasted every person in the room individually, saying that if it took a village to raise a child, it took a whole lot of dedicated people to run a successful restaurant.

As we gathered to chat among ourselves, Tom came up to Jared and said, "Noodletown? Yes? Yes? I want to eat my face off."

"Yes, let's do it. Patrick, are you up for the Noodletown initiation?" he asked.

"Yeah, man. I'm game," replied Patrick.

New York Noodletown is a restaurant located on a slightly grungy corner in nearby Chinatown and is open until two thirty in the morning, making it popular with night owls, chefs, and people who don't make a lot of money. In short, wd~50 staffers.

"You come, too, Lauren," said Jared, nodding in my direction.

We hailed two taxis and I rode along with Tom and Spencer, who both looked exceptionally haggard. The staff had seemed particularly stressed recently, and still unbeknownst to Wylie, Spencer and Claire were both planning to quit in the upcoming weeks. Rumor had it that Jared wouldn't be far behind. The pressure of working in a restaurant of that caliber was getting to everyone, and if you poked in the right places, you'd feel a sense of unease running through the kitchen like electricity on a live wire.

"I'm sick of making no money," Spencer said in the cab.

"How much do you make, if you don't mind my asking?" I said.

"Five hundred and forty dollars a week. Tom only makes a

hundred dollars more," he said, nodding in Tom's direction. Tom replied with a head nod and a semi-raised eyebrow.

"Do you guys get benefits?"

"No," Spencer said with a snort.

I was floored—I was working sixty-hour weeks, and the others got to the restaurant about two hours before I did each day. So they were working seventy-to-eighty-hour weeks for $540, which averaged about $7.50 an hour. Which translated to roughly $.35 above minimum wage.

"Aren't you worried you're going to get hit by a car or something and be screwed without health insurance? God, five hundred and forty dollars...You can make more money in New York babysitting. Or dog walking. Like, four times that amount," I said.

"And I've been cooking for seven years!" exclaimed Spencer. "But it's not always been like this. Three years ago when I was back working in Chicago, I was making forty-five thousand bucks."

"That's not bad," I said, quickly calculating that it was at least $10,000 more than he was making now in New York City. I guess he figured that working at a prestigious restaurant like wd~50 was worth the salary cut in the short run and would substantially enhance his résumé in the long term. Still, though, Spencer had been cooking for seven years. Could I ever make a culinary career profitable and afford to live in a nice neighborhood in New York City?

Our taxi halted at the corner, and we all scrambled out. A neon yellow-and-green sign illuminated the otherwise dark street, and glistening roast ducks hanging upside down and pork bellies with crackling brown skin beckoned to us from the restaurant's window. We plopped ourselves down at one of the large circular tables in the middle of the restaurant and ignored the cups of tea in front of us, opting instead for cold bottles of Tsingtao beer.

Before we could remove our coats, Tom began ordering for the six of us: Spencer, Tom, Jared, Patrick, Patrick's girlfriend Karina, and me. Soon the table was loaded with a plate of juicy roast pork and roast chicken with ginger-scallion sauce, along with wonton soup with plump shrimp dumplings. Then came two orders of jumbo salt-baked shrimp with walnuts and mayonnaise, a small mountain of beef lo mein, roast duck sautéed with flowering chives, two orders of steamed Chinese greens covered in rich oyster sauce, pork fried rice, and the boys' favorite dish, Singapore chow fun. Two orders, of course.

Even though it was my third dinner of the evening, I dug into the food as though it were a race to see who could fill a plastic plate the fastest. Never slowing their brisk pace, Tom and Spencer deftly plucked one shrimp after another from the glass serving platter. As at any great meal, conversation slowed to a crawl as all eyes and mouths focused on the food: rich, salty, slightly greasy, and filling. This was real food, without fuss and intricate plating and knife skills involved—not to mention that the bill for the six of us was about what it would cost one person to dine at wd~50. We ate every last bite and stumbled out of the restaurant, bellies full and wanting nothing more than to fall asleep.

As we waited for taxis to shuttle us home, Jared turned to me and said, "You did good, Shockey. You held your own eating at the table, and we're masters at this. You even exceeded my expectations."

I smiled, for I knew I was now officially one of the group. Or as close to being part of the group as a girl could get. For this brief moment in time, over the bounty of the table, we weren't a ragtag team of stressed-out, hardened kitchen workers; we were friends. I wouldn't say we were now the best of friends, but we were edging closer, particularly because I rarely—if ever—saw any of my other friends, given my long hours during the week and on weekends. But our moment of bonding was fleeting; in just a few hours, we would have to get up, resume our spots on the kitchen hierarchy, and start cooking all over again.

wd~50 at Its Best

The recipes that follow are two of my favorites from the time that I was working at wd~50. As you can see, they are difficult—if not downright impossible—for the home cook. (They are also written in metric units, which are more precise than American units.) But I've included them because they let you see the amount of labor and precision with measurements that goes into making a dish at wd~50. I can't take any credit, though. These are Wylie's recipes through and through. Terra Spice Company (www.terraspice.com) sells the hard-to-find ingredients, while Kalustyan's (www.kalustyans.com) sells lemon confit. Each of these recipes serves a crowd.

EVERYTHING BAGEL; TROUT THREADS, CRISPY CREAM CHEESE

A take on the brunch staple of bagels and lox, this dish expresses Wylie's whimsy and playfulness with ingredients, while making use of several different techniques. Note for home cooks: You'll need a thermometer to measure the water temperature.

FOR THE TROUT THREADS:
25 grams kosher salt
25 grams sugar
250 grams ocean trout
45 grams kombu
2 liters water
Few drops of soy sauce
Few drops of mirin

Mix together the salt and sugar, and liberally cover the fish on both sides. Allow to sit for 2 hours, then rinse and pat dry.

Place the kombu in water in a pot and heat to 170 degrees F for 35 minutes, then place fish in water and cook through, about 8 to 10 minutes. Remove, pat dry, and crumble into small pieces.

Place a few drops of soy sauce and mirin in a large shallow pot over medium heat. Place fish inside and stir. Continue stirring constantly for about 1 hour, until trout becomes dry, light, and threadlike. Remove from heat and allow to cool. Place the threads in a cold smoker, smoke for 2 hours, and cool.

FOR THE CRISPY CREAM CHEESE:
200 grams cream cheese
100 grams water
6 grams methylcellulose (A4M)
1.5 grams kosher salt

Place the cream cheese in a heat-proof bowl. Bring the water to a boil and pour it into a high-quality blender like a Vita-Prep. Add the methylcellulose and salt, and then pour the mixture onto the cream cheese. Mix well and cool to 50 degrees F. Spread the mixture onto a silicone-lined baking sheet and place in a dehydrator set to 125 degrees F overnight. Break into irregular-sized shards and store in an airtight container.

FOR THE PICKLED PEARL ONIONS:
20 grams red wine vinegar
40 grams water
20 grams sugar
5 red pearl onions, peeled and sliced into rounds

Warm the vinegar and water, add sugar, and dissolve; cool mixture. Place onions in a vacuum bag with the pickling liquid and compress. Compress twice more, remove the pickled onions from the bag, and reserve.

FOR THE EVERYTHING BAGEL:
1 quart whole milk
2 everything bagels, toasted and crushed

Warm the milk and steep the bagels for 1½ hours; strain. (This should yield about 400 grams of bagel milk.)

5 egg yolks
50 grams sugar
10 grams glucose sugar
100 grams cream
400 grams bagel milk
.2 gram guar gum
Caramel coloring

Cream yolks, sugar, and glucose. Scald the cream and bagel milk, temper the yolk-and-sugar mixture, and proceed as you would for a classic ice cream. Cool the mixture over an ice bath. Once it's cooled, blend the milk solids and guar gum and churn in an ice cream maker.

Transfer the ice cream into a piping bag, pipe into a silicone miniature savarin or ring-shaped mold, and freeze. Once it's frozen, turn out and spray with an airbrush filled with caramel coloring so that the ice cream resembles a lightly toasted bagel. Store in the freezer until needed.

FOR SERVING:
Poppy seeds
Wood sorrel leaves

To serve, place the trout threads on a plate. Place a small pile of pickled pearl onions next to it. Coat each bagel with poppy seeds and place on top of trout. Garnish with wood sorrel leaves and shards of cream cheese.

LAMB BELLY, EGGPLANT, DATES, SMOKED FETA

This is one of the most complex dishes at wd~50 and one of the most delicious. As you'll see, you'll need a water bath with an immersion circulator to control the temperature, plus a good deep frying or candy thermometer.

FOR THE LAMB BELLY CURE:
200 grams kosher salt
200 grams brown sugar
25 grams Insta Cure No. 2
1 lamb belly, cleaned, ribs removed

Mix together the kosher salt, brown sugar, and Insta Cure, and cover the lamb belly in it on all sides for 24 hours. Rinse thoroughly under cold running water. Place lamb in vacuum bag and seal. Cook in a water bath at 69 degrees C (156.2 degrees F) for 12 hours, or until tender. Rest the lamb and press flat while icing it. After the lamb has cooled, preheat the oven at 250 degrees F. Slice the lamb in a meat slicer on number 5 setting. Lay the lamb belly slices on a silicone-lined sheet pan, place another silicone baking sheet on top, and bake for 1 hour and 15 minutes. Remove from oven and pat off excess fat. Cool and store.

FOR THE CUCUMBER RELISH:
4 cucumbers, seeded
10 grams lemon confit, diced
1 lemon, juiced
Kosher salt and citric acid to taste

Pulse all of the ingredients in a professional food processor. Place in *chinois* or fine-meshed sieve for 30 minutes to allow all excess water to drain; save the drained liquid. Check the seasoning of the relish and store.

FOR THE CUCUMBER SAUCE:
Drained cucumber juice from relish
4 percent Ultra-Sperse 3 (4 percent of cucumber juice weight)
.3 percent xanthan gum (.3 percent of cucumber juice weight)

Place all of the ingredients in a high-quality blender and blend until smooth.

FOR THE EGGPLANT PUREE:
1500 grams eggplant, roasted
75 grams tahini
30 grams honey-garlic slices (thinly sliced garlic that has been
  preserved in honey for at least 3 months)
30 grams honey-garlic liquid
70 grams shallot confit
3 grams lemon confit
12 grams lemon juice
Kosher salt

Prick the eggplant all over, then roast it at 350 degrees F until fully cooked. Discard the top, and place in a blender along with all the other ingredients. Puree until smooth. Season with salt, cool, and store.

FOR THE DEHYDRATED DATES:
250 grams Medjool dates

Press Medjool dates and dehydrate for 6 to 12 hours at 150 degrees F. Once cooled, julienne.

FOR THE SMOKED FETA:
500 grams feta
.5 percent Ultra-Sperse 3 (2.5 grams)

Cold-smoke the feta and blend it with the Ultra-Sperse 3. Roll into desired shape and dehydrate for 2 to 3 hours at 150 degrees F. Cool and refrigerate.

FOR SERVING:
Canola oil

To serve, fry the lamb belly in canola oil at 375 degrees F for 45 seconds to 1 minute. Press the lamb belly flat and pat with a paper towel to remove excess fat. Fry the feta in canola oil at 375 degrees F for 30 seconds, until golden brown. Reheat the eggplant puree. Smear the eggplant puree on the center of the plate in a rectangle. On the left-hand side of the smear, place a quenelle of cucumber relish. Stand three slices of lamb belly on their sides in the eggplant puree and place one slice flat across the top at a 95-degree angle. Place the feta between the lamb belly slices and on top of the flat slice. Dot the cucumber sauce around and sprinkle on the sliced dates. Serve.

Chapter 4

SUNDAYS WERE OUR BIG NIGHTS for going out, but we often hit the town Fridays and Saturdays after work to experience "real people weekends." The Clerkenwell, a British gastropub, had just opened across the street and was quickly becoming one of our regular watering holes. This Saturday, when I walked out of the restaurant to meet everyone, I realized I was the last one.

"Let's go," said Tom. "Without the *stage!*"

"Oh, Tom, you're going to miss me when I'm gone," I replied. Only a few weeks of my *stage* remained at wd~50, two full months having whizzed by.

Claire whispered to me, "You know, he really will."

At the bar, I grabbed a stool next to Spencer, who said, "What's your poison? Whiskey? It's on me."

"You don't have to buy me a drink, but thanks."

"Ugh, Wylie is going to hate me soon. I just don't know when is the best time to tell him about leaving," he said after taking a big swig of his drink. He had just finalized his decision to move back to Chicago come summertime and was holding off telling Wylie.

"You need to do what's right for you. If Chicago's where you need to be, you can't feel bad about that. Plus that's where your lady friend is, right?" I said. Although I had initially considered Spencer as a potential prospect for a kitchen romance, I abandoned the idea when he told me that he had decided to give his relationship with his ex-girlfriend in Chicago another try.

"Yeah, all true. And I'll have my own apartment there, and I'll make more money," he said.

"Do you think that they'll bring Jared upstairs to replace you?" I said.

"Jared's put himself in a tough position because he runs the prep kitchen so well that there's no one really who can replace him. I mean, he could be good upstairs, but he needs to spend more than one day up there," said Spencer. During my time at wd~50, Jared had worked upstairs only once, and even though I was a *stagiaire*, I wondered if maybe Jared was jealous of my being up there so frequently. Jared had told me he was hurt when Patrick was hired to replace Tom on *garde manger* even though Jared had worked at wd~50 for over a year and was ready to move upstairs.

"Yeah, for sure," I said.

"When he was up there, he was so bad he didn't know how bad he was. He was constantly joking around with Tom and didn't know how anything was plated."

"It must be tough, though," I said, wanting to defend Jared. "I was just thinking about how long it would take to train someone to run the prep kitchen."

"You know, Brian asked me and Jared the other day if you'd be interested in that job. But we said we didn't think you were, or are you?"

I was thrilled to hear this but replied, "I don't think wd~50 is the place for me. It's been great working here, but I want a restaurant that focuses more on taste."

This was true, and by now I had decided to head to Vietnam,

to apprentice under Didier Corlou, who (at least from what I'd read and heard) valued flavor and spice first and foremost in his cooking. Was it ridiculous to turn down a job offer to pursue another unpaid *stage*? No, I reasoned. Although wd~50 could teach me technique until the sun came up, that wasn't all there was to cooking. Sure, I was learning about esoteric combinations—eel and Campari, octopus and pine nut, miso and sunflower—but these pairings didn't always impress me. For the most part they worked, but sometimes they just tasted odd. I wanted to immerse myself in cooking by taste rather than chemistry.

"Did you get a lot out of working here?" asked Spencer.

"Sure. I feel like I can walk into any restaurant kitchen and hold my own. I can't believe I didn't know how to hold a knife properly before. How do you graduate from culinary school not knowing how to hold a knife?"

"I remember that. It was like your first or second day and you were holding it like this—" Spencer twisted his knuckle awkwardly around an invisible knife.

"I'm still slow, but not nearly as slow as I was," I said. "And yes, sometimes I wish I had done more cooking, but you guys don't even do that much cooking. It's all measuring out the same ingredients day after day and making the same things over and over."

"Oh, so you've learned the sad, unglamorous truth of restaurant cooking," he said.

⁙~⁚

A FEW DAYS LATER, while waiting for the rest of the cooks to finish getting dressed after service, I went outside to enjoy the cool spring breeze. Jared was leaning against the brick wall, smoking his ritual after-work cigarette. "Lauren, I have to say I'm going to miss you when you're gone. You do good work."

"Thanks, it's really nice to hear that. I definitely feel like I've improved," I said.

"If this is the kind of job that you want, I think you could do it. You just have to really want it," he said.

"Yeah, we'll see," I said, wondering how much Jared wanted it and how much I did.

"But don't do it here."

Jared was alluding to the greatest problem with molecular gastronomy and the reason I had decided I couldn't work full-time at wd~50: It was simply too focused on technique. While the restaurant had innovated some great technique-based dishes—fried hollandaise and mayonnaise, barbecued lentils, aerated foie gras, shrimp noodles—molecular gastronomy is a lot like a party trick: exciting the first time you see it, but far less mesmerizing once the initial novelty has worn off.

Throughout my time at wd~50, I often questioned the lasting impact of this type of experimental cuisine and wondered if most diners preferred an experience that comforts and soothes with flavor or one that surprises and shocks with technique. Which experience is more memorable and which is more meaningful?

I think the answer is that diners do generally prefer a meal that comforts and soothes; when you're paying a significant amount of money on dinner, you want to walk away satiated and pleased. I mean, we're biologically conditioned to enjoy food that tastes good. However, going to a place like wd~50 will certainly be a more memorable dining experience than going to a restaurant to eat seared tuna steak followed by chocolate cake. It's true that not everything is delicious at wd~50, but I don't think that's the restaurant's sole purpose. Wylie pushes boundaries and intellectualizes the meal; his cuisine engenders a timely discourse about food and restaurants.

"I know," I said to Jared. Indeed, the wd~50 experience isn't one that you want every day—as a diner, certainly, but also as a cook. I had wanted so much to work at wd~50 that I waited six months to work twelve-hour days for free. Now I was ready to move on and find a kitchen experience that would constantly excite me and that allowed for a different kind of creative expression.

⌇

ON MY FINAL DAY at wd~50, I arrived in the prep kitchen to find it buzzing with people. Jared was breading sticks of "mayonnaise" (similar to the fried hollandaise cubes but log-shaped and less eggy) for "the Wylie Dog," an homage to Wylie in hot dog form consisting of a fried hot dog with fried mayonnaise, tomato molasses, and freeze-dried onions. These would be served at PDT, a nearby bar where Wylie had a standing weekly reservation. Because the bar didn't have the capacity to make the fried mayonnaise or tomato molasses, we sent them over every week. Mathias, the pastry *stagiaire*, had transferred over to the savory kitchen to take my place and was cutting melon into a tiny dice, while another new *stagiaire* was cleaning the never-ending supply of ramps. Hector sliced cauliflower on a mandolin to make into chips, while Tom cleaned fish for an *amuse* he was preparing. Not a single work space was free.

"Go upstairs this week. See something new. Tell them to teach you some cool shit," said Jared.

I did it. Finally. After three months of sunless days that transitioned seamlessly into nights without my noticing, I was going upstairs. For the *whole* day.

It turned out that working upstairs was much like working downstairs, except that the ingredients were different and we listened to docked iPods blasting The Band or Tom Waits instead of the La Mega radio station's hit list of Spanish-language music (somehow, the top ten songs hadn't changed during my three months at the restaurant). Upstairs, instead of chopping endive, I sliced Asian celery into thin strips and soaked them in ice water so that they magically curled up like Rapunzel's ringlets. I quarted up buttermilk whey instead of long beans. But Patrick and Spencer had me doing some "real" cooking, too, or at least creating components of dishes from start to finish. Using the gram scale (nicknamed Pablo since it was frequently used to measure tiny amounts of white powders), I weighed out the chemical Ultra-Sperse 3 and added it to cucumber juice to form the gel-like sauce served with the lamb belly. I made the Asian celery financier cake from start to finish without a stitch of help, and I learned my way around the wall of chemicals, now fully understanding the difference between gellan high, xanthan, and methylcellulose. (In case you ever get this question on a quiz show: Gellan high helps turn a liquid into a gummy gel, like when we turned the hollandaise base into a gel so that it was easy to coat with bread crumbs but would melt into a liquid when fried; xanthan helps to thicken sauces or foods like the carrot puree, which can stand up on the plate without running all over the place; and methylcellulose turns a liquid brittle and paperlike, such as in the cream cheese paper on the everything bagel dish.) As it turned out, there wasn't much difference between Ultra-Sperse 3 and Ultra-Tex 3; both are just tapioca starches, though the latter is used more when a glossy, smooth, and creamy end product is desired.

Spencer even entrusted me with the task of cleaning the oh-so-expensive lobes of shiny foie gras, showing me how to massage out the bloodlines from the liver with my thumbs. The trick to cleaning foie gras is to first separate the lobes at the natural breaking point, then massage the lobes with your fingertips, pressing around the ruby red bloodlines until they reach the surface. Then you gently place your finger under the bloodline and run it along the bottom until you can lift out the whole bloodline while leaving the lobe intact (albeit somewhat smushed, like Silly Putty under a school desk). If you break the lobe into several pieces, it's more likely that little bits of the bloodline will get trapped inside, which will impact the dish's final flavor and be unsightly for the diner. It took me several tries, and even Wylie himself had to demonstrate how to do it properly. But finally I mastered it, deftly plucking out the unseemly red strands and placing the lobes on a baking sheet, where I seasoned them with cognac, salt, and pepper and placed them in the oven.

Best of all, I cooked on the wd~50 stove, making a sunflower seed brittle for the new cold miso-sunflower soup. Patrick explained the procedure as I took notes, and then he let me be. My kitchen nerves weren't completely gone, but I took my time and double-checked my actions to ensure that everything would go smoothly. I poured isomalt, which is similar to sugar, into a large pan over high heat to melt it. When it formed a clear syrup, I added the sunflower seeds and quickly stirred the mixture, then poured it into a rectangular-shaped pan. The trick with the brittle is to flatten it quickly before it hardens by pressing down on it with another pan so it's uniform in shape. I pressed down hard on the pan, but my brittle wasn't flattening.

"Just stand on it," said Patrick, who was sautéing garlic and onions in a pot next to me.

So I placed the pan on the floor and stood on it, shifting my body weight back and forth as though I were surfing on the kitchenware. Wylie laughed across the kitchen.

"What? Patrick told me to do it this way," I said.

"Patrick, you pick the lightest person in the kitchen for that job?" he said, shaking his head in amused disbelief. But it worked: The brittle came out perfectly. After it had cooled to the touch, I chopped it into small pieces and tossed it in a mesh sieve with a dust made from ground shiitake mushrooms. When finished, the pieces of brittle resembled scraggly rocks and tasted nutty and earthy, with just a touch of sweetness.

My last service was so hectic that it flew by, with two parties of eleven guests each, but it didn't feel any different from any other. The nightly "'Order in, foie, octo, benny,' 'Service, please, two bagels to table eleven,' 'One up on twenty-two,' 'Order in, four tasting,' 'Start plating those scallops and then go on to the eel,' 'Another four, eight all day,' 'Service, please, table thirty-two, benny one, shrimp two,' 'How's table twenty-seven doing with their foie?' 'Start setting up for six scallops,'" played as it did every night in the kitchen, a seamless if chaotic song and dance among cooks and servers. And then it was over, and I found myself wiping down the kitchen for the last time.

While I scrubbed caked-on egg yolk off the counter, Jared appeared and asked, "Do you have a cocktail?"

The keg had been tapped, and plastic quart containers of flat beer were lining the countertop, waiting to be drunk. "A cocktail? No," I replied.

Jared called out to Scott as he was leaving the manager's office, located in the hallway next to the prep kitchen. "Scott, get her a cocktail. It's her last day," he said.

Scott said, "What would you like?"

"Something delicious," I said, intrigued by the expertly prepared signature cocktails, which used intriguing ingredients like beet juice, yuzu, and Cynar.

Scott returned and handed me a martini glass filled with light brown liquor. "A perfect rye Manhattan," he said. It was perfect: clean and smooth, with a tiny brandied cherry resting at the bottom of the glass.

Patrick held up his quart container of beer and clinked my glass. "It was great working with you."

"Thanks," I said, well aware that not all the *stagiaires* got acknowledgments or thanks. Most got slight head nods and a "See you around, man." Some simply got shown the door.

Brian joined us in the kitchen, holding an ice-filled tumbler that held his yuzu cocktail, one of his favorite drinks he had once let me taste.

"Whose is that?" he asked, looking at my half-drunk Manhattan on the counter.

"Mine," I said.

"Who gave that to you?"

"Um, Jared said I could have it," I said, nervous I was going to get in trouble on my last night.

But Brian smiled. "It's already your last day?"

"Time flies in the kitchen." I refrained from mentioning that it's especially true when you're in a windowless basement with no frame of reference to the actual time of day.

Overhearing us, Wylie left his office to shake my hand and bid me farewell. Seeing his outstretched hand, I said, "I wanted to thank you for everything. I know I was really green when I started out, but I've definitely learned a lot. A whole lot."

"You're still green. I'm just sorry you had to work with some of these crazy boys," said Wylie, smiling.

"It's cool. They were the brothers I never had," I said. I took a final look around the kitchen and said to Wylie, "I'm a hugger. Let's hug good-bye!"

After three months, Wylie didn't scare me anymore. Well, maybe I was still afraid of unleashing his ire, and I remained in wondrous awe of his culinary innovation, but I wasn't afraid of him as a person. He was just a dude who cooked for a living. A highly talented dude, of course, but still an average dude. Although I'd spent my first weeks in the kitchen trying to avoid him and praying he wouldn't have an opportunity to point out my errors, I now stood on my tiptoes and flung my arms around him. Working at wd~50 had been a trial by fire, but I had made it through relatively unscathed. And now, no longer intimidated by Wylie—or, even more important, of the restaurant kitchen—I wanted more.

Bringing wd~50 Home

What makes wd~50 a great restaurant is that it offers you food and an experience that you cannot create at home. Not unless your home includes an army of assistants, a bevy of chemicals, and specialty equipment ranging from dehydrators to immersion circulators. And truthfully, at the end of the day I don't want to be measuring out .6 grams of xanthan to add to my carrot puree. The recipes that follow use the flavors and the simplest techniques employed in some of wd~50's dishes and are ways in which I can bring a bit of wd~50 to my kitchen table.

DORITOS CONSOMMÉ, SHRIMP, SMOKED CORN, CILANTRO

Making a gelatin clarification is a laborious process compared with the traditional technique of using egg whites, but the end result—crystal-clear liquid with no trace of egg flavor—is worth it, and you can basically make a consommé out of anything. Anything. Even Doritos. Smoking is another popular technique at wd~50 (Wylie once even made smoked mashed potatoes), but for the home cook who doesn't have a smoker, adding a bit of smoked paprika to whatever you're making will give it that outdoorsy, barbecue flavor.

SERVES 4

FOR THE CONSOMMÉ:
8 cups Doritos Cool Ranch–Flavored Tortilla Chips
10 cups water
½ teaspoon powdered gelatin

FOR THE GARNISH:
⅓ cup fresh corn kernels
½ cup water
2 teaspoons smoked paprika
4 jumbo shrimp
Kosher salt and freshly ground pepper
2 teaspoons vegetable oil
1 tablespoon microcilantro leaves (or regular cilantro leaves)

In a large pot, combine the Doritos with 8 cups water. Bring to a boil, mashing the Doritos with a wooden spoon until the mixture looks mushy. Turn off the heat and let steep for 30 minutes. Strain the soup using a fine-meshed sieve, and discard the solids. You should have about 4½ cups of thick liquid. Wipe out the used pot and return the soup to it. Bring to a boil.

Meanwhile, dissolve the gelatin in the remaining 2 cups of water. When the soup reaches a boil, add the water and stir until the gelatin is dissolved. Pour into a container and freeze until solid, about 6 hours to overnight.

Unmold the frozen soup from its container and place it in a colander lined with two layers of cheesecloth. You may need to break up the block of frozen soup into several pieces. Place the colander in a bowl so that the frozen liquid can drip out. Leave in the refrigerator until the soup has melted completely, about 2 to 3 days. The gelatin will trap all the particulate matter in the cheesecloth, and the resulting liquid will be clear and Doritos flavored. If desired, you can let the colander rest for a few hours at room temperature to help speed up the melting process, but you don't want to exceed more than a few hours since the gelatin may melt as well. Return the consommé to a pot and heat until almost boiling.

Place the corn, water, and smoked paprika in a small saucepan and bring to a boil. Drain the corn and set aside.

Peel and devein the shrimp and season them lightly with salt and pepper. Heat the vegetable oil in a small skillet over high heat. When the pan begins to smoke, add the shrimp and sear on each side for about 2 to 3 minutes. Blot off any remaining oil on a paper towel.

To serve, place one shrimp each in the center of four serving bowls. Fill with the hot consommé, then add a few spoonfuls of corn to the consommé and garnish with the cilantro. Serve immediately.

PICKLED SCALLIONS

This recipe uses wd~50's technique for pickling ramps but substitutes the more readily available scallions. These are great on sandwiches or burgers or as a distinctive canapé at a summertime party. The pickled scallions should keep for several weeks covered in the refrigerator. Feel free to substitute your favorite pickling vegetables for the scallions.

SERVES 4 TO 8 AS A GARNISH

2 cups water
1 cup rice vinegar
1 cup sugar
4 teaspoons kosher salt
2 cloves
2 teaspoons yellow mustard seed
2 teaspoons black peppercorns
2 teaspoons minced fresh ginger
1 teaspoon chile flakes
2 teaspoons coriander seed
1 pound scallions, bottom roots trimmed off (about 3 bunches)

In a large pot, combine all ingredients except the scallions and bring to a boil. Turn off the heat and let steep 1 hour. Strain, discard the spices, and return the liquid to the pot. Bring back to a boil.

Place the scallions in a container and pour the boiling liquid over them. When cool, cover and refrigerate until ready to eat.

SEARED SCALLOPS WITH PARSLEY SAUCE AND PORK RINDS

This recipe plays on the flavors in the scallop dish served on the tasting menu but simplifies the process for the home cook.

Pork rinds can usually be found in the potato chip aisle at major supermarkets or corner delis.

SERVES 4

> 2 tablespoons unsalted butter
> 1 onion, roughly chopped
> 2 cloves garlic
> 1 shallot, roughly chopped
> 1 clove
> 1 bay leaf
> 1 cup white grape juice
> 1 cup chicken stock
> 1 large bunch parsley, stems chopped off
> Kosher salt for seasoning
> 2 tablespoons olive oil
> 1 pound sea scallops
> 1 cup pork rinds
> 1 Meyer lemon or regular lemon

In a saucepan over medium heat, melt the butter. Add the onion, garlic, shallot, clove, and bay leaf. Cook for about 5 minutes, or until the vegetables have softened (but don't let them brown). Add the grape juice and chicken stock, and bring to a boil. Cook until only ½ cup liquid remains, about 30 minutes. Strain and discard the solids.

Bring a small pot of water to a boil, then add the parsley. After a minute, strain and submerge the parsley in ice water to stop the cooking process. Remove the parsley and squeeze out any excess water. In a food processor, combine the grape juice liquid with the parsley and puree until smooth. Season with salt to taste.

Heat the olive oil in a skillet until smoking. Season the scallops with a little salt, then add to the pan and cook until nicely seared, about 1 minute. Flip and cook on the other side. You may need to do this in two batches so as not to crowd the pan.

Spoon a small pool of parsley sauce in the center of each of four plates. Place a portion of the scallops onto each plate, add 2 to 3 pork rinds next to the scallops, and zest the lemon atop each plate.

La Verticale

19 NGO VAN SO STREET

HANOI, VIETNAM

Chapter 5

"SO YOU'RE GOING TO HANOI to learn to cook Vietnamese food from a Frenchman? That seems a little silly, doesn't it? Why don't you just go down to Chinatown to Nha Trang?" my mother asked when I told her and my father about my plans. Nha Trang was our go-to spot for Vietnamese food, and although I loved it, I knew it wouldn't be the same as actually being in Vietnam.

"Mom, I want to learn from the best. Everyone I've asked who knows anything about Vietnamese food has told me to work for Didier Corlou. He is French, but he supposedly has an amazing understanding of the country's flavors and recipes. More than any Vietnamese chef I could find. And it's not like I can speak Vietnamese," I said.

"Ironic, isn't it? I spent my youth trying desperately to avoid going to Vietnam, and now all you want is to go there," my father said.

"Times change. I bet the country bears no resemblance to Vietnam back then," I said.

"You're probably right," he conceded.

"I just don't want you on the other side of the world cooking in some ramshackle hut on the side of some godforsaken road," said my mom in her best mother hen voice, as though she'd forgotten that I had basically been living on my own since college.

"La Verticale is a nice place, Mom, one of the best in Hanoi. I mean, if I could have gone and cooked pho in a hut, I would have. But it's not like I have a way to contact those types of places. I did the best research I could using guidebooks and the Internet, but the corner pho joint obviously doesn't have a website address. Besides, I still have some savings, and the cost of living is going to be much cheaper there than in New York. So it's almost like I'll actually be saving money," I said enthusiastically.

"Almost," said my mother, while my father raised an eyebrow.

"It's what I need right now."

"We aren't going to stop you. Just be careful over there."

And that's how I found myself in the thick of a sweltering Hanoi summer, with two boxes of latex gloves, my knives, a Vietnamese dictionary, and lots of mosquito repellent in tow.

⟢⟿

"YOU NEED TO CALL A TAXI to get downtown to the restaurant. If you hail one off the street, you'll probably get scammed. I'll give you the number for the company I use," said Belinda, the bubbly Australian handbag designer who was my new housemate.

Before leaving New York, I had placed an ad on an expat website for a furnished room for rent. Belinda's friendly response offered me not only a large air-conditioned ("the most essential necessity in Hanoi, from April to September," she wrote) bedroom with an en suite bathroom in a three-story villa, but also an invitation to show me around Hanoi, to meet her social circle, and to navigate the eccentricities of expat life. Hav-

ing moved to Hanoi six months before, she had settled in Tay
Ho, an expat enclave just north of the city center whose quiet,
tree-lined streets of gated villas surrounded the city's largest
lake. Given its Western-style minimarts offering these temporary foreign visitors a taste of home wrapped in cellophane, I
was at first skeptical of the location, but Belinda had explained
that downtown Hanoi was noisy and hectic, and Tay Ho offered
a welcome respite from all that.

I popped into the taxi, which soon sped past brightly lit storefronts filled with a dizzying array of wares for sale in the Old
Quarter. Trees swayed over tangles of phone and electricity
lines, shading the motorbike drivers who perched languidly
across their bikes, which were parked willy-nilly in the middle of
the sidewalk. "Moto! Motorbike!" they shouted to any foreigner
passing by. When we reached the center of town, I saw more
and more signage written in English for tours and day trips to
Ha Long Bay and Sapa, along with the tanned and beer-fueled
backpackers who purchased them. Incessant honking from
the thousands of whizzing motorbikes drowned out the humming of the taxi's air conditioner. But after sitting in traffic for
five minutes in the heart of the Old Quarter, we soon drove by
stately, colonial-era villas and several tranquil lakes, glistening a
magical silver blue under the intense rays of the sun, while old
men played badminton or read newspapers along the banks.

Just south of Hoan Kiem Lake in the city center, Didier's
restaurant, La Verticale, is housed in a lemon yellow villa on
Ngo Van So Street in a quiet neighborhood resplendent with
embassies and a few modern office buildings. Upon entering,
I recognized Didier from the picture on his website and introduced myself. Sweat beads formed a crown around his shiny
forehead, but he appeared affable and much younger than his
fifty-something years.

"Ah, Lauren. Our *stagiaire*. Just starting out your career. An exciting time in one's life. So tell me, what would you like to learn here at La Verticale?" he said to me in French as we sat at a table on the terrace.

"Um, I was working at a restaurant in New York that did a sort of experimental cuisine," I said. Although I knew he had seen my résumé, I doubted he had scanned it for more than a few seconds.

"You mean molecular gastronomy? I don't like that type of cuisine. Food should be able to nourish you. With all those powders, I don't know...," he said, slightly dismayed.

"Yes, it was a great learning experience, but I decided it wasn't the type of food I wanted to specialize in," I said.

"So why Hanoi? Do you have a connection to the place, or any family history here?"

"No, I just wanted to learn to cook in a place that was completely different from New York, and live somewhere I had never been before," I said.

I also wanted to go to a country that hadn't yet been completely tainted by globalization and commercialization. Somewhere that was exotic and a little rough around the edges, where everyday necessities weren't readily available. Perhaps this wanderlust came from my childhood years in Budapest. My parents and I had moved there in the winter of 1993, when Hungary was slowly shaking off its outdated, drab Communist facade. My father's law firm had sent him over to help the Hungarian government privatize its banks and public infrastructure to get the country up to speed with the rest of world that hadn't been locked behind the iron curtain. He had spent the previous year alone there, and when he realized that the project would require another two, my mother and I packed up our New York life and went along for the ride.

While today's Budapest rivals any other European capital, back then, and especially during the interminable winters, a somber grayness blanketed the city. Even grocery shopping proved a daily challenge. On our first full day on our own, Mom and I trudged through the knee-deep snow to the local supermarket at Batthyány tér. When we approached the meat counter, we asked for a *"csirka"* after consulting our Hungarian dictionary for the translation of chicken and were met by the butcher's pasty-faced, blank stare. Undaunted and desperate to provide me with a semblance of an American-style dinner, my mother tucked her hands under her armpits and imitated a chicken's clucking sounds. Finally the butcher grasped what we wanted. He disappeared into a back room, returning with a shorn chicken whose gnarled yellow feet were still attached. He placed it on a sheet of newspaper, wrapped it halfheartedly so that the legs dangled out of the paper, and handed it to her with a grunt. Our search for salad ingredients proved even more elusive, as lettuce wasn't available. We might now embrace the locavore ideals of eating seasonally and locally, but let me tell you, eating Hungary's cabbage—bland, greenish gray, and limp—for nine months out of the year got old really quickly.

As a ten-year-old, I quickly resented Budapest and nagged my mother about what I missed from home: my friends, cable television, stores that were open on the weekends, potato chips that weren't exclusively paprika flavored. Nostalgia, of course, alters our memory, and over time, it's easy to forget the daily aggravations and hardships. I now relish my two years in Hungary as a period that helped shape me, and I see the beauty of living in a country at a crossroads. In many ways, I found parallels between Budapest of the early 1990s and the Vietnam of 2009. Vietnam remains a staunchly Communist country, at least politically, but it has embraced economic market reforms accompanied by a powerful private sector. Daily life in Hanoi, I soon learned, was still slow and fraught with bureaucratic and infrastructural annoyances, but foreign capital was pouring into the country. It was an ephemeral moment in time for a country, and I wanted to be there to see it.

This explanation seemed too complex for me to tell Didier, though, especially in French, so I said, "I was attracted by the fresh flavors of Vietnamese cuisine, and intrigued to see if there were any lasting vestiges of France's culinary legacy. I've read a lot about your influence on Hanoi's food scene and how you helped bring upscale Vietnamese cuisine to new audiences."

Didier nodded approvingly and then led me on a tour of the restaurant. I had read about La Verticale in my trusty Vietnam guidebook, and its description rang true to form: The restaurant occupied a refurbished colonial four-story structure, with dining rooms on two floors and a rooftop bar on top that overlooked the city. As we climbed the staircase that spiraled up the stories, Didier pointed at the framed photographs on the walls and said, "These are all the generations of my family. France and Vietnam, together here. You know, family is very important to me. My wife, Mai, even tastes all my recipes before I put them on the menu."

We wended our way to the second-floor dining room, and he pointed out the orange hanging light fixtures, the white walls, the golden yellow abstract sculptures against the wall, and the black-and-white-tiled floor. "This room is decorated in five colors to represent the five seasons," said Didier.

"There are five seasons?" I replied.

"*Oui, bien sûr.* In the Vietnamese culture, there's also a fifth season, which is known as the transition season. You see, you must have the spirit of the place, of the country, even in the little details like the decor," he said.

"How many days a week do you want me to work?" I asked after Didier showed me the other dining room on the third floor and then the open-air rooftop bar on the fourth floor, whose comfy brown leather chairs and views of the city's rooftops channeled the stately charm of colonial Hanoi.

"This is your *stage*. Make of it what you want," he said, shrugging.

"Okay, maybe lunch and dinner, Monday through Friday?" I said.

"No problem. Do just mornings this week, though. Come tomorrow at ten and we'll see how next week is," replied Didier. It sounded good to me: After the intensity of wd~50, I was ready for something a bit more low-key.

AS I APPROACHED the restaurant the following morning, I saw that it was dark, as were all the shops along the street. "The electricity is out," Didier said after I greeted him. "I think they're working on the street or something, but it's annoying. Have a glass of ice water. You look very hot."

"It's not too bad," I demurred, although I was already dripping in sweat from this furnacelike heat, more powerful than a New York City subway platform in the dog days of August.

"I guess you can stay. You can get dressed in the locker room in the back," he said, leading me into the kitchen, where it couldn't have been any cooler than a hundred degrees, even at ten in the morning. He introduced me to the kitchen staff before leaving to deal with the electricity. Thanh, one of the head cooks, was wide-eyed and welcoming as he shook my hand. He spoke very broken English but smiled as he handed me a daikon radish to peel. Unlike the Swiss peeler I was used to, the Vietnamese peeler was a single blade affixed to the end of a wooden handle and required a peeling motion away from the body. I began peeling the daikon the wrong way, stubbing the white flesh with the blade. Yen, a wisp of a girl who came to my eye level, shook her head at me gently and demonstrated the right way. I thanked her in English, but my face flushed with embarrassment.

Next, two large bowls of shallots and garlic cloves awaited my cleaning, trimming, and mincing. The shallots were the tiniest I'd ever seen, no larger than the size of my pinky nail. The cooks wielded cleavers, but I stuck to my Western-style knives.

At eleven o'clock, Son, one of the cooks whose intense, brooding expression belied his warmth, took off his white apron and announced, "Okay, now we go to lunch." Didier had explained that the staff ate at a canteen around the corner because the restaurant lacked space for a family meal. So the restaurant staff, about fifteen of us, trooped to a dusty storefront that probably dated back to the days before Ho Chi Minh. Didier, though, I would soon learn, ate a light dish from the menu by either Chien or Thanh after the lunch service ended. The staircase leading to the canteen's second floor creaked as we walked, but once we reached the top, a huge buffet of home-style Vietnamese food confronted us. An elderly female server whose face had the texture of a sun-dried tomato and whose smile was punctuated with gummy gaps ladled out rice from a gargantuan pot while clouds of steam rose to the ceiling's wooden beams. I followed Thanh's lead and approached her before hitting the buffet tables. She grinned enthusiastically as she reached in for another scoop, but I shook my head no. One mountain of rice on the plate was all I could handle. I skipped over a tray containing a heap of small, pearly white ridged creatures that I was certain were fried maggots and spooned up boiled daikon, banana leaf salad, tofu with tomato sauce, and three balls of ground pork wrapped in betel leaves.

"Nem, nem," said another server, accosting me before I could sit down. She resembled the older woman, and I figured this was probably a family-run restaurant with all the generations pitching in. She placed two fried spring rolls on my plate.

"So, Lauren, tell us about you," said Son in clear English as I joined him and Thanh at a small table. Luckily, the electricity worked at this eatery, and a lazy fan stirred the stagnant air, sweeping the pungent aromas of chile-flecked fish sauce under our noses.

I told them the basics: growing up in New York, going to school in Chicago, and my experience working at wd~50. Then I quickly shifted the conversation back to them. "Are you from Hanoi?" I asked. I was curious about their lives, how they had ended up as cooks, and whether culinary career trajectories differed significantly here from back in New York.

"No, from the country," said Son.

"How long have you worked at La Verticale?"

"Almost two years, since it opened."

"Do you eat lunch here every day?"

"Yes, and dinner, too. But dinner, it is not as good as lunch because this restaurant is for businessmen and at night they go home," he explained.

"Is it easy to buy a gun in a store in America?" Thanh asked out of the blue.

"I don't know. I think so, especially in rural areas. But I don't know anyone who owns a gun."

"America, lots of gangs, very dangerous," he said.

"Well, sometimes," I said. The news is censored in Vietnam, and its citizens are treated to highlights about the benevolence

of the reigning Communist Party along with occasional dia-
tribes about Western immorality. My new co-workers asked me
if I had been in New York on September 11 and why I wanted
to learn how to cook Vietnamese food in Hanoi. They peppered me with questions about the weather and the difference
between a state and a city.

"What are your hobbies?" asked Son.

"I play squash, and I like to cook, and I like to go to the movies," I said.

"Movies? I like romantic comedies. And action films. And
learning English is my hobby," Son said proudly, without any
tinge of irony. I had already sensed that these were good, genuine people, not as hardened and stressed as wd~50's cooks, and I
hoped we would become fast friends.

Before I knew it, the half hour had passed, and we headed
back to La Verticale to set up for the lunch service. Didier's
lunch menu featured a set three courses for $13, which included
an appetizer, entrée, dessert, and glass of wine, although it was
possible to order just an entrée plus appetizer or dessert for
$11 or simply an entrée for $8. Like most upscale restaurants
in Hanoi, La Verticale quoted its prices in U.S. dollars, clearly
catering to the town's expats and tourists. The contemporary
Vietnamese (with some French accents) menu changed weekly
and included dishes like fish salad with coconut milk, chef's
pâté with three peppers, or a spicy seafood soup flecked with
local mushrooms and seaweed as appetizers; entrées might
be veal three ways with lime or Hanoi's famous bun cha pork
dish, served "Verticale style." Didier offered an à la carte menu
at lunch and dinner, but since it was more expensive, people
rarely ordered from it at lunch, although it featured what I'd
gathered were Didier's specialties: wild prawn spring rolls, Da
Lat artichokes with clams, ocean escabeche, and beef yin-yang.

During the first day's service, I mostly observed to understand the working rhythm, reading the handwritten tickets that came in (which, like the menu, were written in English) and watching as the female cooks warmed the bread in the oven before preparing the appetizers and sending them out, at which point the male cooks started the hot entrées. After Didier's okay and final garnishes, they were good to go, and then the girls would take over once again and assemble everything needed for the desserts. When at the end of service I asked Didier about the gender divide, he shrugged and said, "Oh, you know, the girls don't like to get too hot making the entrées, and they are also not as good with the wok."

"Oh, okay. So should I come at the same time tomorrow morning? Are you sure you don't want me to work the afternoon shift, then?" I asked Didier while the staff began piling all the dirty dishes in the kitchen's two small sinks.

"No, no. You should ease into the *stage*. See what's going on, observe. Vietnam is not just about La Verticale; it's about the streets, the people...La Verticale is important, of course, but you should explore and visit the markets or see how herbs and spices are used at the local hospital that specializes in Eastern medicine, go eat lots of street food. That's where you'll find the true Vietnam."

Over the next several days I submerged myself in kitchen life, this one worlds away from wd~50. I missed dishwashers, large cutting boards, higher countertops (even for someone as short as me), air-conditioning, and the ease of asking a question and having it understood and answered on the first go-round (since only three of the eight cooks spoke any English beyond what was written on the menu tickets). However, I was relieved to be away from Tom's critical eye and the precision required at wd~50. No one at La Verticale cared about proper attire; the chefs wore jeans and chef jackets and slip-on sandals with socks, which gave me visions of cleavers decapitating toes. Here, knife skills weren't important. The cooks wielded cleavers, both big and small, and they wouldn't have known a *brunoise* from a jardinière shape. Assigned shallot chopping, I began crosshatching them until Son instructed me to throw a bunch of them together and hack away until they formed small pieces. *Take that, Wylie!* I attempted to work with the cleavers during my first two days but couldn't master the proper way to hold them, so I continued to use my own chef's knife. One of the waiters took it and waved it in the air, pretending to be a samurai warrior, and we all laughed—no translation needed.

"Lauren, come see. Do you know how to make fried rice?" asked Son.

"Sort of, but not really. I know that you need to use old rice because if you use just cooked rice, it'll stick to the pan, right? Basically you fry it in a very hot wok in a bit of oil, right?"

"Yes, yes. How do you make it in American restaurants?"

"Usually it's made with pork," I said.

"Little cut-up pieces?"

"Yes, and eggs, and scallion, and peas. And sometimes mushrooms. Are those lotus seeds?" I asked as he added small ivory-colored balls to the wok.

"Yes, lotus seeds," he said, stirring them into the rice, which was already studded with chopped shiitake mushrooms. He added fish sauce and minced scallions to finish it off before noting, "See, very easy. I think Vietnamese version is the best."

"Yes, very easy. Even I can make it!"

"Yes, yes. You can make back home," he said. Then, abruptly, "Do you have a boyfriend there?"

"No," I said. Chase was out of the picture, although he still e-mailed me, even saying he was thinking of coming for a visit.

Yeah, right. I was enjoying being in this new place so much that the opposite sex wasn't foremost in my mind, which felt liberating. I was much more excited about the prospect of finding the tastiest pho and bun cha restaurants than about finding a man.

"Oh, are you married?"

"No. Not yet," I said. Even after only a short time in Vietnam, I was used to this question. If you are a female between twenty and fifty, everyone will immediately ask you this upon your arrival in Vietnam. If you're thirty or older and the answer is no, you will receive a pitying look. I was still in the safe zone. Never before had my love life, or lack thereof, been such an important topic in daily discussions, but never before had I been so relaxed about it.

"You should marry a Vietnamese man," said Son, giggling.

I smiled. "Maybe. We'll see how things go."

"Vietnamese men, they're not tall, but kindhearted. You can make them fried rice."

⟶

"THERE'S A WINE TASTING and then a pool party at the Hilton this weekend. You can come with me," said Belinda.

"Great," I replied. Belinda was upholding the reputation of the friendly Australian.

"My friend Lucy is going to come along, too, and I invited that American girl, Suchi, whom I met in the supermarket earlier this week," said Belinda, as though it were completely normal to make new friends at the supermarket. In all my years of supermarket shopping in New York, I had never once spoken to anyone except to ask a store clerk what aisle held the paper towels, and I loved the ease of making social connections here.

So on Saturday, Belinda, Suchi, Lucy, and I found our way to the wine tasting in the basement of an upscale Vietnamese restaurant. Suchi was Indian but had been educated in America and was in Hanoi conducting research. She was twenty-eight and beautiful, with strong, angular cheekbones, wide-set eyes, and a tiny, elegant, birdlike frame. Lucy, meanwhile, was tall, blond, and very British, enthusiastic about everything. "Lovely" and "brilliant" were her two favorite words. She was a nonpracticing lawyer, and now, forty-three and single, she was living in Vietnam in order to adopt a baby here. I liked them both instantly, although I liked the wine, a cheap Italian import, a lot less, and after an hour we left for the Hilton hotel, located next to the opera.

At first, I had scoffed at the idea of a hotel pool party, but Belinda explained that many of Hanoi's social events, especially for expats, were held at hotels. The night air was saunalike, and the damp heat clung to our skin like leeches. We sipped our vodka-spiked frozen lemonade and perched on padded lounge chairs, trying to avoid the shiny brown cockroaches that scurried along the pool's edge. Belinda knew everyone and introduced me to all her friends. But in contrast with a typical New York party, here we didn't talk about job promotions or new apartments or recent status symbol purchases. We talked about food and restaurants and how expat life could be both thrilling and aggravating.

"I'm going to go for a swim," Lucy said. Fueled by several glasses of white wine, she promptly took off her dress and dove into the warm turquoise water.

"Is she really in her underwear?" asked Belinda, mouth agape.

"It looks like it," I said.

"She must be drunk!" said Belinda.

"It's lovely in here," Lucy called as she backstroked across the pool.

A swaggering young Brazilian man in a white linen shirt inched his way into our group and began flirting with Suchi.

"Fabio, she's married," said Belinda.

"Oh, are you?" he asked me.

"No," I said. He immediately sat next to me, then suddenly grabbed my back and scooped his arm below my knees, picking me up like a baby.

"No!" I shrieked. And with a ceremonial splash, he threw me in, shoes and all, as Belinda and Suchi gasped.

"Don't worry, at least it's cool in here," I said, teeth gritted into a half smile. Fabio reached down to lend me a hand.

"Pull him in!" cried Belinda.

I tried, but I wasn't strong enough, so I climbed up the railing, my diaphanous blue dress clinging to my body as water dripped down my legs. I grabbed my floating shoes.

"So sexy," said Fabio. Belinda retrieved a towel, which Fabio grabbed and used to dry me off, caressing my legs with it.

"I've got it," I said.

I found a bathroom, where I dried off my dress under the hand dryer. When I returned, Fabio had disappeared and the girls fluttered around me, complimenting me on my grin-and-bear-it attitude. Lucy and Suchi decided to call it a night, but Belinda and I went to Face Bar afterward. After all, a little wet dress wasn't going to rain on my Vietnamese parade.

⟵⟶

THE FOLLOWING MONDAY MORNING when I got to work, Son was already preparing a massive hunk of pork belly, rubbing it all over with a marinade of garlic, soy sauce, and fish sauce. As I peered over his shoulder, he turned, tapping his bare arm, and asked, "What is this?"

"Arm? Or arm hair?" I said.

"And this?" He pointed to his leg hair.

"Leg hair."

"And this, pig hair?" asked Son, chuckling, poking the few coarse black hairs sticking out of the marinating pork belly.

"Yeah, I guess so," I said.

Unlike Wylie, Didier rarely worked in the kitchen, and at first I worried about communicating with the other cooks. But Son had a good command of English, and Thanh and Chien scraped by. While I rarely spoke to the female chefs (except for Luyen, who occasionally spoke to me in French), the male chefs and I started a language exchange. I mastered counting to ten and basic phrases for greeting people in Vietnamese, while Son and Thanh scribbled English kitchen terms in their pocket-sized notebooks.

"Lauren, what is this?" asked Thanh.

"Ladle. L-a-d-l-e," I said.

"And this?"

"Whisk."

"And this?"

"Strainer."

"And this?"

"Flattop."

"What?"

"Flattop."

"No, no. Come—" He led me into the office and pointed to the computer. "This, flattop?"

"Ah, no, that is a laptop. This is a flattop," I explained as Thanh burst into a fit of laughter.

"I think you say this is laptop!" he said, smacking his palm against his head. "And what is sheril?"

"I don't think sheril is a word. Can you write it down?"

Thanh got out his notebook and wrote out "c-h-e-r-v-i-l."

"Oh, chervil. It's an herb. You say it like sure-vil," I enunciated.

"Same as parsley?"

"No, it's not the same. It's milder and has smaller leaves."

"Yes, I think it is the same," he said, drawing the leaves on his notebook.

"Okay, it's same-same, but different."

At this, we both erupted in laughter, because "same-same, but different" was one of the unofficial slogans of Vietnam. It was particularly useful in explaining the nuances of the English language, as when Son asked me the difference between the words *tired* and *fatigued.* I simply explained that they were "same-same, but different." Why you needed the second "same," I didn't know, but you did. Outside of our vocabulary lessons, though, the slogan was often used for scamming tourists. You might book a hotel room at one place, but when you got there, it would be full to capacity; however, they would offer you a "same-same" room at their "sister" hotel down the road. Of course, that room would not be same-same. It would be worse.

Although I bonded with the men, most of the female cooks unfortunately gave me the cold shoulder. So much for sisterly solidarity in the kitchen. Maybe they saw me as a threat, or perhaps they didn't want another girl to hog the spotlight. Or maybe they were intimidated by me. But one day while changing into my uniform, Yen, the spritely female cook who was the resident expert at making the prawn summer roll appetizers, said in broken English, "I'm happy you are at La Verticale, and I want to be your friend."

"I want to be your friend, too," I said, and she gave me a big hug.

Son and Yen then began chatting in Vietnamese. Son told

me, "She wants to know what makeup you use to have your skin stay so white. She wishes her skin was as white as you."

"I don't use anything. But you're so beautiful!" I said to Yen, who shook her head.

"Not like you," she said, stroking my face.

Son diplomatically changed the subject. "So, Lauren, do you take taxi home tonight?" he asked.

"Yes, I think so."

"Taxis are very expensive," he replied. "How much do you pay for taxi?"

Money was a hot topic with the Vietnamese. Everyone at La Verticale watched me take a taxi home every night as they chugged off on their motorbikes. Having grown up in New York City, I didn't learn how to ride a bicycle until I was sixteen years old (at which point my parents, never athletic types, hired someone to teach me in Central Park), so riding a motorbike in Hanoi was basically an instant death wish. By the end of my first week, the staff had peppered me about the cost of my airplane ticket, my rent in Hanoi, my salary in New York, and how much I paid for everything else in Vietnam (to which they always responded, "Lauren, too much!"). By Vietnamese standards, I was wealthy, and I began to tell white lies because I wanted my fellow cooks to see me as a compatriot and not as a rich dilettante.

"Forty thousand dong," I said, although the real price was 65,000 dong, or almost $3.

"Yes, very expensive. And you take in morning?"

I also took a taxi to work every morning. I reasoned that taking taxis weren't much more expensive than commuting via the New York City subway, and I didn't really have many expenses in Vietnam, since my meals were either free or next to nothing and my rent was 400 percent cheaper than in New York City (for a space that was probably 400 percent larger). A *xe om*, or motor-bike taxi, was about 15,000 dong, but I didn't want to endure a hot and sweaty ride at morning rush hour, during which I'd be inhaling pollution for twenty minutes straight, even if I wore the ubiquitous cotton face mask. So I took taxis, but I couldn't shake my sense of guilt, and I made the taxi driver drop me off two blocks away from the restaurant so no one would see me.

"No, I take the bus," I lied.

"You should get motorbike, like Valentin," said Son, referring to the twenty-three-year-old French manager who had started working at La Verticale a few months before I did. Because Valentin was the manager and always busy with front-of-house responsibilities, he and I didn't become close the way I thought we would as two Westerners in Hanoi; instead we maintained a professional relationship.

"I don't think that will happen. I am not a good bicycle rider. I think I would die on a motorbike," I said, mimicking the twist-ing and turning motion of imaginary handlebars.

"Oh, oh," said Son, chuckling. "Then tonight I take you home?"

"You want to drive me home tonight? But I live very far away." I doubted Son lived in Tay Ho.

"No problem," he said.

And after work, we flew through Hanoi on the back of his motorbike, the lights of storefronts blurring into one electric rainbow and the wind pushing our hair back behind our ears and flapping it up against our plastic helmets.

"Okay. See you tomorrow. Bye-bye," he said when we got to my front gate.

Son, Yen, and Thanh continued to drive me home occa-sionally, not because they had to, but because they wanted to. Because we were now more than co-workers; we were friends.

☙

DURING THE FIRST FEW WEEKS of service, I was responsible for warming the bread in the oven and for preparing the rice and potato sides that accompanied the fish and meat dishes. The fried rice was pretty traditional, flavored with fresh lotus seeds and shiitake mushrooms, but the potatoes were one of Didier's more fusion dishes. With a nod to France, thinly sliced potatoes were boiled in a mixture of water and chicken stock and topped with bread crumbs before being placed under a salamander for a quick broiling—a sort of lighter potato gratin. But Didier added turmeric, star anise, and large strips of cinnamon to the chicken stock, which colored the potatoes a bright, school bus yellow and subtly flavored them with the sweetness of Vietnam.

I quickly learned that everyone had an assigned role: The girls (Luyen, Nu, and Yen) prepared the appetizers and desserts, Con was responsible for the prep work for the entrées, Son cooked the entrées, Thanh plated them, and Chien, the sous-chef, alternated between cooking and plating the entrées. No one ever strayed from an assigned job. Didier primarily supervised and added sprinklings of salt or spices at the last minute to the entrées that the other chefs cooked. He also spent a lot of time when he was in the kitchen discussing cooking and his culinary philosophy with me. I wasn't sure if he was trying to imbue me with his personal philosophy and steer me away from my molecular gastronomy origins, or if he was just so excited about Vietnamese ingredients and flavors that he couldn't help sharing.

"See this? Simple, good flavors. That's all you need. I'm so against molecular gastronomy. You destroy the food's integrity and you just play around with it," he reiterated yet again, pointing to the warm chocolate cake nesting in a black bowl, still hot from the oven. We made a large quantity of batter but kept it in the refrigerator, filling small ring molds and baking them only as needed, so that each diner could enjoy an individual-sized cake. The cinnamon-spiked aroma swirled into the damp, humid breeze drifting in from the open door leading to the porch.

I nodded as he looked in my direction, as though to ascertain that I understood that *this* was the *real* way to cook. And here in the La Verticale kitchen, I was becoming more convinced by his philosophy; although his cuisine might have lacked Wylie's intellectual elements at wd~50, I was learning the importance of using local ingredients at their freshest, how to make a few simple ingredients pop with flavor by adding a single freshly picked herb or a pinch of exotic spice—and, most important, that cooking isn't a precise science. You don't need to follow a recipe to a tee; it's more important to trust your taste buds and other senses, because foods aren't static products but change from day to day.

"And the visual is important," he added, cutting a stalk of lemongrass and adding it to a glass filled with orange-flavored gelatin. "But taste, that's what matters. I believe in the five flavors. Sweet, salty, sour, bitter…Do you know what the fifth one is?"

"Spicy?" I ventured.

"*Fade,*" he said, referring to the French word for blandness. "The Japanese, though, they think differently."

"Right, umami," I said, referencing the flavor profile that's best described as savory or meaty and is found in foods like soy sauce, Parmesan cheese, and anchovies.

"But it's all about balancing flavor. Here's a question for you: What is the profile of vanilla?"

"Sweet," I said.

"Yes. And chocolate?"

"A little sweet and a little bitter?"

Pleased he had stumped me, he shook his head. "No, it's not sweet, just bitter. We add sugar to it. But some things, like tomatoes, are both sweet and sour. You know, I spend one to two hours a day learning about new ways to use flavor, and then I experiment in the kitchen. As a chef, you always have to be evolving, and there's always more to learn."

Didier's passion for flavors was obvious in the moment you set foot in La Verticale, since the entrance to the restaurant opened into a spice shop that spanned the front of the ground floor. Large glass apothecary jars lined the walls, filled with star anise, curled cinnamon sticks, and bright red chile powder, while Didier's own salt and spice blends were displayed in neat rows along the counter. He also stocked rare Vietnamese spices, including exotic ones that I'd never before encountered, like musky-scented talaluma, floral-noted ambrette, and minorities' spice, which came from the northern highlands of Vietnam, near the Chinese border, where many ethnic minorities lived (and presumably cultivated these spices). And although you can't walk into a restaurant in Hanoi without encountering nuoc mam, or fish sauce—the lifeblood of Vietnamese cuisine—Didier sold a special version that had been aged for fifteen years. Didier might not have been Vietnamese by birth, but he was Vietnamese by choice, and that was evident in his culinary knowledge, a fact that further reassured me that I had made the right decision to learn about Vietnamese food from a non-Vietnamese.

"On Friday, you should come to my house. First, you can

help prepare for the buffet that we are catering, and then you can sit in on the cooking class that I'm giving," said Didier. He wore many culinary hats: In addition to the restaurant, he ran a catering business, preparing food for private parties and take-away, and also taught cooking classes for tourists.

So that Friday morning I took a taxi to Long Bien, a suburb of Hanoi located across the Red River. Lush, flowering potted plants surrounded a small swimming pool, and a caged bird chirped from the veranda. Didier's wife, Mai, petite and slender like almost all the Vietnamese women I'd met, greeted me and led me down a winding path to the back of the house. Didier's home featured an industrial kitchen in addition to his personal one, and it was huge, with a walk-in refrigerator, bread ovens used for La Verticale's triangular-shaped rolls, and tons of counter space.

Three members of the kitchen staff were already busy chopping mushrooms and skewering meat. They murmured hello, and the sounds of cleavers tapping against the cutting boards echoed across the room.

Mai handed me a bag of wriggling shrimp. "You must get them alive," she said in heavily accented French. She grabbed one from the bag, beheaded it deftly, and peeled off its shell.

"Place the shells here. For stock," she said, spreading out an empty plastic bag. "Pinch the shrimp just below the head to stun it, then twist off the head in one motion, and peel off the remaining shell."

I had never worked with live shrimp before, and while I felt bad about inflicting these crustaceans with a beheading crueler than Marie Antoinette's, I appreciated how truly fresh they were. When you buy shrimp at the grocery store, you really have no idea how fresh they are. Surely it's more aesthetically pleasing and desensitizing to buy a bag of shelled, cleaned, and cooked shrimp, but working with fresh, live products was giving me a greater understanding of the source of our food.

After I peeled all the shrimp, I wedged a bamboo skewer through each one so that when boiled, they would remain elongated, making them easy to wrap inside a summer roll. The technique works for any foods that curl up when cooked, like squid or lobster tails; simply boil or steam or grill until done, then slide off the skewer.

When my task was completed, Mai beckoned me over. *"La sauce satay,"* she said. "Do you know how to make it?"

"I've had it, but I don't know how to make it," I said.

"Easy. Shallots, peanuts, peanut oil, turmeric juice, coconut milk, lemongrass, chiles, galangal. You know galangal?" she asked, holding up a pink, knobby rhizome that looked almost identical to ginger. I nodded and watched as she placed all the ingredients into a blender. The peanuts, shallots, and coconut milk formed the base of the sauce in relatively equal portions, about a cup each, and she added the other ingredients by taste, not measuring, though each was about a few tablespoons' worth except for the chiles, which was just a pinch.

After smearing the sauce on skewered pork, we began to prepare steamed fish in lotus leaves. Mai made a marinade of fish sauce, pepper, and turmeric juice, and we dipped the fish in the sauce before placing them in cut pieces of leaf along with dill sprigs, thinly sliced carrot and scallion, and several lotus seeds. "You can also do this with banana leaves," she said. Everything was uncomplicated, seasoned by intuition and with discriminating taste.

I began mincing onion, mushroom, carrot, and sweet radish for the fried spring roll filling, and each chopping motion transported me back to wd~50 and once again rekindled my love of my home kitchen's mini–food processor. When finished, we spooned the vegetables into a bowl and added pork, wood ear mushrooms, and bean thread noodles.

"Mix with hands," said Mai, working the mixture into a cohesive stuffing. She showed me how to place a large spoonful in the middle of a dampened sheet of rice paper and to roll it up, folding the ends toward the center and then rolling again, forming a tight, sealed parcel.

We broke for a lunch of rice, preserved mustard greens, roast pork knuckle, crunchy Thai eggplants in fish sauce, and a clear soup of greens and itsy-bitsy clams, which had been prepared by Mai and an assistant earlier in the morning. After I finished my rice, Mai immediately offered me more, saying, "You don't eat anything. I've already had three bowls of rice."

"I'm fine," I said. The Vietnamese appetite for rice never ceased to amaze me. No meal in Vietnam was complete without rice. Lots and lots of fluffy, steaming rice.

We returned to work, and then at two o'clock, Mai told me to get changed so that we could drive to meet Didier at the restaurant for the cooking lesson. While swerving through the Hanoi traffic, she asked me, "So, you want to be a chef?"

"Yes, I think so," I said.

"It's a hard life, especially for a woman. I couldn't do it," she said.

"Yes, I know." I thought of her and her children. Even though Didier wasn't working the line at the restaurant, he was there every morning and evening except Sundays and probably returned home after his two sons' bedtime. Maybe he saw them in the morning before school, but when you're growing up, that's not always enough.

Mai and I made small talk until we reached the restaurant,

where Didier was conversing with a woman in her mid-fifties whose coiffed hair and fashionable scarf screamed French haute bourgeoisie.

"Lauren, this is Chantelle," said Didier. "Her husband is working in Hanoi for a few months and she will be taking the cooking class today. Chantelle, this is Lauren. She is in Hanoi for two months to do a *stage* with me and learn more about Vietnamese cuisine, so I invited her to come along for the lesson."

Chantelle smiled, and we chatted in French while Didier made final preparations for our market visit. A German film crew in town to shoot Didier for a television program followed us with their cameras. Even in Berlin, it seemed, Didier had culinary clout.

With a midafternoon drizzle under way, we hopped into Didier's van and headed to the Hom market. Once there, we saw prepared goods lining the walkway to the central part of the bustling market: everything from basins filled with swimming carp to designer knockoff shoes. Pointing to the rows of wrapped sausages, plump like thighs in a Rubens painting, Didier exclaimed, "And here we have Vietnamese mortadella and pâtés. You can see the French influence in foods like these..."

As we wended our way into the heart of the market, Didier paused occasionally to highlight his favorite ingredients. "Dried shrimp, young rice...Ah, do you know what this is? Buddha's hand. You use the rind. It is so fragrant." He held up a gnarled green fruit as we inhaled the grassy citrus notes.

"Why are they green? Aren't they ripe yet?" I asked.

"No, not yet, but when they are, you can use the rind to make marmalades. It's much more fragrant than lemons or the citrus fruits you can find back home," he said. We walked through the market, passing a few kiosks selling kitchenwares, including cleavers fit for giants and, of course, the frustrating, difficult-to-use Vietnamese vegetable peelers.

Passing stool-lined counters serving noodles and papaya salad, we snaked our way to the back of the market. Coal black eels squirmed in galvanized tubs, while gray shrimp fluttered in circles, performing a synchronized death swim as their antennae intertwined. We saw stands selling every conceivable cow part carved into shiny slices alongside glistening white brains and maroon livers. I cringed at the cage filled with live frogs ribbiting loudly and clamoring for space as they sat one on top of the other. Sticky, primordial smells of fresh blood and guts filled the air, masked only slightly by the mild aroma of steamed glutinous rice being sold by a crouching woman wearing a *non la*, the traditional Vietnamese conical hat.

Didier stopped and picked up a large striped orange crab, its claws tied underneath its body. "This is how you tell the difference between male and female crabs. If it forms a point, then it is a male, and if it is curved, it is female," he said, noting the design of the white underside.

"And the females are better, right?" I asked.

"Yes, they are a little bit sweeter, so when you go to your fish markets back home, you should look for that. Oh, look at this. I will make a tempura with a bit of orange juice for an *amuse* before the meal," he said, now reaching into a large bucket crowded with white baby squid.

"Now *this* is Vietnamese cooking," he continued as we reached a small stall dedicated to herbs.

Large bamboo baskets displayed multitudes of herbs packaged in small parcels tied with wooden string, like an artist's palette in shades of green. Didier reached down and snapped off a feathery leaf tinged with purple. Holding it, he said, "Perilla. And that is cilantro. And dill. Ngo herb. Lemon balm. Do you know what this is? This is rau ram, or Vietnamese mint." He encouraged us to inhale the grassy scents of each leaf before we tasted them as the video camera zoomed in.

Once the market tour concluded, we returned to Didier's house along with the cameramen. When we arrived, cups of hot, fragrant tea greeted us.

"Your house is beautiful," said Chantelle to Mai, admiring the black-and-white family photos on the wall and the Asian antique furniture that stood beside modern Western accent pieces, much like the East-West blend of Didier's cuisine. "Where else in the world has Didier worked?"

"Malaysia, Tunisia, Thailand, Bora Bora...," said Mai with a trace of wonder, as though Didier had lived a whole life before her.

"Are you going to move anywhere else?" Chantelle asked.

"No, Didier has his roots here now. I'd like to, maybe, but he's done."

We ambled to the kitchen, where the film crew was adjusting the lighting and setting up microphones. From our seats at the central island, I spied four generous bottles filled with homemade rice wine and fruit-infused liqueurs and brandies, and in front of us was a tray filled with standard Vietnamese ingredients and spices. "Action," said one of the cameramen, and Didier commanded center stage like the maestro at the Metropolitan Opera.

"Herbs, herbs, herbs. They are the king of Vietnamese cooking. And nuoc mam, the famous fish sauce made from anchovies, it is the connecting force between northern, central, and southern Vietnamese cooking, which are all very different, you know. The food in the North is simpler, more refined and unadulterated, while in central Vietnam the food is spicier, and in the South it's much sweeter and ornate. Northern pho is pure, just broth and noodles with maybe a touch of green onion, but in the South it's like salad with all the herbs and sauces they shower into it," he said.

"Which version is better?" I asked.

"Why, northern, of course. Any Hanoian will look down on southern pho. But in the South, they think our pho is bland and that theirs is far better."

Didier handed Chantelle and me a folder containing his classic Hanoian recipes. Pho didn't make the cut, but he had included recipes for other local favorites, including banana flower salad, bun cha barbecued pork, grilled chicken skewers with lemon leaves, sautéed pumpkin branches, and fried spring rolls. Mai, a seasoned home cook, joined Didier as he began to prep ingredients. "We'll start with the marinades for the meat. Raw meat must be marinated, to give it extra flavor and to make it more tender, but don't let it marinate for too long. Just an hour or two is good," Didier said, adding the fish sauce, turmeric juice, minced shallots, thinly sliced lemon leaves, oil, salt, and pepper that had already been prepped. He placed them in a bowl with the chicken.

Chantelle and I observed his technique, scribbling notes onto our recipes.

"And for the pork bun cha, we have fish sauce, chopped shallots—and they must be chopped with a knife to keep their juice—chives, sugar, pepper, caramel. You make the caramel by cooking water and sugar together until very dark, and then you immediately add cold water so that you have liquid caramel. But don't add salt, because you have the nuoc mam. And you must have small morsels of meat, because, of course, you eat with chopsticks in Vietnam," he said while Mai sliced pork shoulder into bite-sized pieces.

As the meats marinated, Mai and Didier began preparing nuoc cham, the fish sauce–based dressing to accompany the bun cha and nems.

"You add salt and sugar and a little lime juice to help soften the vegetables and draw out the water," Didier explained as Mai cut green papaya and carrot into delicate slivers and plopped them into the bowl of sauce.

He continued, "Green papaya, it is excellent. You can boil it and make a puree, or you can have it fresh in a spring roll with herbs. With this spring roll, you can do anything. You can make it with seafood, but then make sure you add fewer vegetables and a bit of ginger. But you have not been to Hanoi until you have had nem."

Once he rolled the nems into tidy parcels, we tackled the banana flower salad, ubiquitous in Vietnam. "This is the flower from the banana tree, but you can make this recipe with cabbage, or whatever you have, since the banana flower has no flavor," he said. "You want to have the spirit of the salad. But Vietnamese salad, it has no salt, no vinaigrette, no oil, and it is perfect." After Didier had demonstrated all the dishes and left for the restaurant's dinner shift along with the camera crew, Chantelle and I were presented with the afternoon's bounty. We sat like empresses at the long dining room table, where we were served the dishes in succession. We relished the salad's cool crunch, the pork's sweetness, and the crispness of the fried spring rolls, the herbal intensity of the lemon leaves, and the freshness of the sautéed pumpkin branches. Everything was filled with flavor and passion: *This* was the food of Vietnam. *This* was why I had come.

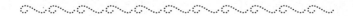

An Introduction to Vietnam

These recipes, which typify some of the classic dishes you'll find in Vietnam, have been adapted from Didier Corlou's cooking class to make them fairly easy to replicate at home. You should be able to find most ingredients at Asian grocery stores.

FRIED SPRING ROLLS

You cannot talk about Vietnamese food without mentioning spring rolls, which are called nems in Hanoi and cha gio in the South. Although they are served primarily with bun cha (see page 141), I ate fried spring rolls all the time, particularly as part of my lunch meal at the commissary. As Son said, "All foreigners like nems." It's true. For this dipping sauce (as well as subsequent dipping sauces), I like to use a Microplane grater for the garlic, which results in a fine paste that dissolves easily into the liquid.

SERVES 4 AS AN APPETIZER

FOR THE SPRING ROLLS:
½ ounce dried wood ear mushrooms
½ ounce dried shiitake mushrooms
2½ ounces cellophane or rice noodles
2½ ounces bean sprouts (about 1 cup)
2½ ounces onion (about 1 small)
6 ounces ground pork

(continued)

1 egg
Large pinch of freshly ground black pepper
16 rice paper sheets
Vegetable oil for frying, about 2 to 4 cups depending on the size
    of your pot

FOR THE SAUCE:
½ cup water
2 tablespoons fish sauce
1 tablespoon lime juice
1 tablespoon sugar
½ teaspoon rice vinegar
½ teaspoon minced or grated garlic
¼ teaspoon finely minced Thai chile

FOR SERVING:
1 head of lettuce, or about 16 lettuce leaves, for serving (large,
    flat leaves like green leaf or Bibb work best)
Herbs for serving, including mint and cilantro (optional)

Soak both mushrooms in hot water until soft, then rinse off any grit or dirt. Discard the shiitake stems, and mince the mushrooms. Meanwhile, soak the noodles in hot water until soft, about 10 minutes, then drain. Return the noodles to the bowl and, using a pair of scissors, cut into small pieces, about ¼ to ½ inch. Mince the bean sprouts and onion, and combine in a large mixing bowl along with the mushrooms, noodles, pork, egg, and pepper. Mix until fully combined.

Moisten a piece of rice paper with a little water, rubbing the water all over both sides. Place about 2 tablespoons' worth of filling at the base of a piece of rice paper, and form into a log shape, leaving about an inch of space from the sides of the rice paper. Begin rolling the rice paper over the filling until you've used up about half the sheet. Fold in the sides over the center and roll all the way up so that your enclosed parcel measures about 4 inches by 1 inch. Repeat with the remaining rice paper rolls and filling.

Pour enough oil into a heavy-bottomed pot or wok so that you've got at least 2 inches' worth of oil. When the oil is shimmering, add a few of the spring rolls. (You can test to see if the oil is hot enough by dropping a small piece of moistened rice paper into the oil; if it floats and bubbles, you're ready to fry the rolls.) Fry until browned, about 3 minutes. Let dry on paper towels to absorb the oil, and continue frying in batches.

Meanwhile, combine all ingredients for the sauce in a small bowl, and mix well.

To serve, wrap a lettuce leaf around the hot spring roll and a few sprigs of fresh herbs, and serve with the sauce for dipping.

BUN CHA

After pho, bun cha is one of Hanoi's most famous dishes and is a delicious summertime lunch or light dinner. In Hanoi, you'll know you're at a bun cha stand by the smoke wafting from the charcoal grills. Living in New York City, I don't have the luxury of cooking pork on a charcoal grill, but my stove's broiler works just fine. For some reason, my local bun cha joint in Hanoi served foreigners pork patties while the locals got pork patties and grilled pork belly—but on my last day in Hanoi, when I went for a farewell lunch, I was served both. Coincidence? Maybe, but I like to think that by then I was considered a local. This version uses only pork patties, but feel free to add sliced pork belly to the marinade and grill both.

SERVES 4

FOR THE PORK:
2 tablespoons sugar
5 tablespoons water
1 pound ground pork
1 large shallot, minced as small as possible
3 tablespoons fish sauce
¼ teaspoon freshly ground black pepper

FOR THE SAUCE:
2 tablespoons fish sauce
2 tablespoons rice vinegar
1 teaspoon brown sugar
1½ cups water
½ teaspoon minced or grated garlic
1 red Thai chile, minced
2 tablespoons green papaya, cut into small, thin slices,
    about ¼ inch (optional)

FOR SERVING:
1 pound thin rice noodles
Selection of Asian herbs, including any of the following:
    cilantro, perilla, mint, sawtooth coriander, ngo herb
    (for a total of about 2 loosely packed cups)
½ head red leaf lettuce, torn into small pieces

In a small saucepan, combine the sugar with 3 tablespoons water and cook over high heat until a dark brown caramel forms, about 8 minutes. Remove from the heat and add 2 tablespoons cold water, swirling the pot.

In a large mixing bowl, combine the pork, shallot, fish sauce, caramel sauce, and pepper, and marinate in the refrigerator for 1½ hours.

Meanwhile, combine all ingredients for the sauce in a large mixing bowl.

When the pork is through marinating, remove from the refrigerator and shape into small patties, about 15 to 20 in all.

Heat a charcoal grill or a broiler to high. Bring a pot of water to a boil and cook the noodles according to the directions on their package. Drain, then rinse under cold water to halt the cooking process.

Meanwhile, grill or broil the pork patties until fully cooked and slightly charred, about 4 minutes per side.

Spoon the sauce into four bowls, then place the pork patties over the sauce. Place the herbs and lettuce in one large communal bowl and the noodles into another large communal bowl.

To eat, dip some of the noodles into the sauce and eat with the patties and herbs.

SAUTÉED GREENS

We made this dish with pumpkin shoots, which are easily found in Hanoi but less so in America. Instead, you can use Chinese broccoli, bok choy, watercress, spinach, or any other variety of Asian greens. You will need to blanch a larger green with thick stems like Chinese broccoli or bok choy, but if you're using a leafy green like spinach, there's no need.

SERVES 4 AS A SIDE DISH

1 pound Chinese broccoli or other Asian greens
2 tablespoons vegetable oil

(continued)

1 tablespoon chopped garlic
2 tablespoons fish sauce
Pinch of freshly ground black pepper

Bring a large pot of water to a boil and add the Chinese broccoli. Blanch for 1 minute, then drain.

Meanwhile, heat a wok over high heat and add the oil. When it starts to shimmer, add the garlic and sauté until softened but not browned, about 30 seconds. Add the greens and sauté until tender, about 2 minutes. Add the fish sauce and pepper, and stir until coated, about 30 more seconds. Remove the greens to a serving platter, leaving any liquid that remains in the wok. Serve hot, as an accompaniment to any entrée.

Chapter 6

"LAUREN, DO YOU KNOW how to make cha ca?" asked Son one evening after the dinner rush had ended and we were about to begin cleaning up.

Cha ca is a Hanoian specialty of fish marinated in a turmeric-based sauce and fried with scallions, dill, and peanuts served over rice noodles. Unlike pho or goi cuon—the cooling summer rolls filled with rice noodles, shrimp, and lettuce—it's rarely the first dish foreigners think of when they consider Vietnamese cuisine, but Cha Ca La Vong, a famous old restaurant in Hanoi's Old Quarter, specializes in the dish, and over the years it's become an unofficial requirement for visitors to sample while visiting Hanoi. I had yet to try it, so I shook my head no.

"Okay, I will teach you now," he said excitedly.

"Right now?"

"Yes, you come to Vietnam to learn Vietnamese food, so I teach you. You can eat it after," he said.

He pulsed a small handful of sliced galangal in the blender, an outdated cream-colored model that was stained yellow from turmeric-based sauces and roared like a jet engine, and spread the puree over several fish filets in a blue plastic bowl. From the lowboy refrigerator below his workstation, he retrieved a small plastic bottle filled with a murky purple liquid. "Shrimp sauce," he said, then reached for another plastic bottle filled with bright orange turmeric juice.

After adding these ingredients, he opened a plastic bag filled with a white paste and held it up to my nose. I inhaled the acrid smell, flinching but returning for another whiff, since I was clueless. Yeasty, sour notes bombarded my nasal passages.

"Fermented rice," Son explained.

"Ah," I said.

"Do you have that in America?"

"I don't think so. Maybe you can find it in Chinatown, where there are a lot of Vietnamese markets, but I've never seen it," I said as he added a few spoonfuls to the fish.

"Oh. It's not popular?"

"No. It smells a little funky, so I don't think Americans would like it that much or know what to do with it. So you add it to the sauce, and then how long do you marinate everything?"

"About three hours, but for you, now, only five minutes," said Son, shrugging. In Vietnamese cooking, precision wasn't that important. Things were done when you needed them to be done.

"So now I will teach you cha ca and you will eat it after. Very Vietnamese dish. You can make it back at home. You be the cha ca expert of New York," Son said as he heated the oil in the wok to a boil and gently dipped in the scallions using a slotted spoon. He followed suit with a few sprigs of dill so that they wilted but retained some crunch. He lowered several pieces of the marinated fish into the oil, which immediately bubbled and splattered. Once the fish were fully cooked and had turned the color of summer honey, he swirled his perforated spoon into the wok, scooped out the fish, and placed them on paper towels to drain. He took fresh rice noodles out of a bag and placed them in a serving bowl, then added a few fried prawn crackers. On a long black plate, he arranged the fish next to the cooked scallions and dill and poured chile-flecked fish sauce into a small dipping dish.

"For garnish, you want to make the green onion look pretty. Use the light green part only, and, holding in the middle, make many slits into the top and bottom using a small knife. You see, it looks pretty. You try now," he said, handing me a few scallions. Following his instructions, I quickly transformed them into garnishes that sort of resembled bicycle handles adorned with streamers. We added them on top of the fish, and Son garnished the whole plate with a handful of crispy fried shallots. One complete meal, all in under ten minutes.

"Okay, Lauren! Eat!" said Son.

"Thanks. It looks delicious," I said.

"Go eat out there." He motioned toward the front room of the restaurant, which served primarily as the spice shop but had a single table in the middle.

"No, no, it's okay, I can eat in the kitchen," I said, not wanting to draw attention to myself. But Son was adamant, so I took my plate and sat at the table, catching Didier's glance when I walked in.

"Son made this for me," I explained before he had a chance to speak.

"Ah, cha ca. Good. Do you want some wine?" he said, pulling up a chair next to me.

"No, I'm fine."

"Have some wine. White wine?"

I gave in. "Sure."

"One glass of white wine for Lauren and a glass of red for me," Didier said to one of the servers. Then he turned back to me. "So you have been here for some time now. What do you think?"

"Everyone has been great. I'm teaching them some English and they're teaching me Vietnamese. I've learned how to use lemongrass and fish sauce and all the Vietnamese herbs, how to use the wok, and now, how to make cha ca."

"Good, good. Eat," he said, pointing to the fish.

I lifted my chopsticks and ate a piece of fish with the rice noodles. "When did you open La Verticale?" I asked between mouthfuls. Although I had done some preliminary research on Didier and the restaurant before I arrived, I didn't know why Didier had left the esteemed Metropole Hotel, his previous employer. It was the nicest hotel in Hanoi, if not in all of Vietnam.

"In 2007," said Didier, adding that it took time to get the restaurant up and running. "But I think 2010 will be our year. But you know, sometimes there are issues with the staff... You know how it goes in Vietnam."

"Mmmm...," I murmured, not entirely sure what he meant.

"You really have to train the staff well. It's not Paris or New York here, but you want the level of quality to be there. That's why we brought in Valentin. I always want young people, too. I wouldn't want another European chef in the kitchen. There would be too much conflict, and the restaurant wouldn't have my spirit," he said, knocking his knuckles together.

"I can understand that," I said. Everyone knows too many cooks spoil the broth.

"And you know, I'm not going to pay the workers all the same wage and be a socialist. No, they do different amounts of work, and some are better than others. But I share the tips with everyone. The front-of-house staff, they don't like that, but I think it's only fair to the kitchen. Some people tip twenty or thirty dollars, which is enormous for here, since Vietnam is not really a tipping culture."

I admired his egalitarianism, since I also benefited from

these tips. By the time they got distributed to the whole staff, I received about 150,000 dong, or a little less than $10; though that's not a lot in America, in Vietnam it's ten bowls of pho. I felt that Didier wanted to reassure me that he knew things were different elsewhere in the world. But as much as I liked being the chef's confidante, it made me a little uncomfortable as he talked about the staff. These were my new friends, after all.

"Do you make much money from the spice shop?" I asked, trying to change the subject. The shop sold not only Didier's spice blends, but also his cookbooks and postcards with his recipes.

"No, not really, maybe forty American dollars a month. But it creates the esprit. I want to teach people about *my* spices and cuisine and to share *my* knowledge," he said. While Didier didn't work the line each night, he was nevertheless represented in each of the recipes, and he did add the finishing touches to dishes before they went into the dining room, ensuring that they met his standards. And there was no denying that Didier Corlou was embodied in all aspects of the restaurant. The name *Didier Corlou* boldly branded everything in sight, from the *C* of his last name intersecting with the *c* in La Verticale on the restaurant's outdoor signage to the *DC* embossed on the bottom of every plate and bowl.

Still, I kept flashing back to Wylie sautéing fish filets for hours on end nearly every night in the wd~50 kitchen. He was so much more in touch with the day-to-day workings of his restaurant; but I began to wonder if it was really so wrong for a chef to take a backseat from cooking if his spirit was still present in the restaurant. Or did there come a point later in life where a chef's priorities changed, and it simply became less important to be working the line each night? I wondered what this would mean for me in the future. As much as I wanted to take the Wylie approach, it seemed more practical to take Didier's.

JUST AS DIDIER had encouraged me (although I needed little encouragement, if any), I supplemented my formal training at La Verticale by applying myself to the study of Vietnamese street food culture. I trawled the streets of Hanoi during my off-hours for authentic dishes, stopping whenever I saw eager customers poised on miniature blue plastic stools, chopsticks in hand. Because I lived far away from the restaurant, I never returned home between the lunch and dinner shifts like the rest of the staff but wandered around until I got too hot or tired. Most eateries specialized in one dish, almost always written on their signs, so ordering wasn't too difficult, especially since my Vietnamese culinary vocabulary was growing quickly. And if a waiter approached me and said something I didn't understand, I simply nodded, figuring he was offering me the restaurant's specialty. So far no mishaps, although pausing at one crowded spot, I was glad I knew that "trung vit lon" meant cooked embryonic duck egg, once described by a friend as "the most vile thing I have ever put in my mouth." I had come to Vietnam to push my boundaries, but I wasn't ready for that. Yet.

Thus I chanced upon a bun bo Hue stall on Quang Trang, a busy street near La Verticale. Bun bo Hue is the official soup of Hue, the former imperial city in central Vietnam. Pho may be the blood that runs through the veins of Hanoi, but frankly it pales in comparison with bun bo Hue. While the general condiments for the two beef noodle soups are identical, bun bo Hue packs a punch with lemongrass, shrimp paste, and chiles instead of the delicate spices of cinnamon and star anise found in pho. The former is a soup whose bold, expressive flavors represented what I loved about Vietnamese food.

And tucked away in the Hom market, I found a new favorite

in banh bot loc, small cold tapioca flour dumplings stuffed with shrimp and pork and served with fish sauce and herbs. The dish was a harmonious combination of textures, flavors, and colors: chewy dough with crisp herbs and crunchy shallots, unctuous pork fat with fish sauce, the bright greens of the herbs contrasting with the pale pinks of shrimp filling. Food wove a spell over me in Vietnam, and as Didier had promised, the most important foods weren't in restaurants; they were in storefronts with unsteady plastic tables and child-sized blue stools spilling out onto the streets and where bowls of steaming soup were ladled out of waist-high metal stockpots.

However, not every dish was a success; I wandered all over Hanoi in search of banh mi sandwiches like those Chase and I had feasted on in our ethnic food outings in New York, but to no avail. One sandwich was an air-filled baguette lightly smeared with pâté and pickled green papaya, while another was basically an omelet inside of a baguette with pork pâté and scallions, served with pickled cucumbers, cilantro, and hot sauce.

"Today, I ate bun bo Hue, and banh beo," I said to Son as I helped him marinate tuna in passion fruit sauce one evening. I liked telling him all the different things I sampled in the streets and sought his advice on those foods I hadn't yet tasted.

"Oh, bun bo Hue, very spicy. From Hue, in the center of Vietnam. Yes, good! Oh, Lauren, you eat so many different things in Vietnam. You eat more kinds of Vietnamese food than me," he said with delight. I was an outsider, the white female foreigner, but I wanted to convince Son and Thanh that I had come to Vietnam to learn about and embrace *their* food culture and that I wasn't like the other tourists or expats who kept their refrigerators stocked with balsamic vinegar, pasta sauces in jars, and other Western goods. After all, it was easy enough to avoid Vietnamese food; McDonald's and Starbucks, emblems of Western "progress," had yet to arrive, but the local alternatives, Lotteria and Highlands Coffee, were always packed with foreigners. Even Belinda rarely ate Vietnamese food. Our housekeeper, Lan, came five days a week and made dinner for Belinda every night while I was at work. Although Lan occasionally made vegetarian summer rolls or tofu sautéed with lemongrass, Belinda usually left her a recipe, often for a Western-style salad or vegetable stew that she had printed from an Australian food website. I found it odd that Belinda lived in Vietnam and rarely ate Vietnamese food, but I guessed that she wanted a reminder of home. I wanted to show Son and Thanh that I was different, but perhaps they didn't need convincing. Maybe I simply needed to convince myself.

⌒

"LAUREN, what do you do after lunch? You go home?" Thanh asked at work.

"Usually I walk around Hanoi, or sometimes I eat at restaurants or go to cafés and read," I said.

"Next time can I come with you?"

"Yes, of course."

So the next day after lunch, I changed into my street clothes and met Thanh on the terrace. "Okay, we go eat ice cream. Here, here," he said, handing me a motorbike helmet.

We got on his bike and zigzagged through the Old Quarter, a labyrinth of curving streets. Many of these were devoted to a specific kind of store, either toy, or lanterns and paper, or sunglasses. En route, Thanh pointed to an Italian restaurant called Pane e Vino. "This is where I work before La Verticale," he said.

"Oh, cool. Do you like working at La Verticale more?"

"Yes, yes," he said. But I wasn't sure. Was he merely being

polite, or did he actually prefer Didier's kingdom? I sensed that cooking was more of a job for Thanh and the rest of the La Verticale staff than a true passion, the way it had been for the chefs at wd~50.

We slowed down once we reached Kem Trang Tien, an ice cream shop which I had seen but not yet tried. We sped into the motorbike parking lot located in the back.

"Great. I've been wanting to try this place," I said to Thanh.

"This ice cream, very famous. Anytime someone come to Hanoi, they come here. Very good because not so expensive. Poor people can come here," he said.

"Do you come here a lot?" I asked.

"Sometimes. Now, stay here," he said, indicating that I should remain to guard the bike. "What kind you want? Coconut?"

Pleased that he had remembered my favorite ice cream flavor, I smiled and nodded, then watched as he headed to the counter. He returned with two ice pops on sticks, mine as white as milk and his cream-colored with a few beige splotches. "What kind did you get?" I asked.

"Bean. Better than the sweet rice and corn flavors. But coconut is good, too. I will bring my child here next month when he comes to visit. My child, he lives in my countryside because it is too expensive to buy a house in Hanoi," he said.

"So it's only you and your wife here, and your son is in the country?"

"Yes, I miss him. But too expensive." I instantly regretted letting him pay for the ice cream.

We ate our ice pops in the motorbike park underneath a trellis of fake pink and red hibiscus flowers. A television projected an animated movie on one of the walls, and kids chased one another, high on sugar. "Okay, now we eat ice cream cup," said Thanh, pointing to the soft-serve station a few steps away.

"No! You'll get me fat," I protested. "You have one, and this time let me buy it for you." Despite my insistence, he refused. "No, I pay. One for you, one for me."

"No. Really." I was struck by Thanh's genuine good-heartedness and vowed to be a kinder person myself.

"Okay, then, instead we go to market?" Thanh said after we had finished our ice pops.

"Sure."

He steered the motorbike to the Dong Xuan market, a treasure chest for the bargain hunter. We walked through jam-packed stalls selling fake designer clothing, souvenirs, trinkets, and rolls of fabric. We stopped at one on the ground floor displaying plastic magnets of Hanoi. Thanh picked out a pale blue one depicting Hoan Kiem Lake and took out his wallet. After a spirited negotiation with the seller, he paid and handed me the magnet.

"You didn't have to do that," I said, touched.

"But it's your birthday tomorrow, yes?" asked Thanh.

"Yes, I'll be twenty-five. How did you remember? It was over a month ago that I told you my birthday."

"My birthday is July twenty-first. Almost same-same."

"Oh, what will you do for it? Drink some beer?" I joked.

He laughed. "My wife, she will make dinner."

"What will you have? Cake?"

"No, no cake. We have rice and fish."

"What kind of fish?"

"Little fish, the kind you had at lunch today. Good because not too expensive. Okay, we come back," Thanh said as we reached the end of the market, confusing the "go back" and "come," as the kitchen staff did nightly when they said, "Okay, Lauren, come back home."

Later at La Verticale, while I filled small ceramic bowls with fried rice, Thanh said, "Lauren, come here."

I signaled to him that I was working, but he called out again. "When you go back to America, you don't want to tell people you learned to make rice and potatoes. Potatoes not important for Vietnam." He flicked his hand in mock disgust. "You work on meat, you can take back. Make your style."

"Okay, sounds good, boss. I will make beef in America," I said, pleased to see plates in their final stages.

"Yes, yes. My style, always same-same, though. My style is Didier Corlou," he said with a note of disappointment, and it saddened me that Thanh or the other chefs here probably couldn't afford to open their own restaurants or wouldn't have a real chance to develop their own cooking styles. I joined Thanh at the stove to begin the dinner shift. The differences between our lives were still pronounced, but now, as we stood side by side behind the stove's burners, the distance didn't feel as wide.

A Taste of the Hanoi Street

Vietnam is filled with delectable treats, but the following recipes particularly recall summer days in Hanoi.

GREEN PAPAYA SALAD

Green papaya salad is ubiquitous in Hanoi and is generally served with thinly sliced dried beef or sometimes quail. I've made this salad with cooked shrimp, and I've added shredded carrots and scallion, but personally I think it's at its best when it's just green papaya with a few added flavorings. Green papayas can be found in Asian markets, but if you don't live near any, just search for an unripe regular papaya at your grocery store. This salad is also great with green mango. If you don't have a mandolin, you can cut the green papaya into thin strips using a knife; just be forewarned that it will take a bit longer.

SERVES 4 TO 6

> ⅓ cup Chinese peanuts (or regular peanuts)
> ½ cup loosely packed mint leaves
> ½ cup loosely packed cilantro leaves
> 1 to 2 red Thai chiles
> 3 tablespoons fish sauce
> 3 tablespoons water
> 1 tablespoon rice vinegar
> 1 tablespoon lime juice
> 1 tablespoon sugar
> 1 large green papaya, about 1½ pounds

Preheat the oven to 350 degrees F. Bake the peanuts for about 10 minutes, or until golden brown, then chop them roughly and set aside. Chop the mint and cilantro leaves, and slice the chiles into rings as thin as possible (if you want to avoid touching the chiles, use a pair of scissors to cut them into rings), then set aside.

In a small bowl, combine the fish sauce, water, rice vinegar, lime juice, and sugar, and mix well.

Cut the top and bottom off the papaya, then peel it and cut in half. Use a spoon to scoop out the seeds and inner membrane, then slice each half into quarters. Using a mandolin, slice the papaya into thin strips about 1 to 2 millimeters thick. Place the papaya into a large mixing bowl along with the peanuts, mint, cilantro, and chiles. Pour in the dressing and mix well. Let sit for 30 minutes, then mix again before serving.

FRIED FISH WITH DILL AND TURMERIC (CHA CA)

The two main places to eat cha ca in Hanoi (besides the upscale version at La Verticale, of course) are Cha Ca La Vong and Cha Ca Thang Long. The following recipe is my approximation of the dish. Don't balk at the amount of oil used; it's supposed to be like that, as the spice-infused oil forms a sauce for the fish.

SERVES 4

FOR THE MARINADE:
2 teaspoons minced or grated ginger
2 tablespoons ground turmeric
2 tablespoons fish sauce
¼ teaspoon finely minced Thai red chile
¼ cup vegetable oil
1 tablespoon sugar

FOR THE FISH:
1 pound tilapia or other mild, firm-fleshed fish, skinned
   and boned and cut into 1-inch chunks
⅓ cup Chinese peanuts or regular peanuts
12 ounces thin rice noodles
¼ cup vegetable oil
5 scallions, sliced into 2-inch pieces
1 bunch dill, roots cut off, cut into 3-inch stems

Combine all ingredients for the marinade in a small bowl. Add the fish and coat well. Let marinate, covered, in the refrigerator for at least 2 hours.

Preheat the oven to 350 degrees F. Roast the peanuts for 10 to 12 minutes, or until golden brown, then roughly chop and set aside.

Bring a pot of water to a boil and cook the rice noodles according to directions on the package. Drain, then rinse under cool water for a few seconds to halt the cooking process. Divide the noodles among four bowls.

In a large frying pan, heat the vegetable oil over medium-high heat. When the oil starts to shimmer, add the fish. Sauté for about 5 minutes, or until the fish is almost fully cooked, making sure not to stir too frequently. Add the scallions and cook for another minute, then add the dill, stirring until just wilted.

To serve, spoon the fish and herbs over the noodles along with a spoonful of the oil. Sprinkle generously with the peanuts.

REFRESHING LIME JUICE

The Hanoi summer is a scorcher, and nothing beats the heat like a big glass of limeade, which the Vietnamese call "lime juice." I like to add lemongrass for a Southeast Asian flavor, but it's great without it, too.

MAKES 1 PITCHER (ABOUT 6 TO 8 SERVINGS)

1 cup sugar
7 cups water
Pinch of kosher salt
1 (6-inch) piece lemongrass, smashed with a mallet
1 cup freshly squeezed lime juice (from about 6 to 7 limes)
Ice

In a small saucepan over medium heat, combine the sugar with 1 cup water, salt, and lemongrass, and cook until the sugar has dissolved. Remove from the heat and steep until room temperature.

Pour the lime juice and remaining water in a pitcher and add the syrup, making sure to discard the lemongrass. Stir well and serve over ice.

Chapter 7

BOTH BELINDA AND SUCHI were out of town on my birthday, but Lucy convinced me that my quarter century was worthy of celebration. We headed to Jo Jo's, a centrally located wine bar popular with expats. Jo Jo's was celebrating its own anniversary, and the all-you-can-drink wine for 200,000 dong (a little over $10) was flowing like Niagara Falls.

"There was a little girl there, and she was lovely. I brought some soap bubbles with me, and we spent time in the yard, blowing bubbles together," said Lucy, describing her orphanage visit that day. The adoption process was clogged with red tape and required a lot of energy on Lucy's part, and I knew it must be difficult for her.

"How old was she?"

"See, that's the thing. She's three. But they found her abandoned and walking down the street alone. She probably hadn't eaten anything in days, poor child."

"You wanted a baby, right?"

"Yes, but I don't know for sure. There was a girl, too, who was about eighteen months, but she has an older brother, and if they have siblings, you have to take them both."

"You don't want a boy?"

"No, it's not that. A boy really needs a father figure, and I can't give him that. And the reason they're in the orphanage is that their parents were drug traffickers. The father was sentenced to life and the mother ten years. So what if she gets out and then wants to claim her children..." She trailed off, her voice tinged with apprehension.

"Can you hire someone like a fixer to help you speed up the process?" I asked.

"You can, but it's very expensive, and I also don't want to do that," she said, implying that she didn't want to buy a baby like a new car. "I'm going back again next week, so we'll see. Do you have any plans for the week?"

"Just working. But if you're not sick of me, would you like to come to dinner with me at La Verticale tomorrow? Didier invited me as a thank-you because he's leaving for vacation in France next week and won't be back before I leave. He said I could bring a date, and I thought you'd be a great dining companion."

"I'd love to," Lucy exclaimed.

I arrived at La Verticale the following evening right at seven, and Didier welcomed me personally. *"Bonjour, ça va...* Yes, I make you little menu," he said, and returned to the kitchen. Ushered upstairs, I waited alone for Lucy in the high-ceilinged room on the second floor.

She soon breezed in and said, "I've never been here before. It's gorgeous!"

Our waitress brought us wet towels for our hands and faces, a necessity in the middle of a Hanoi summer, and explained that Didier was offering us the $28 "Hanoi Journey" set menu.

Valentin greeted us, and after I introduced Lucy, he launched into the menu. "So there is the artichoke, it is from Da Lat in the South, it is one of our most popular, very nice... Or the mackerel, it is spirit of Brittany; you know, the chef, he is from

Brittany, and it comes with rhubarb and clams... And then the ocean soup, it is a little spicy, more *Asiatique*... The duck, it is very French in style if you like that. And the farm piglet is very popular... The fish, it is light... The passion cake is also one of our most popular, the lychee also more *Asiatique*, but very refreshing and with almond jelly..." Finally he stopped and caught his breath.

"Wow!" Lucy said after Valentin had left.

"You are ready to order?" asked our waitress a few minutes later.

"Yes, I'll have the artichoke and the ocean soup and the piglet and the passion cake," I said.

"You know, that sounds so good, I'm going to have the same thing," Lucy told the waitress. She turned back to me. "Oh, this is so lovely. You know, back at home I led a fairly posh life, but I never do anything posh like this in Hanoi. There's really no need, is there?"

"You're right," I said. In New York, new restaurants are eagerly awaited, and gossiping about the newest hot spot is a way of displaying cultural capital. But that sort of hypercompetitive foodie culture didn't exist here. I had already dined at a couple of the "nicer," touristy restaurants in town with Belinda, and to me the food was mediocre and overpriced. I put my money into eating in the markets and at the local stands for a cheaper and more authentic experience. Although, I admit, on those stifling hot nights when the air was as thick as molasses, I relished dining in air-conditioned restaurants.

Lucy and I worked our way through several *amuses*; the first was a small bowl of sliced cucumbers accompanied by chile salt, a tiny shot glass of fish sauce, and a deep-fried squid's egg topped with passion fruit sauce, resting on a soup spoon. The second featured a duo of soups, creamy pumpkin and chilled tomato, with a small quenelle of Didier Corlou's eponymous goat cheese—the first cheese ever to be produced in Vietnam, I told Lucy.

A small group of Australians soon sat down two tables away. "Do you know who those people are? They look familiar," I asked Lucy.

She glanced over, concentrating. "Oh, I know. I met her at Belinda's birthday party." She turned toward their table and said, "Excuse me, you're Larissa, right?"

"Yes," said the blond woman.

"Right, we met at Belinda's party. I'm Lucy," she said.

"And I'm Lauren, Belinda's flatmate," I said, adopting the local term even though my instinct was to say "roommate."

"Oh right, how are you? Where's Belinda?"

"She's in Hoi An at the moment with Sinan." Sinan was Belinda's Turkish boyfriend, whom she'd met a month before. The relationship was doomed since he was moving to Russia shortly, but they were making the most of it and had jetted off for a romantic weekend together.

"Oh," said Larissa, exchanging a subtle look with her boyfriend, whom I had also met at an expat barbecue my first week in Hanoi.

"I hope you weren't supposed to keep that quiet," Lucy murmured.

"Oh, crap, I didn't think of that," I said. I'd forgotten that gossip traveled like wildfire in the expat community here. Even if you met someone new at a party or restaurant, it was guaranteed that you had someone, if not several people, in common. Hence, you constantly had to watch your mouth when talking about other people, especially their love lives.

"Mmm, this 'all part of farm piglet' dish is divine. Let's hope your dog meat tomorrow night will be as tasty. I still can't believe you're actually going through with it," Lucy exclaimed.

"I'm already nervous, but I told my friend Hung that I'd at least try it. Who knows, it could be really tasty," I said, hearing the doubt in my voice.

"Unlikely! Just be careful you don't get 'the cholera,'" she warned me. "A man at my office was out for a month because he ate dog and then came down with it."

Indeed, only two months earlier, a cholera outbreak had socked Hanoi. It was first attributed to the fermented shrimp sauce served alongside dog meat, but then later it was determined that the dogs themselves were carriers of the bacteria that cause cholera. Although the outbreak had forced many dog meat restaurants to close, officials were able to contain it, and the restaurants were once again bustling. And I had a dinner date at one of them tomorrow with Hung, who was a friend of a friend in New York.

"In any case, I'll tell you all about my dog dinner afterward," I said as we finished our entrées.

Lucy groaned. "Do you know how they kill them? They bludgeon them to death to raise their adrenaline levels because that's supposed to make them taste better. Please don't tell me about it. I don't want to know. Let's eat our desserts and talk about happy things."

⌒

I HAD MET Hung two weeks before, when he had taken me out to lunch at Quan An Ngon, a bustling open-air restaurant that served the best of Vietnam's street food. It's popular with locals and tourists alike, particularly those who are eager to sample the bounty of the street but aren't quite ready to plop down on a miniature plastic stool in the middle of a crowded sidewalk. Hung was wide-eyed and cheerful, eager to show me all that his city had to offer. On our way back from lunch, he took me on a motorbike tour of Hanoi and shared his favorite places. Slowing the bike as we rolled past a stretch of restaurants, he explained, "These restaurants, they serve dog meat."

"Oh. What does dog meat taste like?" I said.

"You want to try dog meat? Ooooh! I will take you next time I see you. Very good for American girl to want to eat dog," he said, chuckling. I didn't tell him that I just wanted to know what dog meat tasted like; I wasn't sure I wanted to try it myself.

"Um . . . I guess so?" I replied.

"Yes! We will go in two weeks," said Hung, squealing with delight.

So the day after my birthday dinner at La Verticale with Lucy, Hung and I headed toward a very different kind of restaurant: Tran Muc, the famed dog meat restaurant fifteen minutes north of central Hanoi, situated in a dilapidated stilt house, one that you could describe as "rustic" or "authentic" at best. Under the hazy mauve sky, a large illuminated billboard in front blazed, *Nha hang dac san thit cho*" ("Restaurant specializing in dog meat").

We climbed the rickety wooden stairs single-file to an open-air room covered in bamboo mats embossed with a red pattern. Mud-splattered shoes cluttered the entranceway, and Hung and I slipped off our own, then walked barefoot toward the hostess.

"In dog restaurants, you eat on the floor," Hung explained as we followed the waitress to an unoccupied space on the floor marked by an unfolded newspaper doing triple duty as table, seat, and place mat.

"Why?"

"I don't know. Dog restaurants, you always sit on the floor. And you know, dog meat, it is good for sexual power. You see the couple? They eat dog meat and they get closer together," Hung said with enthusiasm, pointing to a young couple a few feet to our left. I smiled, shifting my body a few inches away from Hung. I was one of only three women, not to mention the only non-Vietnamese person, dining in the restaurant, and I was suddenly unsure of Hung's intentions.

Before my dog dinner date with Hung, I had trolled the Internet to learn more about the importance of dog meat in Vietnamese cuisine. Apparently, eating dog meat is thought to bring luck and prosperity, but only during the second half of the lunar month. Consuming dog during the first half is considered very unlucky; consequently, many dog meat restaurants close during that time. Although dog meat is more commonly eaten during the cold winter months because it is considered a "warming" food according to traditional food classification, Tran Muc was nevertheless crowded, filled with clusters of men in their twenties and thirties dressed casually in T-shirts and slacks, laughing and swilling glasses of vodka like Vladivostok pros in the dead of winter.

The most traditional way to sample dog in Vietnam is in a set of dishes known as cay to 7 mon, in which a whole dog is used and prepared seven different ways. We knew that would be too much food for us, though, so without consulting any sort of menu, Hung ordered a plate each of steamed dog, grilled dog, and dog stew.

Our waitress soon brought out a plate filled with lemongrass stalks, basil leaves, and a large-leafed Vietnamese herb called la mo that was grassy-tasting and covered in a light fuzz; a plate of cucumber spears with chile salt, sliced chile peppers, and lime wedges; a large sesame-studded rice cracker; and a small bowl of purple fermented shrimp sauce whose potent smell and taste are supposed to help mask dog meat's strong flavor.

The steamed dog pieces were placed before us; several slices of fatty, pinkish gray meat resembling boiled leather slumped one atop another on a small white plate. The olfactory mirrored the visual—the scent wafting through the air recalled wet cardboard in a slaughterhouse. My stomach clenched.

The grilled dog placed in front of us, however, looked more appetizing than the steamed dog. The bite-sized chunks of meat were covered in a paste made from galangal and had been grilled on skewers until lightly charred. The dog stew closely resembled a vegetable-free beef stew and followed next in a bowl.

"The dog stew might not be fresh, so we aren't going to eat it," said Hung, examining the bowl with a medical eye like the doctor he was. Why he hadn't decided that before, I wasn't sure, but if the local expert wasn't going to take chances, I would follow his lead.

Chopsticks in hand, I reached for the grilled dog. Hung instructed me to wrap it in herbs and dip it in the murky shrimp sauce. After a deep breath, I slowly nibbled the meat. It was chewy and fatty, with a strong animal taste like squab or venison, but not as succulent. The minced galangal and subtle charcoal flavor were pleasant enough, and the meat itself was reminiscent of beef—if you closed your eyes and didn't think about it too much.

While Hung lapped up the meat, I nibbled on the cucumber spears, dipping them into the chile-flecked salt. Seeing that I wasn't going for the steamed dog meat, he placed a piece in my bowl and smiled. I hesitantly wrapped it in herbs and told myself that it *had* to taste better than it looked. Yet as soon as I began to chew, my visceral reactions took over and my throat closed. All I wanted to do was gag, but somehow I swallowed.

I tried to force a smile as Hung watched my every move with gleeful anticipation. The steamed dog meat packed a primordial punch; it was strong and complex, but also extremely earthy and wild, like nothing I'd ever tasted. I can say with authority that steamed dog meat is an acquired taste, and one that I hadn't acquired—nor was likely to.

"Hung, can you ask our waitress what kind of dogs they use?" I asked after we had finished our meal, Hung having eaten the majority of it.

He flagged her down, and they conversed for about five minutes in Vietnamese. "She says local dogs," he said after the waitress had cleared our plates. "She tells me that Western dogs do not taste good. Neither do old dogs. Adolescent dogs taste the best."

"Who would have guessed," I said, trying not to appear too disgusted.

I excused myself to find the bathroom, which ended up being a single, empty tiled room with an angled floor leading to a hole in the ground, further adding to the restaurant's rustic charm. Restrooms in Vietnam weren't always up to Western standards, but this was the worst I'd encountered. Hoping there was another option, I began to explore. I accidentally stumbled upon the basement-cum-kitchen and spied a large cage to my left. The room was dark, dimly lit by a single fluorescent lightbulb far in the back, but I caught the reflection of two eyes enshrouded in black fur looking in my direction. While I had come to terms with the idea of dog meat itself, seeing this caged, living dog primed for dinner turned my stomach. I met its eyes, then quickly retreated upstairs to Hung.

I insisted on paying the bill, which amounted to the equivalent of a reasonable $6, and Hung asked me, "So, did you like dog dinner?"

"It was interesting, although I'm not sure I'll be eating dog again soon," I said.

Indeed, my Tran Muc dog dinner did not figure into my top five most delicious meals. Or top ten or twenty or hundred. But hands

down, it was the most unforgettable meal I'd ever eaten, and it was part of why I'd wanted to come to Vietnam in the first place. In Hanoi, I was out of my culinary comfort zone, eating foods and shopping for ingredients I had never encountered before. While most of my expat friends in Hanoi shunned street food and stuck to upscale, Western-type restaurants, I was busy exploring every storefront that offered me something new. Not everything I ate in Hanoi was delicious or a culinary revelation, but everything was exotic and magical to me, and I was too sated with wonder to care. In sweltering Hanoi, I had found my place at the table.

"Hanoi Moment" Recipes

These dishes are all adapted from Didier Corlou's recipes and highlight some of my favorite dishes at La Verticale. No recipes for dog meat here.

SAUTÉED CLAMS WITH CURRY SAUCE AND ARTICHOKES

This dish is somewhat labor-intensive, but it's well worth the effort. You can also make this without the artichokes and just serve plain or over white rice if you want to save time.

SERVES 4 AS AN ENTRÉE OR 6 AS AN APPETIZER

Juice of 1 lemon
3 to 4 artichokes (about 2⅓ pounds)

(continued)

3 tablespoons vegetable oil

1 medium onion, finely chopped

1 tablespoon curry powder

1 ounce dried shiitake mushrooms, rehydrated in warm water
  and finely chopped

1⅓ cups chicken stock

½ teaspoon kosher salt

¼ teaspoon freshly ground black pepper

3 tablespoons unsalted butter

2 tablespoons fish sauce

1 teaspoon cornstarch dissolved in 1 cup water

4 pounds Manila clams

2 shallots, minced

½ cup dry white wine

2 teaspoons tamarind paste

4 scallions, minced

Bring a large pot of water to a boil. Lower the heat to a simmer and add the lemon juice and artichokes and poach, covered, for 45 minutes.

While the artichokes are cooking, heat 2 tablespoons vegetable oil in a wok or pot over high heat. Add the onion and sauté, stirring frequently, until it begins to soften. Add the curry powder and sauté another minute. Add the mushrooms, chicken stock, salt, pepper, butter, and fish sauce, and bring to a boil. Then add the cornstarch-water solution, and boil until the mixture thickens to the consistency of oatmeal, about 20 minutes. Set aside.

Drain the artichokes, then remove the petals from the artichoke hearts. Scoop out the fuzz inside the heart and discard, then trim off the peel from the stems. Cut the heart into small cubes.

Scrub the clams and let sit in cold running water for at least 10 minutes to get rid of any sand.

Heat the remaining oil in a wok, then add the shallots and sauté until soft. Add the clams, white wine, and tamarind paste, and sauté until the liquid has almost evaporated. Add the curry sauce and bring to a boil. Cook over high heat, stirring frequently, until the clams have all opened, about 5 minutes. Add the cubed artichoke hearts and the minced scallions to the clams and stir until combined.

Divide the artichoke petals among four bowls, arranging them in a circular pattern around the inside of each bowl, petals facing upward. Spoon the clams evenly among the four bowls and serve immediately.

TUNA WITH PASSION FRUIT SAUCE

Fresh passion fruit can be hard to find, but many Hispanic grocery stores carry frozen packages of the pulp, which will work perfectly. Serve with rice and sautéed Asian greens like bok choy.

SERVES 4

¾ cup passion fruit pulp
2 teaspoons honey
1 tablespoon fish sauce
1 tablespoon soy sauce
Pinch of freshly ground black pepper
1½ pounds tuna, cut into 4 steaks
3 tablespoons vegetable oil
1 large shallot, minced
½ red Thai chile, seeds removed, and minced

In a large bowl, combine ¼ cup passion fruit pulp, 1 teaspoon honey, 1 teaspoon fish sauce, the soy sauce, and the black pepper. Add the tuna and marinate for 10 minutes.

Heat 1 tablespoon vegetable oil in a small saucepan over medium heat. Add the minced shallot and cook until softened but not colored. Add the remaining passion fruit pulp, honey, and fish sauce, then add the minced chile and cook until thickened, about 5 to 10 minutes.

Meanwhile, heat the remaining 2 tablespoons vegetable oil in a large skillet over high heat. When hot and nearly smoking, add the tuna. Cook on each side about 2 minutes for rare, longer for medium. Transfer to plates and top with passion fruit sauce.

HANOI FRIED RICE

There are two types of starch lovers: those in the noodle camp and those in the rice camp. I'll take noodles over rice any day, but after living in Hanoi, I've come to respect rice. Fried rice with mushrooms and lotus seeds was a staple side dish at La Verticale, but I personally like to jazz up Didier Corlou's version a bit with protein for a complete meal. One essential thing, though, is to make the plain rice a day ahead of time so that it dries out overnight and will fry well and not become sticky and clumpy. As for lotus seeds, I prefer dried seeds over canned. If you use them, soak ¾ cup dried seeds in water overnight, then cook in boiling water until soft, about 20 to 30 minutes.

SERVES 4 AS AN ENTRÉE OR 6 AS A SIDE DISH

*¾ cup dried shiitake mushrooms, rehydrated in warm water
(about 1 to 1½ ounces dried)
3 scallions*

1 egg
5 to 6 tablespoons vegetable oil
½ teaspoon minced or grated garlic
1 cup cooked lotus seeds
4 cups cooked, cold rice (about 1½ cups' worth uncooked)
1 cup cooked, shredded chicken
2 tablespoons fish sauce
Cilantro leaves for garnish

Discard the mushroom stems and chop the mushrooms into small pieces, roughly ¼ inch on all sides. Slice the scallions as thin as possible.

Whisk the egg in a small bowl. Heat 1 tablespoon oil in the wok over high heat. When the oil begins to shimmer, add the egg and fry until fully cooked, about 1 to 2 minutes. Transfer the egg to a cutting board and roughly chop into large pieces.

Wipe out the wok with a paper towel, then add 2 tablespoons oil and turn up the heat as high as possible. When the oil begins to smoke, add the garlic, mushrooms, and lotus seeds. Stir constantly until the lotus seeds start to get a hint of color, about 3 minutes. Add the remaining oil along with the rice, chicken, and egg, and stir frequently until well combined. If the rice is sticking to the wok, you can add a little more oil. When the rice and chicken are hot, about 5 minutes, add the fish sauce, stirring until combined. Add the scallions and cook for another 30 seconds. Transfer to serving bowls and garnish with the cilantro.

Chapter 8

BY THE SECOND HALF OF JULY, Didier had abandoned Hanoi for his annual summer holiday in France, leaving us cooks happily to our own devices. Belinda's romance, too, was winding down, since Sinan was preparing to leave the following week for Russia. "He wants me to go to Russia with him, but I'm not going to sit around as someone's girlfriend in a hotel there. It's not even like he's going to Moscow or St. Petersburg, where I could maybe find a job. He's being transferred to somewhere in the middle of nowhere," she complained.

A friend of Sinan's was throwing him a going-away party, and Belinda and Sinan invited Lucy and me. Belinda and I made dinner for all of us, a not very Vietnamese meal of bean burritos and a green salad, and the four of us jumped into a taxi, even though the party was a five-minute walk away. When it's that humid and muggy, and a taxi costs only sixty cents, you take one.

"Liam lives in the penthouse," Sinan told me as we got into the elevator of a remarkably modern building on the edge of Tay Ho Lake. Like several of the Tay Ho complexes, this building featured full-serviced luxury apartments, which were usually rented to business travelers or expats by their company.

"Oooh, fancy," we cooed collectively.

"And he's single," Sinan added.

"Great. Just my type: single and rich," I joked.

"My gosh, this is fantastic," Lucy said when we walked into the penthouse apartment. The living room was two stories tall and decorated with modern furniture. Liam, the host, was an affable blond with a square jawline and enough confidence to wear a pink, flower-print shirt. He was sandwiched between two striking Vietnamese girls in bright satiny skintight dresses.

"Shall we have a drink, girls?" said Belinda.

"Yes, let's," I said. We poured ourselves champagne and then offered some to the Vietnamese girls, who were the only other guests at this point.

"No, we have orange juice," one of them said. I found it funny how the tables were covered with bowls of Doritos, pretzels, and Lay's potato chips instead of local treats, but I knew not everyone shared my love of Vietnamese food. And I was also aware that I was a temporary visitor and my culinary experiences in Hanoi were limited to only three months. Perhaps when you've been an expat in Vietnam going on three years, the novelty of the foreign cuisine wears off and you just want a taste of home, even if it is one that is shrink-wrapped and artificial nacho cheese–flavored.

Eventually more guests flowed in, many coming from a wine tasting. The crowd ranged from young expats in their twenties like me to Michael Michalak, the American ambassador to Vietnam. I joined Lucy and Liam in the kitchen and helped myself to a glass of imported champagne. "So, Liam, how did you end up in Vietnam?" I asked.

"Before this I was in Dubai for a few years, and before that I spent two years traveling the world as an auditor. It was a good job, and people wanted all these glamorous places like Paris or

London, but I said, 'Where else do you have?' So I went to Panama, El Salvador, Brazil, Amsterdam, Kazakhstan, Azerbaijan, twenty different countries over the course of two years."

"That must have been hard," said Lucy.

"No, it was great. The company gave us money to travel on the weekends, and we would lose it if we didn't use it, so we went to some new city or country every weekend. It's probably the only time in my life where I can remember exactly what I did every single weekend."

Maybe it's a by-product of being an expat, but I was getting the impression that Vietnam attracted eternal wanderers. Belinda had lived in Hong Kong and wanted to move to Tokyo; Lucy had come via Hong Kong and was contemplating Dubai next. At the party, I met a couple who worked at the American embassy and were heading out on a mysterious-sounding mission to Cuba the following week, while Sinan had worked in Dubai before Vietnam and was now bound for Russia. It made me dizzy, but perhaps those bitten by the travel bug felt that the grass was always greener elsewhere and that each new locale presented an opportunity for self-reinvention and testing one's limits.

"I don't know if I could do that, move somewhere every few years and have to start all over," I said later to Belinda. As much as I could see myself temporarily packing up and heading out into the unknown, I was comforted to know that I could always call New York home.

She said, "Yeah, you know, I was upset the other day because my life hasn't gone exactly how I thought it would. Hong Kong didn't work out professionally and romantically, and now Hanoi hasn't really either. But I suppose you can meet interesting people, people you wouldn't necessarily be friends with at home. It makes you think about your preconceived notions of people, doesn't it?"

"Definitely," I said. Indeed, Lucy and Belinda were so different in terms of age and background from most of my friends back home, nearly all of whom I had met through school or were friends of friends, but we had quickly formed strong bonds. On the few occasions where I was home with Belinda on a weekend and we didn't feel like going out to dinner, she'd make us a light soup and salad or sautéed vegetables over rice. She didn't do it to impress me by showing me that she, too, knew how to cook. She did it because she wanted to, because here, abroad, we were like a little makeshift family.

"Soooo, what do you think about Liam?" said Belinda, smiling.

I glanced at him. "Do you really think he's flirting with me?"

"Yeah! Was he holding your hand just then?"

"Yeah." Okay, he *was* flirting.

"Lauren, go back there! Go talk to him! Think of this apartment. This is as good as it's going to get in Hanoi!" said Lucy.

"What should I say? I'm out of practice being flirty," I said.

"Say, 'I didn't know which of the wines I should open and can you come and help?'" said Belinda.

"Maybe I'll take a beer and ask if he needs a refill. I'm nervous, though! I haven't been out on a date in forever, since working in New York halted all chance of a dating life and here I just haven't bothered," I said.

"Don't overanalyze it, just go!" But before she could shoo me away, Liam trooped into the kitchen with a posse and a bottle of whiskey.

"Shots!" they said, and glasses were distributed. Liam handed me one and we clinked plastic cups. Somehow the conversation turned to dating.

"Yeah, well, the Western girl has it worse off," I said. "Western guys are all off with Vietnamese girls, and Vietnamese

guys aren't interested in Western women because the power
dynamic in the relationship is different than if they're with a
Vietnamese woman."

"Let's go outside," said Liam. He grabbed me by the hand,
and we walked to the terrace.

"So what are you doing here in Hanoi?" he asked.

"Cooking, taking a break from New York...," I started.

"Cooking? That seems rather bizarre."

"Well, it's what I'm passionate about, so it's not that bizarre.
Do you like *your* job?"

"Do I like my job? I'm not going to lie and say I love my
job, but it lets me live in places like this. But all jobs basically
suck. No one would work if they didn't have to. If you were,
like, here's a pile of money, take it, or here's a pile of money but
go do x, y, and z first, I tell you, no one's going to choose the
second option..." He paused and smiled at me. "Come on, let's
stop talking and dance."

We started dancing to the music, an odd amalgam of songs
from the past decade, and, fueled on French champagne and
American bourbon and a steamy Vietnamese summer night,
he leaned in to kiss me. And kiss me again.

◌⌇⌁

"LAUREN, we take photograph after work, okay?" said Son.

It was my last day in the kitchen, and I was sad to leave the
kitchen staff, but I was looking forward to having a break and
traveling for two weeks with my friend Coreen, who was coming to visit from California before starting law school in the
fall. Once the lunch service ended, the staff crowded around
and presented me with a bag. The day before, I had given them

a box of See's chocolates that I had asked Coreen to bring so that the Vietnamese cooks could have a small taste of American candy.

"We wanted to give you a present," said one of the barmen. I opened it and saw two Vietnamese figurines, as well as a small wooden box filled with chopsticks and a set of bamboo place mats.

"Now when I'm home, I can eat as if I'm in Vietnam," I said as they all giggled.

"Now pictures," said Son, ushering us out to the patio.

I posed for photos with each of the staff members, and then we all posed for a group photo, in which I towered over the girls but stood at about eye level with the guys. For the first time in my life, I was one of the tall ones in a group photo.

"So, Lauren, now we drink a coffee or a beer together. Which do you want?" said Thanh.

"Either is fine by me," I said.

"Beer is more funny," said Son.

"Yes, beer is more funny," I agreed.

The whole kitchen staff—minus Luyen, who had never warmed to me and perhaps decided I wasn't worth spending an afternoon with—headed for their motorbikes, and I leapt onto the back of Thanh's. We soon pulled up to a small bia hoi joint that was pretty empty. Bia hoi is a type of local beer; because it's unpasteurized, it needs to be consumed right away and is thus sold at dirt cheap prices. A glass is about 4,000 dong, or around twenty-five cents. Usually it's a predominantly male activity, which was why I had gone out for bia hoi only a few times, though it's popular with both men and women on the tourist circuit.

We crowded around a table in a small room that looked as though it hadn't been refurbished in about forty years. Its peach-colored paint was chipped, and the dark gray carpet cried out for vacuuming, but we didn't care. Shortly after we ordered the beers, our waitress came back with four two-liter jugs of bia hoi. Everyone began conversing in Vietnamese, and Son explained, "They are just very excited because we do not usually have the opportunity to drink beer with a foreigner."

Drinking bia hoi required clinking glasses with everyone at the table no fewer than ten times. Okay, this wasn't a set rule, but after every ten minutes, or after anyone finished a glass, we all raised our glasses anew and cheered.

"Drink, Lauren," said Thanh.

"I am drinking. I don't want to end up too drunk!"

"You tell me yesterday that you can drink five glasses of beer. You must drink five glasses."

"Okay, I'll try." I was thankful not to be returning to work for the evening shift but worried for any customers whose meals would be whipped up by my soon-to-be-drunk colleagues.

A menu was passed around, and I tested my new Vietnamese vocabulary. "Okay, so moc, that's squid, and ech, that's frog, right?"

"Yes, yes. Good. You speak Vietnamese now," said Son.

"See, this is dish I tell you earlier. You want to try it?" Thanh said, indicating the bo cuon la cai on the menu. Earlier that day, he had explained that it was a popular food to be eaten with bia hoi, but that girls generally didn't like it because it was too spicy.

"Sure, I like spicy," I said, which was true, though I also wanted to refute the idea that girls couldn't handle the heat.

In the center of the table, our waitress placed a large circular platter holding piles of vegetables that formed a brilliant kaleidoscope: thin slices of red chiles, yellow pineapple, orange carrots, spears of green cucumbers, branches of ngo herb, and earthy shiitake mushrooms, all next to the cooked, cold sliced beef.

"What's that?" I asked, pointing to a mound of greenish brown vegetables next to the pineapple.

"Green banana," said Thanh. He placed a mustard green leaf on top of a sleeve of rice paper and topped it with a few vegetables and a few slices of beef. After rolling it up tightly but leaving the ends open, he dipped it in the thick brown sauce and handed it to me.

A rush of fire exploded through my nostrils as I took a bite. The wasabi in the dipping sauce was way stronger than I had anticipated. My eyes teared up, and the whole table giggled at the sight of the Westerner getting a real taste of Vietnam.

Once the burning subsided, I pried open my eyes. "Yes, that was definitely spicy," I said, and everyone laughed. Our waitress then brought out a plate of deep-fried corn kernels that were crunchy and sweet and tossed with melted butter like movie theater popcorn, but a hundred times better. Next we dove into a whole carp nestled under a bed of pickled cabbage and stewed tomatoes, pausing occasionally to refill our glasses and toast one another. It didn't matter that most of the conversation was in Vietnamese—I felt right at home.

⌣⌢

I SPENT THE NEXT TWO WEEKS in central and South Vietnam with Coreen, and we basically ate our weight in food. In Hoi An's central market I inhaled bowls of cao lau, a local specialty of chewy, textured noodles in a soy-based broth, while two young Vietnamese girls with toothy smiles showed me how to add vinegar for extra flavor. On the beaches of Nha Trang, I ate spiny lobster with sweet chile sauce served by little old ladies pedaling portable charcoal grills. I wound up with sticky fingers and a full belly after eating crabs in a pool of sugary tamarind sauce in Ho Chi Minh City, where I also slurped down bowls of mi quang and glasses of che in the central market.

But I was excited to see Liam again in Hanoi. We had spent time together before I went on vacation, and I was happy. I had texted him the day before I got back to Hanoi and hadn't heard back, but I figured he was busy with work. Even though I was soon leaving Vietnam, I felt there was a spark between us, and I'd even told my mother that I'd met someone special.

The Friday night I returned to Hanoi coincided with a monthly event called Friday Night on the Terrace, which was held at the Press Club, a restaurant and lounge frequented by expats. I had dinner with Lucy and some of her friends, then headed to the Press Club to meet Belinda. As the elevator opened up to the bar, I immediately spotted Belinda sitting on a bar stool, sipping champagne and chatting with an older gentleman.

"Your boyfriend is over there," said Belinda, jerking her head toward Liam.

I spotted him amid the jostling bodies and made my way over. "Hi. How are you? How was Thailand?" I asked, leaning in to kiss his cheek.

He paused for a moment. "Oh, yeah, my vacation was good...yeah..."

"Oh. That's good, I guess," I said, confused and feeling uneasy. Why wasn't he happier to see me?

"Yeah...how was Hanoi?"

"I was actually in the South, remember?"

"Oh, yeah, I think I remember you said something about that..."

We stood in silence, an awkwardness separating us like two opposite poles of a magnet. Why was he being so cold?

"Okay, I'm going to get a drink," I said. As I turned away, he walked toward a group of people across the room.

I gulped down my champagne and rejoined Belinda. "He wouldn't talk to me. He completely brushed me off and acted all weird. I don't get it," I said, my voice cracking. I had let down my guard and now I was paying for it.

"Just forget him. He looks like a weirdo anyway," she said.

"But why would he ignore me?"

"Because he's weird! Because he's a man, and men are assholes."

Though I appreciated Belinda's loyalty, I couldn't shake how hurt I felt. Was it me? Was it him? How do you go from being so hot to so cold? When my mother called me a few days later to ask about my trip with Coreen, she also asked about Liam.

"I don't want to talk about it. It's too upsetting," I said.

"Why? What happened?"

"Nothing happened. That's the point. It's over," I said.

"I'm sorry. What a jerk."

"Why can't I just find someone who likes me?" I said, on the verge of tears.

"Daniel liked you," said my mother, referring to my first serious boyfriend. She still believed that he was pining away for me, despite the fact that he was now living with a new girl-friend in Philadelphia.

"Mom, that was over seven years ago!"

"Still."

"Mom, that's not helping. I've always worked hard to achieve what I've wanted, but it doesn't work like that with love. What if I end up alone? Why can't everything just work out perfectly and I'll be happily married?"

"Honey, is that what you really want right now? You know that you don't need to have your entire life figured out just yet.

Look at me, I changed careers after fifty and now I'm happier than I ever was as a corporate slave. You're only twenty-five. Give it time."

"It seems like everyone else has their lives all sorted out."

"Lauren, that's ridiculous and not true. Look, you're only in Vietnam for two more weeks. There's no need to let this asshole ruin things. Think about what you've learned and the fun you've had."

"Okay," I muttered.

"Your future will happen when you no longer plan it out in advance. Think about the present. Vietnam's been special," she said gently.

She was right, and with the exception of this Liam thing, I was happier than I had been in a long time. I loved my job and co-workers and felt a true kinship in the kitchen. I liked that at La Verticale I didn't have to crosshatch the shallots or *brunoise* the chile peppers—rough chopping was fine. I learned how to appreciate taste and flavor and was in an environment that valued those aspects of cooking over technique. I always smiled when Thanh greeted me with, "Hello, my teacher!" or when Yen grabbed my stomach in what I hoped was a sign of affection. I would miss the friendliness of both the Vietnamese people and the expat community, and of course, I loved eating Vietnamese food all day, every day. I liked that I wasn't always measuring myself against my friends and that I wasn't defining my worth by my job, social status, or apartment address. It was reassuring that other people here, Didier Corlou among them, not only didn't think it was weird when I explained I'd chosen Vietnam simply because I'd felt inexplicably drawn to it, but had come themselves for the same reasons.

Before Didier had left for France on vacation, he had asked me, "Did you have a good experience here?"

"Yes," I replied without hesitation. I had come to the country to be seduced by its food, but I was leaving it having also been seduced by the people behind it—by Didier and everyone at La Verticale, by all the street food vendors who doled out bowls of noodle soup, by Hung and his gleeful enthusiasm for dog meat, and by Lucy and Belinda, who had been both dining companions and friends who had taken to the kitchen for me when all I needed was a good home-cooked meal.

"Good," he had said. "Because, you know, a *stage* is not just a culinary experience, it's also a human experience."

My (Almost) Vietnamese Cuisine

Under Didier Corlou, I analyzed my own style of cooking and how to incorporate the Asian flavors and ingredients I had so grown to love. Didier's food combines East and West. The recipes that follow take the same approach, with a nod to the new American school of cooking.

CRAB-AND-PERILLA SUMMER ROLLS

Didier made summer rolls using a single large shrimp wrapped inside a thin slice of mango in a dramatic presentation. But I love the taste of crab, and I was inspired by the flavor combination of California sushi rolls when inventing this dish. Perilla (or shiso, its Japanese version) can be hard to find outside of Asian markets in major cities, but basil leaves are a fine alternative.

SERVES 4 AS AN APPETIZER

FOR THE SAUCE:
½ cup water
2 tablespoons fish sauce
1 tablespoon lime juice
1 tablespoon sugar
½ teaspoon rice vinegar
¼ teaspoon finely minced Thai chile

FOR THE ROLLS:
2 ounces thin rice noodles
1 avocado
2 large lettuce leaves (either green leaf or romaine
*   is a good option)*
8 rice paper roll sheets
8 large perilla leaves (or 16 small leaves)
½ pound lump crabmeat

Place all the ingredients for the sauce in a small serving bowl and mix until well combined.

In a pot of boiling water, cook the rice noodles according to the directions on the package until done. Rinse under cold water and place in a bowl. Slice the avocado in half and remove the pit. Slice lengthwise into ¼-inch-thick strips and remove the slices from the peel. Slice the lettuce leaves into thin strips.

Working on a kitchen towel, moisten a rice paper roll sheet with a splash of water and rub both sides of the rice paper with the water. When pliable (about 30 seconds later), place a perilla leaf on the bottom half of the rice paper sheet. Place 1 ounce of crabmeat on top of the perilla leaves in an even row. Place 1 or 2 slices of avocado next to the crab. Add a small amount of noodles, about 1 ounce, on top of the crab. Place a small amount of lettuce on top of the avocado.

Fold the bottom of the rice paper over all the filling and begin rolling about halfway to the top. When the side with the avocado and noodles is facing upward, fold in the side flaps and then continue rolling until you reach the top. Repeat seven more times with the remaining rice paper sheets. Serve with the dipping sauce.

SUMMER TOMATO SALAD

This is a salad you will want to serve during the late summer months, when tomatoes are at their prime. If you can find them (check your local farmers' market), use a variety of different-shaped and -colored heirloom tomatoes for a bright and festive salad.

SERVES 4

FOR THE SALAD:
1 pound tomatoes (heirloom, if possible)
¼ pound watermelon
2 tablespoons chopped basil leaves
2 tablespoons chopped perilla leaves
1 teaspoon chopped mint leaves.

FOR THE DRESSING:
1 tablespoon lime juice
1 tablespoon olive oil
2 teaspoons fish sauce
1 teaspoon sherry vinegar

Core the tomatoes and cut into wedges, then place in a large serving bowl. Cut the watermelon into ½-inch chunks, discarding the rind, and add to the bowl. Add all of the chopped herbs to the bowl.

In a small bowl, combine all the ingredients for the dressing. Pour over the tomatoes and mix until well coated and evenly distributed. Serve immediately.

DUCK PHO

Pho is quite possibly the national dish of Vietnam and a source of culinary contention between the North and the South. Beef pho and chicken pho are the most common types you'll find in Vietnam, but the warm spices like cinnamon and cardamom found in the beef broth immediately led me to think of duck pho. Instead of buying a whole duck and breaking it down to get the bones and breast meat (reserving the leg meat for another use), I find it easiest to buy a 1-pound package of duck wings from my local Asian supermarket and then purchase a single duck breast separately.

SERVES 4

FOR THE BROTH:
1 pound duck bones
2 large shallots, cut in half
1 (2-inch) piece ginger, peeled
2 garlic cloves
1 cinnamon stick
2 pieces star anise
1 black cardamom pod, crushed
6 black peppercorns, crushed
10 cups water
Kosher salt (about 1 teaspoon, as desired)

FOR THE SOUP:

1 duck breast, about 6 ounces

1 tablespoon vegetable oil

12 ounces thin, flat rice noodles

2 scallions, sliced into thin rings

1 large shallot, sliced as thinly as possible

¼ cup cilantro leaves, roughly chopped

1 lime, cut into wedges

1 to 2 red Thai chiles, cut into thin rings

Preheat the oven to 400 degrees F. Place the duck bones in a roasting pan along with the shallots, ginger, and garlic, and roast until the bones begin to brown, about 40 minutes. Place the bones, shallots, ginger, and garlic in a large stockpot along with the cinnamon, star anise, cardamom pod, and peppercorns, and add the water. Bring to a boil, then simmer for 2 hours. Skim off the fat, then strain the stock using a paper towel–lined fine-meshed sieve into a large bowl, discarding the solids. Add the salt (if desired) to the broth and rinse out the pot, then return the broth to the stockpot.

Now that you have your broth, prepare the rest of the soup's components. Discard the layer of fat on the duck breast. Heat the oil in a skillet over high heat, then add the duck breast. Cook for about 2 minutes on each side. The meat should be just browned on the outside but still rare inside. Slice the meat as thinly as possible.

Bring a pot of water to a boil and cook the rice noodles according to the directions on the package, until al dente. Divide among four bowls and top with the duck meat, scallions, shallot, and cilantro.

Return the broth to a boil. Ladle the broth over the noodles and duck, and garnish with the lime and chile to taste. Serve immediately.

Carmella
Bistro

46 HATAVOR STREET

TEL AVIV, ISRAEL

Chapter 9

JUST AS I LEARNED how to cook Vietnamese from a Frenchman, I made the equally perplexing decision to master Israeli
cooking at a non-kosher restaurant. Or so I initially thought.
But then I discovered that there actually aren't many kosher
restaurants in Tel Aviv, and those that are generally aren't that
tasty. So after researching online while in Hanoi and reading guidebooks about Israel, I found my way into the kitchen
of Carmella Bistro, a charming restaurant located a few steps
from the Carmel Market in southern Tel Aviv. Carmella's cuisine, created by chef and owner Daniel Zach, was influenced
by the Mediterranean region, and the restaurant itself is always
featured in guidebooks as being the most romantic spot in the
city.

I didn't know much about the geography of Tel Aviv, but I
knew I wanted to live within walking distance of Carmella.
While in Hanoi, I'd found an apartment on Craigslist on
nearby Mazeh Street and took it sight unseen, valuing con-
venience and location over anything else. Unlike my pristine
villa in Vietnam, the apartment I landed in Tel Aviv was in dire
need of repairs and a thorough scrubbing; but the bedroom was
sunny and had a small balcony that overlooked the street. As a
paranoid New Yorker, I frowned at the balcony door's broken

windowpanes, and whenever I complained to the landlord, he grunted and promised to fix them but never did. It was technically a three-bedroom apartment (with no living room) in one of the white Bauhaus-style buildings ubiquitous in Tel Aviv. My landlord told me I would be alone until he could find two additional subletters. I refrained from suggesting that he might find additional tenants if he actually repaired the other broken doors, television, and washing machine and repainted the mustard yellow, peeling walls. My initial hopes for home cooking were also shattered since the kitchen consisted of a refrigerator, a table, and two hot plates on a counter. But the apartment was only a ten-minute walk to the restaurant, so I was content.

Carmella occupied one of the oldest buildings in Tel Aviv. In addition to the main dining room, the restaurant had two smaller, semiprivate rooms closer to the kitchen and an outdoor terrace framed by potted plants and trees. Multicolored painted tiles and framed drawings of architectural buildings adorned the interior walls, while wall sconces and small wrought-iron balconies wrapped around the building's exterior. I had met Shai, one of the sous-chefs, and Nimrod, one of the managers, the day before, but that meeting had basically consisted of their telling me what time to arrive. So at one p.m. on the following day, I arrived, calm and collected. I wasn't nervous about entering a new kitchen. Now I knew the ropes and how the game was played.

After making my way into the kitchen, I spotted Shai, who introduced me to the guys: Vlady, tall and lanky, with dark eyes and a faint mustache; Hamoudi, whose chubby frame was topped by a shiny bald head; and Eli, elflike and wearing bright red clogs. Shai then ushered me into the adjoining pastry kitchen.

"Hi, I'm Lauren," I said, shaking hands with the pastry chef, who was the only woman and who looked about my age.

"I'm Nitzan. Yay, girl power," she said in accented English. She took me upstairs to the large storeroom pantry, where Carmella's uniforms shared space with dried pasta, nuts, and bottles of oils and vinegars. We rifled through a shelf strewn with a mishmash of clothes, looking for a small pair of black cotton pants and a shirt. "I bring my own a lot since these are all big," she said.

"Here's a medium. I'll go try it on," I said, holding up a black short-sleeved shirt, the color perfect for disguising spills and stains.

After a quick kitchen tour, Shai pointed out where the meat, fish, and vegetables were kept. As at wd~50, the containers were clearly labeled with the name and date of the product, except I couldn't decipher a single character of the Hebrew script. In fact, my Hebrew vocabulary was limited to "shalom," I never had a bat mitzvah, and I hadn't even gone to Hebrew school or belonged to a synagogue. My affection for Christmas (though without the Christ aspect) might even be greater than that for Hanukkah, and my father is an atheist after having disavowed a Presbyterian childhood. But why hadn't I thought about this before now? In Hanoi it hadn't mattered that I couldn't read Vietnamese, since none of the containers was labeled and nearly everything was brought in fresh daily from the market, with very little prepared stuff carrying over to the following day.

"Get a cutting board," said Shai. "We use the blue or yellow ones for fish, and the red for meat and green for produce." I grabbed a blue one, thinking how smart it was to color-code cutting boards to avoid cross-contaminating them inadvertently.

As I arranged my knives, he brought over some fish. "Lokus, or grouper, for carpaccio. Do you know how to clean the fish and skin it?" he asked.

"Yes," I said, thrilled to be handling fish on my first day of work. No more mincing shallots for me!

"Okay, so it's very easy to make a carpaccio, and you can do this with any fish. First cut the cleaned fish into little pieces, but you don't need to be that precise. Just make sure you first cut out the bloodline since you don't want to eat that. Then measure out one hundred grams' worth, and put that in a small mound between two pieces of plastic. Then use this metal pounder and pound the fish, starting in the middle and working your way outward in a circular motion like a snail shell. Then just keep pounding until you have a flat circle that's about the size of this plate," said Shai, pointing to a medium-sized, flat white plate.

"So I should do all of the fish that's here?" I asked.

"Yeah, we need about sixteen portions, so do all of it," he said. "And then just leave the carpaccios in the plastic and stack them all on a plate. We finish them to order by removing the plastic and flipping them onto the plate. You'll see later on."

Preparing the carpaccios was easy, and I was instantly comfortable filleting and pounding the fish. After I'd finished and tidied up my station, Shai asked me to cut orange segments. "Show me," he said, and I did. He nodded in approval. Score another point for me!

Later in the early evening, I met the other sous-chef, also named Shai. I nicknamed him Blue-Eyed Shai, while the Shai from the morning became Brown-Eyed Shai. He and Vlady showed me how to plate the appetizers when orders came in. At first I used my pocket notebook to scribble down the ingredients for the composed salads and carpaccios, but the kitchen vibe seemed laid-back, and by the end of the evening I was working in a rhythm alongside Vlady, asking for help only occasionally.

"Good work," said Vlady, inspecting my plates and giving me a thumbs-up.

The menu at Carmella was Mediterranean/Israeli, with some added French and German influences. It was a bit of a hodge-podge but guided by a market-driven philosophy, which made sense since the Carmel Market was the biggest produce market in Tel Aviv and only steps away. The restaurant's entrées were mostly grilled or seared meats with vegetable garnishes. It was simple, uncomplicated food with little embellishment—and I was ready for that, especially after wd~50's complicated plating and Didier's many garnishes and sauces at La Verticale.

A few days later, Daniel Zach joined the staff at the two rectangular tables where we ate family meal in the dining room. I hadn't met him yet, but he knew I was there. After a summer of eating in the workers' canteen in Hanoi, I was happy to return to an intimate and convivial family meal, one that included the entire kitchen crew plus one or two front-of-house staff from the afternoon shift. The hot line cooks prepared the entrées, usually roast chicken drumsticks or fried cutlets along with leftover rice and mashed potatoes from the lunch shift. But we also ate homemade falafel, crispy and spring green from a handful of minced parsley, and that day's menu featured pasta Bolognese. I had even been in charge of making a salad of my choosing, using whatever ingredients we had on the station. As I was eating, I zoned out amid the Hebrew chatter, but suddenly Daniel turned to look at me from across the table and switched to English.

"Lauren, how are you doing?" he asked.

"Great. Everyone has been really helpful, explaining things to me and translating."

"Do you speak Hebrew?"

"No, but I'd like to learn. I might try and do *ulpan* while I'm here." *Ulpan* is an intensive Hebrew school for new arrivals to Israel. I wasn't sure how I'd fit it into my schedule, which I'd been told would vary from week to week, but I wanted to learn a little Hebrew so I could better understand what was going on around me and feel like part of the community.

"Well, you've come at a good time. You've come between the wars," he joked.

"That's one way to look at it," I said.

"But you're Jewish, right?"

"Yes. My mom is Jewish and so I was raised Jewish."

"And what do your parents do?"

"My father's a lawyer and my mother teaches English as a second language."

"So you're a Jewish American princess, then?" he stated, looking directly into my eyes.

"No, I don't think of myself that way," I said, slightly offended. Although we were comfortable, I was brought up understanding the value of a dollar.

"You know, in Israel we are very direct about things. Don't take it personally," he said.

"Right."

"Well, if I hear you are doing a good job, and I already have, I may start paying you," he said.

"You don't have to do that," I said, and regretted the words the second they left my mouth. After all, why shouldn't I get paid? I was doing the same work as the paid employees. The only difference was that I was an American without an Israeli work permit and at the restaurant for just a fixed period.

Over the past few months, I'd been thinking more and more about the amount of unpaid labor in professional kitchens. I suppose it's not much different from other industries (media, fashion, and advertising, to name a few) with unpaid or very poorly paid internships. Maybe this is a business model that has to be in place for an enterprise like a restaurant to function successfully and profitably, but it also made me wonder about some of the labor practices within an industry already notorious for its hiring policies. I hadn't encountered it, but I'd heard stories from other chef friends about restaurants that regularly employed undocumented workers and paid them lower wages under the table in an effort to control costs.

"I'll be the one to decide that," Daniel said in a no-nonsense tone, adding, "But you're having a good time working here so far?"

"Yes, everything has been great," I said.

"Good, because the most important thing is for you to be having fun," he said.

Really? My having fun was the most important thing? I could get used to this.

⟡

"YOU MUST COME to La Champa with us. We're so excited to meet you. Any friend of Hannah's is going to be a friend of ours," Kate said after I introduced myself over the phone. Hannah, an old friend and neighbor of mine, had just returned to New York after spending a year in Tel Aviv and suggested that I call her Israeli friend Kate. So I did, happy to make local friends outside of work.

"What's La Champa?" I asked.

"It's a great little tapas bar on Nachalat Benyamin. They specialize in cava, the Spanish sparkling wine, so everyone buys bottles and spills out into the street with their glasses of wine and it's a really fun time. Hannah tells me that you're a cook. We'll have to talk shop. I'm not a professional cook or anything, but I love cooking, so do come tonight at nine. Hannah's shown me a picture of you, so I'll find you at the bar," said Kate.

Indeed, when I arrived at La Champa, throngs of revelers were already leaning against cars while precariously balancing glasses in their hands. I pushed open the door and saw a narrow bar, mirror lined and with only a few bar stools, while a massive cured ham sat on full display in what seemed to me a direct mockery of kosher laws.

Kate waved to me from across the room. "Hi, Lauren! I'm so glad you could join us. This is Asher, who is my roommate, and this is Alex and Sharon. Asher and Alex are American and went to college together, and Sharon's originally from Argentina," she said, pointing to the guy and two girls sitting next to her.

"Hi, everybody," I said.

"Here, let's get you a glass. Oh, I'm so excited for you to be in Tel Aviv. We're going to cook together all the time," said Kate.

"Except Kate doesn't eat anything she cooks," said Asher, who was loquacious and dramatic, with dark eyes and a crooked smile.

"You don't? Why not?" I asked.

"I'm vegan. But it's a health thing, not an ethical thing. So I make Asher meat dishes all the time." Kate certainly had the frame of a vegan, with delicate bone structure and the long, lean limbs of a prima ballerina.

"How do you know if the food you make is good?"

"By smell. Or by asking Asher to taste it."

"And that works out?"

"Yeah, totally. You'll have to taste my cooking soon and let me know what you think. Speaking of, do you have plans.for Rosh Hashana? We're going to have a big dinner at our house."

"No, not yet." I had been in Tel Aviv for only a few days, hardly enough time to sort out holiday plans. Not that I had anyone else to spend the holiday with, but I didn't see the point of announcing that to the group.

"Well then, you're coming to dinner at our house. We can plan the menu together!" said Kate.

"Yeah, that would be great," I said, sipping my cava, excited to be spending the Jewish New Year with new friends. We drank our cava late into the night—the first of many such nights, I hoped.

⌁

"DO YOU KNOW how to make gnocchi?" Eli asked me at the restaurant a few days later.

"I made it in school, but that was a while ago," I said.

He pulled out a container of potatoes from the refrigerator. "Okay, I'll show you. Some people, they like to make it with boiled potatoes, but we make it with, how do you say, it's like how you make dim sum..."

"Steamed potatoes?"

"Yes," he said, and I nodded, knowing that steaming potatoes yielded lighter gnocchi than boiled potatoes because the starch content was slightly lower. "So you grate the potatoes until you have three kilos. Then add twelve hundred grams of flour, two hundred grams of Parmesan cheese, twelve egg yolks, and a handful of salt. You can use the gram scale that's in the pastry kitchen."

I jotted down the recipe in my pocket-sized notebook.

"Then you take the mixture and rub it between your fingers until it is like salt. And then you form the dough into logs, and make like five or six logs, and then cut with this," he said, holding up a pastry scraper.

"Okay. Got it. If I have any questions, I'll find you." Secretly, I was elated that the other Carmella cooks trusted my culinary judgment. At wd~50, Tom or someone else always watched my every move. To be fair, though, I now had more culinary experience under my belt.

As I kneaded the dough, Brown-Eyed Shai came over to check on my progress. "See, every day it's something new to do. And at the end you'll decide to move to Tel Aviv and become a cook here."

After I finished the gnocchi, I handed them to Yosko, one of the cooks who worked the grill station, to parboil. He inspected them and said, "For first time making gnocchi, good job."

"Thanks," I said, delighted. I cleaned up my station and began to help set the table for family meal.

After each family meal, the kitchen staff migrated to the terrace for about twenty minutes, smoking cigarettes and relaxing. I always joined them, savoring the calm before the dinner storm. Hamoudi looked at me and exclaimed, "You don't smoke?"

Smoking hadn't been a big thing among the staff in Vietnam, which surprised me at first because it was commonplace in Hanoi for men to smoke. But here, every single person except for me and Blue-Eyed Shai smoked. Even Nitzan smoked along with the boys. As the only other female in the kitchen, she was friendly to me, but we hadn't bonded because she was often buried in the pastry kitchen. So I hung out with loud, sarcastic, macho boys.

While they were generally good cooks, they often abandoned dirty cutting boards when starting a new task or failed to clean their counter space. I now appreciated wd~50's efficiency more than ever and how rare it was to have a chef who cooked regularly in the kitchen, like Wylie. Daniel was rarely in the kitchen, even less often than Didier. When we returned to the kitchen, I asked Eli, "How often does Daniel cook here?"

"Not much. I think I saw him here once. And he wasn't even really cooking; he was mostly watching."

I found this interesting, particularly after my experience with Didier Corlou. I wondered why neither chef spent much time in his own kitchen. Was it something about restaurant cooking that made chefs burn out and want to step away from the stove? As much as I was enjoying gaining restaurant experience and confidence in the kitchen, when I examined the situation I saw that it was always the younger sous-chefs who actually ran most kitchens. Daniel Zach obviously cared about running a great restaurant and was responsible for creating its menu and culinary style, but I found it increasingly disheartening that so many chef owners were more businessmen than cooks, abandoning their cooking career when they no longer had the stamina and drive to be on their feet for fourteen hours a day. I was also beginning to consider how this dynamic affected female chefs. Think about how difficult it must be to run a kitchen while pregnant! Or of the guilt that must come at seven o'clock at night when you're feeding a restaurant full of customers but can't be home to put dinner on the table for your children. These weren't immediate concerns for me, but as I thought about my future, I wondered how the work–life balance plays out when you're a top female restaurant chef. The more I saw, the less it seemed to be a real possibility.

"WE'LL GO to the market first and get all the ingredients, and then we'll start the cooking. Well, you'll do the cooking and we'll watch," said Asher.

At the last minute, Kate had acquiesced to her parents' request and decided to spend Rosh Hashana with her family in Modi'in, a suburb forty minutes away. I was sorry to miss out on her cooking, but she assured me there would be plenty of other times to sample her food. And since I was a professional cook, Asher reasoned, I could make the dinner! *Of course I would want to prepare dinner for six with less than a day's notice!* Though daunted at first, I figured I could pull out all the stops and, the way a woman cooks for a prospective boyfriend, seduce my new friends with the pleasures of the table.

"We'll help out, we promise. Just tell us what to chop and peel. We're good at that," said Mati, Asher's boyfriend.

We ambled through the Carmel Market, which was a food lover's dream, hectic and crowded, featuring stalls filled with fragrant herbs, bright red pomegranates and blushing purple figs, creamy feta-style cheeses cut into large, milky cubes, and rows of cured olives floating in shallow pools of golden green oil. The menu was ambitious for the amount of time we'd allotted, but the boys were confident I could do it. For hors d'oeuvres, I wanted something simple and Israeli, like hummus topped with fried onions and sautéed mushrooms. I planned a salad based on Carmella's famous herb one, capturing the spirit of the holiday by adding pomegranate seeds in lieu of toasted cashews. Alex, Asher and Kate's friend whom I'd met at La Champa, had requested brisket, so I opted for a red wine–braised version that I'd serve with onion-rice pilaf and store-bought circular challah bread to represent the cycle of the New Year. For dessert, I planned to make an apple-honey tart, combining the two most symbolic foods of the holiday, evoking the hope for a sweet year to come.

Once we got back to Kate and Asher's place, which was only two blocks from my own apartment, we immediately sprang into action. Ironically, having worked almost nonstop in restaurants since graduating from culinary school, I rarely found myself in a home kitchen. When you work as a restaurant chef, you're on duty during normal mealtimes and don't necessarily feel the urge to cook on your days off. But here in Kate and Asher's spacious, open kitchen, without the chaos of the restaurant, I took charge. I had forgotten how much I enjoyed being in a home kitchen and was undaunted by the amount of cooking to be done over the next five hours.

"Asher and Mati, if you want to prep the vegetables for the hors d'oeuvres, that would be great and I'll get to work butchering the meat," I said.

Six pounds of beef covered with layers of white, bulbous fat awaited me. I began slicing off heavy clumps of fat and pitched them into the garbage. Once the brisket was completely trimmed of fat, I seasoned it generously with salt and pepper.

"That's a lot of salt," said Mati, raising an eyebrow.

"Yeah, it looks like a lot, but it really helps add flavor. That's why restaurant food often tastes so much better than home-cooked food. They add handfuls of salt. I've never made brisket, though, so I hope it works out," I said.

"You're a chef, so I'm sure it's great," said Asher.

"I'm really more of a cook than a chef," I replied.

"Same difference, really," said Asher.

"Not to a chef."

When the pan began smoking, I placed two of the four slabs of meat in it. "You also don't want to crowd the pan, since you'll lower the temperature of the pan too much. And then the meat won't brown properly," I said. *Wow*, I thought, *I actually know more than I realized about cooking.*

"Okay, I guess I'll do the soup after this. If you guys want to peel the sweet potatoes, I'll chop some of the vegetables and get the other stuff ready after I'm done with the meat," I said once all the meat had browned and I'd placed it in the oven.

I had planned to make a butternut squash soup, but at the last minute Asher said he had a glut of sweet potatoes. I wanted to incorporate Israeli flavors into the soup and thought immediately of a combination of feta cheese and olive oil infused with zaatar, a Middle Eastern spice mixture made from dried hyssop, sumac, thyme, and sesame seeds. Its warm and savory flavors, coupled with the dramatic dark green and white popping out against the bright orange soup, seemed appropriately festive.

I quickly assembled a mirepoix, which is a base of chopped onion, carrot, and leek to give depth and flavor to a sauce, soup, or stock, and began sautéing it in a large pot. Delicious aromas began to swirl through the air as the vegetables softened.

"Ooooh, this is so exciting!" exclaimed Asher, peering into the pot.

"I hope so! I'm a little nervous. What if it all turns out terribly? You guys would have to be fake nice about it so I wouldn't get sad."

"That actually would be really funny," Asher said. "We'd be like, 'Oh, mmm, this is so good,' and when you ask if we want more, we'd be like, 'Oh, no, it's very filling.'"

"You know what we need? Wine. I always cook better with a glass of wine in my hand," I said, chopping herbs for the salad.

We were ahead of schedule, and as I made a mental note to turn the brisket in half an hour, I realized that I'd planned and prepared this entire dinner without a single recipe. I realized I didn't *need them* anymore. This was the kind of cooking I truly enjoyed: guided by touch, smell, and intuition, without the need for a gram scale or three dozen ingredients. Surely wd~50 had been an excellent first restaurant experience; it had taught me how an efficient kitchen runs and the passion and discipline required to be a great chef, in addition to honing my palate, knife skills, technical precision, and speed. But I hated that I could never teach Mati and Asher the actual recipes and dishes I had learned there. Molecular gastronomy cannot be translated to the home kitchen. Still, when I arrived in Vietnam I was very focused on measuring out every ingredient precisely, but Son and Thanh quickly dismissed these as time wasters. After all, Vietnamese cuisine isn't about being precise; it's about being fresh, flavorful, and fast.

Home cooking, too, follows this principle, focusing on nourishment, not wowing your audience. When you host a dinner party, you are, of course, hoping to display your culinary skills and impress others, but the ultimate point of the meal is to eat and share a meal *with* friends. When I've played the parlor game of "What meal would you want to be your last on earth?" I've rarely—if ever—encountered a response about seeing caviar or a truffle-and-foie-gras terrine. Instead, people want roast chicken, meat loaf, poached eggs and bacon, lobster grilled simply with drawn butter, a slice of German chocolate cake. As I prepared this meal, I found my culinary ambitions being drawn away from the restaurant and toward the simpler, comforting foods that I could prepare with others at home.

Two bottles of wine and three hours later, we sat down with our guests to the soup course.

"Oh, my God, this is so good!" said Asher. Indeed, the soup was good. *Really good.*

"So what are everyone's goals for the New Year?" Asher asked as he served the salad course.

"I'd just like to make Asher happy," Mati said without a trace of sarcasm.

"I'd like to focus on my studies and have a good school–life balance," said Alex, who was starting a program in conflict resolution at Tel Aviv University.

"I'd like to get fit and to start dancing again," said Asher, whose recent knee surgery had halted his professional ballet career.

I thought about Belinda and Lucy and Son and Thanh and my new friends here, all so welcoming in bringing me into their circle and breaking bread with me. "I guess I'd like to focus on surrounding myself with good, quality people. I'd like to improve my knife skills and get cooking experience for sure, but more important, I'd like to take advantage of my time here in Israel and focus on being happy."

"Well, if this dinner counts for anything, I think you're off to a good start," said Asher.

"I agree completely," I said.

Recipes to Impress New Friends

The following recipes were highlights from my Rosh Hashana dinner. They are what I would call modern Israeli: familiar flavors with hints of the Mediterranean, Middle East, and beyond.

HUMMUS WITH OLIVE OIL AND FRIED ONIONS

How can you start a festive meal without hummus, the ubiquitous chickpea dip found all over the Middle East? Serve with wedges of warm pita bread, crackers, or your favorite crudités.

SERVES 6 TO 8 AS AN HORS D'OEUVRE

2 (15-ounce) cans chickpeas, rinsed under cold water
4 tablespoons lemon juice

3 tablespoons water
¼ cup tahini
1 garlic clove
¼ teaspoon cumin
2 teaspoons plus a pinch of kosher salt
¼ cup plus 3 tablespoons olive oil
Vegetable oil for frying (about 2 cups)
1 yellow onion

In a food processor, combine the chickpeas, lemon juice, water, tahini, garlic, cumin, and salt, and blend. With the motor running, slowly add ¼ cup olive oil and blend until smooth. Pour into a serving bowl and make a small well in the center using the back of a spoon. Add the 3 tablespoons olive oil in the well.

Heat the vegetable oil in a small to medium-sized pot over medium-high heat. You want enough oil to fill at least 1 inch of the pot. Slice the onion into ¼-inch-thick rings. Test to see if the oil is hot enough: Drop 1 onion ring into the oil; if it begins to bubble rapidly and float to the surface, the oil is hot enough. Add the remaining onion rings and fry until brown, about 8 minutes. Using a slotted spoon, remove the onion rings and let dry on a paper towel. Sprinkle with a pinch of salt. Scatter the onion rings on top of the hummus surrounding the olive oil well and serve immediately.

POMEGRANATE-HERB SALAD

This bright-green-and-red salad is inspired by the herb salad with toasted cashews served at Carmella. Plus, it utilizes the best trick I learned at Carmella: deseeding pomegranates in a snap. Since herbs have a tendency to darken when cut, make sure they are completely dry after washing them (the best way to wash them is to leave them tied in bunches and let them soak in cold water for a few minutes, swirling the water occasionally to remove any dirt) before slicing. And don't worry if you have uneven or whole leaves; that's part of this salad's charm.

SERVES 6

> 2 pomegranates
> 2 bunches parsley (about 6 cups' worth of leaves)
> 1 bunch cilantro (about 2 cups' worth of leaves)
> ½ bunch mint (about 1 to 1½ cups leaves)
> 4 cups baby arugula leaves
> ½ teaspoon kosher salt
> ¼ cup plus 1 tablespoon olive oil
> 2 tablespoons lemon juice

Slice the pomegranates in half lengthwise. Make five to six incisions at a 20-degree angle into the base of each half. Over a bowl, place the pomegranate half seed-side down into your palm and whack the top of the fruit with a spoon. Repeat until there are no more seeds left in the fruit. Remove any yellow pith that might have fallen out along with the seeds. Place the seeds into a large salad bowl.

Cut the parsley, cilantro, and mint: Leaving the herbs tied in bunches and using a sharp knife, thinly slice the herbs starting at the top of the bunch. Once you reach mostly stems, discard the bunch. Add the herbs to the bowl.

Take the arugula and form it into a ball. Using the same single slicing motion, cut the arugula into small pieces. Add to the salad bowl along with the salt, olive oil, and lemon juice. Combine well and serve immediately.

SWEET POTATO SOUP WITH
FETA AND ZAATAR OIL

This is a really simple soup, warming and autumnal and gently flavored with hints of the Middle East. Zaatar is a spice blend that combines dried hyssop, thyme, and sesame seeds and can be found at Middle Eastern grocery stores or other specialty stores.

SERVES 6 TO 8

¼ cup plus 2 tablespoons olive oil
2 tablespoons zaatar
1 tablespoon unsalted butter
1 onion, diced
1 carrot, diced
1 small leek, diced
5 small sweet potatoes, peeled and chopped in 1-inch cubes
6 cups water
2 cups chicken stock
1 bay leaf
1 tablespoon kosher salt
¼ cup feta cheese

In a small pot, combine ¼ cup olive oil and the zaatar. Cook over medium heat until hot, but take care not to burn the zaatar. Set aside for at least 1 hour to cool and infuse.

In a large pot, heat the butter and remaining olive oil over medium-high heat. When the butter has melted, add the onion, carrot, and leek, and cook until softened, about 5 minutes. Add the sweet potato cubes, and sauté for another minute. Add the water, stock, and bay leaf, and bring to a boil. Once the soup begins to boil, lower to a simmer and cook for 30 minutes.

Check to make sure the sweet potatoes are completely soft. Add the salt to the soup.

Remove the bay leaf and puree the soup using a regular or immersion blender. If the soup is too thick, add a little water or stock until a desired consistency has been reached. Ladle the soup into individual bowls. Crumble the feta into each bowl and drizzle with the zaatar oil.

RED WINE–BRAISED BRISKET

Brisket is a popular choice for the Jewish holidays, and although the meat can frequently be tough, the trick is to cook it for a really long time over a very low temperature so that the fat and collagen break down and the meat becomes fork-tender. This is great served over a bed of creamy polenta or mashed potatoes. The 5-to-6-pound brisket is the weight before the fat is trimmed off; after the fat is trimmed, the yield should be about 3 to 4 pounds of beef.

SERVES 8

1 medium to large yellow onion

4 carrots

1 leek, white part only

2 ribs celery

1 beef brisket, about 5 to 6 pounds before trimming

1 tablespoon kosher salt

¼ teaspoon freshly ground black pepper

3 tablespoons olive oil

6 cloves garlic

2 bay leaves

6 sprigs thyme

2 cups red wine
2 cups beef stock

Preheat the oven to 320 degrees F. Cut the onion in half vertically, then cut each half into quarters. Cut the carrots, leek, and celery into 2-inch pieces.

Trim and discard all the fat off the brisket, including the center layer of fat. Cut the brisket into three pieces. Generously season the brisket pieces with the salt and pepper on all sides. Heat 2 tablespoons olive oil in a large skillet over high heat. When the oil begins to smoke, place one piece of the brisket in the pan and sear on each side for about 2 minutes, or until a dark golden crust forms. Remove from the pan and keep warm. Repeat with the remaining two pieces of brisket. Add another tablespoon of olive oil to the pan, and sauté the garlic, onion, carrots, leek, celery, bay leaves, and thyme until the garlic begins to turn golden. Transfer the vegetable mixture to a Dutch oven or other heavy-bottomed baking dish. Place the beef atop the bed of vegetables.

Add ½ cup red wine to the skillet and deglaze the pan, scraping up any bits that may be stuck to the bottom. Once you have reduced the wine by half, pour over the meat. Add the remaining wine and the beef stock to the skillet, and bring to a boil. Pour over the meat and vegetables. The liquid should come halfway up to the meat but should not submerge it completely.

Bake, covered, for 4 hours, basting and turning the meat every half hour. The braising liquid should be at a gentle boil the whole time. If the liquid is boiling rapidly, lower the heat to 315 degrees F. If there is a lot of liquid remaining in the pot, cook with the lid slightly ajar for the last hour. The meat should be tender enough when done to be cut with a fork and should fall apart easily when handled with tongs. Let sit for about 10 minutes before serving.

Divide the brisket among bowls and serve with some of the vegetables and braising liquid.

Chapter 10

ONE OF THE DAYS I was most looking forward to in Israel—Yom Kippur—was actually the most somber in the Jewish calendar. Yom Kippur is the Day of Atonement, when Jews repent for their sins of the past year. And I was excited for all the wrong reasons: While many Jews spend the day reflecting by fasting, I was already guilty of thinking about the pre- and post-fast meals I'd be eating at Kate and Asher's house, for we were reconvening to cook and eat together.

Back in New York, I rarely fasted on Yom Kippur, but several of my new friends in Tel Aviv were going to, so I decided to join them on the principle of "When in Rome," although I allowed myself drinking water. Kate and Mati, though, ironically the two people who had lived in Israel the longest, weren't going to fast. Though Jewish and somewhat observant, they didn't see the point.

While taking a short midshift break at work the day before, I had asked Mikhael, "What do you do on Yom Kippur?"

"Sleep, and drink, and smoke," he said without hesitation. Mikhael, who was my age but twice my size, with spiky brown hair and an equally brash attitude, worked next to me at the appetizer station. Like many of the Israelis I encountered, he was abrupt, almost confrontationally so.

"Oh," I said, surprised.

"Some of my friends, they go to synagogue on Yom Kippur, but I find that depressing. And I walk around the streets near my home. The streets are empty, so people walk and ride their bikes. But you don't want to go near B'nei Brak. It's very religious, how do you say, with the black robes?"

"Hasidic?"

"Yeah. If you drive a car there during Yom Kippur, they will stone your car. Even a bike if you ride a bicycle."

"Seriously?" I said, making a mental note not to go there.

"Yeah, it's crazy." He shook his head.

I was surprised at how secular and laid-back Tel Aviv proper was, for a city located in a country known for eternal political and religious conflict. Despite my initial trepidation, living in Israel never made me nervous; in fact, I felt as if I were living in Southern California: The beach was only ten minutes from my house, and the weather was perpetually warm and sunny. The overall vibe in Tel Aviv was extremely relaxed and casual; you were more apt to see someone in the supermarket wearing a swimsuit top, shorts, and flip-flops than you were to see someone dressed in Hasidic robes.

When we got back to the kitchen, I was surprised to see Daniel there. He usually buried himself in his office upstairs, making sure everything was in order businesswise (or so I assumed), and left the cooking to his sous-chefs. Now he was demonstrating a new special of sautéed crabs that he wanted to add to the menu. Shai took over at the stove, and Daniel said to me, "Do you have somewhere to go for Yom Kippur?"

"Yes, I'll be going to my friends' house," I said.

"Good. It's important not to be alone for the holidays. This year I will be in Eilat, but Yom Kippur is my favorite time to be in Tel Aviv. It is so quiet, and so magical. You are lucky to be here for it," he said. Eilat is a popular beach resort in the southern tip of Israel, and although I hadn't been yet, my guess was that Yom Kippur dress there was probably a bathing suit and people would more likely be lifting a gin and tonic to their lips than the customary prayer book.

When I got back to our station, Mikhael held the prep list in his left hand. "Lauren, tonight we are going to be very busy, so I want you to fill all of our *mise en place* containers up to the top. The very top," he instructed.

Vlady had left Carmella two weeks ago to work at another restaurant closer to his home, so Mikhael and I were running the appetizer station. He normally took the morning shift, which ran from nine to five, did the majority of the prep work, and ran the lunch service, while I handled the evening service from three to eleven thirty and was responsible for cleaning the kitchen at the end of the night; we overlapped for a few hours at the end of the afternoon. While Vlady's departure initially meant more work for me, it also signaled a lot more responsibility. Maybe Daniel was going to hire someone to replace Vlady, but then when the sous-chefs saw that I was competent, they gave me the job instead. At least that's how I'd like to think it happened.

How far I had come from nervously following Spencer's orders during service at wd~50. Now I was in charge! Well, so to speak. Even though I had run the station alone—and efficiently—over the past few days, Mikhael's comment had come across like a command and an expression of hierarchy. I refrained from saying, "Look, buddy, I'm not getting paid, but I know that all the containers need to be filled. I don't need you to add that things need to be at the very top. I get it, okay?" Maybe he treated me differently because I was a woman and he knew that I was less likely to talk back to him or tell him to fuck off the way the other male cooks would. I knew that I was every bit as skilled as he was, but I could tell that he thought I was just a silly girl who liked to play around in the kitchen.

"Refill the squeeze bottles, and make sure they are clean, and put a new paper towel on the bottom of the tray when you clean them," he added.

"I know," I said. *No shit* the oily paper towel needed to be changed. I didn't need to be reminded of things in the kitchen. Not anymore, at least. And certainly not by him.

⁘⸰

"DO YOU WANT to go to the Carmel Market with me? I need some fruits and vegetables. We should go early 'cause it's going to get hectic with everyone buying up stuff for Yom Kippur," Kate said to me over the phone.

"Sure, I'd be happy to come along," I said.

"Great, I'll wait for you on Rothschild Boulevard and then we can walk down together."

Although it was the early morning, the market was already humming with shoppers stocking up, since all stores—really all of Tel Aviv—would be closing for two days beginning at sundown. Although she wasn't fasting herself, Kate had planned starch-heavy dishes to give the rest of us energy, so we bought bags of yellow onions for kugel, which is a hearty baked noodle pudding, and tomatoes and cheeses for tonight's quiche and spinach lasagna.

"Oooh, are you familiar with baklava?" she asked, seeing a vendor selling an array of amber-colored pastries, some dotted green with pistachios.

"Yeah, it's good, but it's usually too sweet for me," I said.

"I want to make a dessert that uses this kind of dough. The

Hebrew word for it means 'hair,'" she said, pointing to the wispy, threadlike dough wrapped around each tiny square of baklava.

"That would be awesome," I said.

"Don't you think? I want to make them into little baskets and have a mascarpone ice cream in the middle with some kind of syrup on top."

"Maybe a pear syrup?" I suggested. Considering she never ate the food she cooked, Kate's keen sense of culinary know-how continued to impress me.

"I wonder where we can find the hair dough," she said, brown eyes scrutinizing the market stalls.

"Over there?" I said, spying a modest storefront hidden behind a fruit vendor. Multicolored cans of preserved fish and bottles of yellow and green olive oils flanked the walls. Kate left me with our pushcart and went inside, emerging triumphantly a few minutes later holding a plastic bag. We peered inside at the white mass, which resembled a loofah sponge. "I don't really know how it will work since I've never cooked with it before," she said.

"It's dessert. People will like anything if it's laden with enough sugar and butter," I said.

We returned home and began prepping. Since it was Kate's kitchen, I let her be the chef and I assumed the role of sous-chef. Dinner was scheduled for a quarter to four, since services were at a quarter after five, and as the afternoon sun slowly descended, the guests began to arrive. Alex and Sharon came with a salad, joined next by their friend Michal and her boyfriend, Max. Their friend Josh followed, while Kate, Asher, Mati, and I completed the family circle.

We set plates of food on the table. "Do we say a prayer?" asked Michal.

No one knew a specific prayer for the Yom Kippur pre-fast meal, so Asher took charge and delivered an impromptu version. "Rub a dub dub, thanks for this grub. Yay, God," he said authoritatively.

"Amen," we said collectively.

"Yom Kippur is such a depressing holiday, if you think about it. Having to atone to God and repent," said Mati as Michal cut the lasagna into squares.

"No, I think the holiday is more about doing right by others rather than doing right by God. You know, you're supposed to apologize to everyone you've wronged before Yom Kippur. But even if they don't forgive you, it's still okay because you did your part," said Kate. I liked the idea that it wasn't just about religion or repentance.

"What do you do, Lauren?" asked Max, seated across from me.

"I work at Carmella Bistro," I said.

"As a waitress?" he asked, repeating a question I often got when I told people I worked in a restaurant, as though the idea of a female chef hadn't occurred to them.

"No, in the kitchen." I smiled to hide my annoyance at his question.

"Did you make *Aliyah?*" Josh asked me, referring to the Hebrew word meaning "ascent," which is a tenet of Zionism and Jewish thought that encourages moving to Israel. For some Jews, it represents the ultimate commitment to being Jewish, even if one is not religious.

"No," I said.

Of the eight of us at the table, the only ones besides me who hadn't made *Aliyah* were Josh and Michal, who were both spending a few months in Tel Aviv trying to figure out their respective life plans. Although she was a native-born Israeli, Kate had spent her childhood in Vancouver and returned to Israel at age twelve, and Mati had moved from Hungary at age eight with his family following the fall of communism. Alex and Asher had each come alone three years before.

I chose Israel as a country where I wanted to live and cook, at least briefly, because I was intrigued by this idea of a personal calling to a place. Yes, I was interested in its food culture, a melting pot of ethnic cuisines ranging from Russian and Eastern European to Arabic, one that utilized the bounty of the land and the tradition of its past. During my time in Tel Aviv, I met many people who had come because they believed in the idea of Israel or because they felt called in a deeper, more spiritual way that they belonged here.

"What do you do?" I asked Max, who was British by birth.

"I write for *Ha'aretz*, the newspaper. Mostly on politics and national security. Today was great, because I generally like to add a bit of color to my stories, and today I was able to add the line 'And on the eve of Yom Kippur...' to everything. Like today I wrote, 'On the eve of Yom Kippur, a clash broke out in Jerusalem...'"

"Jerusalem is so intense," Sharon interjected. "That's why I like living in Tel Aviv. It feels so free and removed from all of that."

"Living in Jerusalem is a lot like living in a museum. You have to be careful about what you touch and where you go. And who wants to live in a museum?" said Kate.

"If it were the Air and Space Museum at the Smithsonian, I would," said Asher, grinning.

Tel Aviv's secularity continued to surprise me. Sure, many stores closed on Friday night through Saturday for Shabbat (the Sabbath, which signaled a time of rest and reflection), but for each one that did, another nightclub thumped away into the wee hours of the morning. In Tel Aviv, religion was an afterthought to many people, and Kate said her family never attended synagogue.

Max turned toward me. "So you're really a chef? What do you think about the food in Israel?"

"It's good. There's a lot more Western- or European-style food than I expected, but it's interesting to see all the different food cultures coming together," I said.

Whenever I told people that I was living in Israel to learn more about its cuisine, I mainly encountered confused looks. "Why would you come to Israel?" I was once asked by my Israeli friend Natan, whom I met shortly after I arrived. "Israel has no food culture. Hummus, falafel, we stole that from the Arabs. The only truly Israeli food is chicken schnitzel."

Indeed, chicken schnitzel is hugely popular in Tel Aviv, brought over from Europe during the post-Holocaust immigration influx. It's been reappropriated (chicken swapped for the traditional veal), and the many schnitzel shops populating the city serve it with hummus, tehina (a creamy sauce-like condiment made from ground sesame seeds), pickles, and a cucumber-and-tomato salad inside a pita or baguette. In more upscale cafés or restaurants, the fried cutlets are served alongside pureed potatoes and sometimes a simple chopped salad. While chicken schnitzel is more representative of everyday fare than haute cuisine, it illustrates why I wanted to experience Israel. Like a teenager trying to figure out his personality, Israel doesn't lack a food culture so much as it encompasses many different culinary traditions while trying to define what constitutes its own cuisine.

Many people would probably identify Israeli cuisine as Jewish cuisine, and there's certainly a great deal of overlap. However, when people think of Jewish cuisine, they almost always think of the Ashkenazi culinary tradition, with its matzoh ball soup, brisket, and gefilte fish, and not the Sephardic Jewish culinary heritage, which is steeped in the rich flavors and spices of the Mediterranean and Middle East. As more and more Jews from all over the world immigrated to Israel, they brought along their former home's culinary heritage and precious recipes, ultimately integrating them into the Israeli culinary landscape like leftover squares of fabric woven into a patchwork quilt.

Sabich, one of my favorite Israeli dishes, is a great example. Sabich is an Iraqi Jewish dish made by stuffing cold, fried eggplant slices into a pita along with preserved hard-boiled eggs, tehina, hummus, chopped salad, and amba (a mango pickle thought to have been brought to the Middle East by spice traders in India). Sabich was traditionally eaten for Shabbat breakfast because all the ingredients were cold and prepared the day before—a necessity, since observant Jews aren't supposed to perform any working tasks on Shabbat, including lighting a stove. When the Jewish population fled Iraq, many trooped to Israel and brought sabich with them. Over time, sabich became a popular street food and is now found throughout Tel Aviv.

Similarly, in Tel Aviv two popular breakfast dishes are jachnun, a traditional Yemenite dish of rolled dough served with grated tomatoes and spicy pepper paste, and shakshuka, a dish of poached eggs in tomato sauce originally eaten in North Africa and brought to Israel by Tunisian Jews. And the ubiquitous dish of chopped cucumbers and tomatoes tossed with oil and lemon may be known as an Israeli salad but is widely considered to have originated within the Arab culinary tradition, along with other "Israeli" favorites like hummus and pita.

More sophisticated restaurants in Israel, like Carmella, still exhibit a French or European influence. Lacking a distinct Israeli food culture in the early years of statehood, upscale chefs embraced generic continental cuisine. But the food scene is quietly evolving in Israel as chefs depend less on outside influences and more on the foods indigenous to Israel and which grow best in its climate. So we are beginning to witness a cuisine that draws on olive oil, fresh fruits and vegetables, fish, and grains. Pomegranates, dates, figs, and olives are taking center stage in today's new Israeli cuisine, just as they did in biblical times.

This was part of Israel's draw; I wanted to learn to cook there because I wanted to be part of a movement defining a national cuisine. While Carmella unquestionably retained a few flourishes of continental cuisine, it offered distinctive examples of contemporary Israeli fare. Its herb salad, although simple to make, was packed with flavor from a trinity of mint, cilantro, and parsley. The halloumi—a soft cheese that was pan-seared until crispy—and beet salad were tossed with honey-based dressing infused with zaatar. I liked how Daniel had reinterpreted shawarma, the local fast-food staple, with his sliced lamb with fried cauliflower and roasted potatoes in tahini sauce, and I had never thought of combining roasted eggplants with mashed potatoes until I saw—and swooned over—his version, which accompanied a simple seared, herb-crusted fish.

"Okay, enough. We have to go. We're already late," said Asher, pointing to his watch while we scrambled to finish dessert and rush out the door.

Because most synagogues in Israel are Orthodox and quite traditional, we chose to attend services at a nearby community center, located in Meir Park, which focused less on God and more on community. In New York City, you have to purchase tickets to attend services, but that wasn't the case here. But because we arrived late, every seat was already filled, and we had to stand against the wall in the back of the auditorium. The windowless room was stifling and the air was stale, so Kate and

Sharon left after ten minutes. Mati and Asher found two seats in the back row, and Michal, Max, and I inched our way to the right side of the room, where the only free seats were in the first row by the rabbi, a tall, bearded man in his late forties with broad shoulders that swayed back and forth with the melody of the songs. I hoped he wouldn't focus on me, clueless and attempting to hum along with the songs and ancient chants.

The community center's auditorium was two stories high, with a narrow wraparound balcony on the second level, which was left empty. Instead of religious iconography, a large poster of a tree hung from the rafters behind the elevated, gray-carpeted stage. The gilded Torah rested in a modest wooden ark no more than two or three feet high, placed on a folding metal table in the center of the stage. Two drooling toddlers had escaped their mothers and were crawling around the stage, occasionally making faces and gurgling noises. The rabbi paused now and then from reciting the prayers to smile at them or to pick them up and rock them in his arms, shrouded under his blue-and-white embroidered silk prayer shawl. When the children got bored, they hoisted their chubby bodies and crawled over the tops of our shoes while we smiled politely at their mothers, who appeared unconcerned about the cleanliness of the Formica floor.

Michal and Max shared a prayer book, but even they got lost occasionally in the flood of mumbled Hebrew. It didn't matter, though, as the beauty of the songs and being together made the actual words less important. Even though I had grown up in New York City, few of my close friends were Jewish, and my family's celebrations of the holidays (initiated by my mother, endured by my father) were always more of an excuse for a festive meal and plenty of wine. When we went to services on holidays like Rosh Hashana and Yom Kippur, it was only my mother and me. Today, I found comfort in sharing the experience of this day with my new friends. I might not yet have embraced all the religious tenets of Judaism, but I appreciated the sense of community it brought.

The following day, Yom Kippur proper, Tel Aviv had shut down to a post-apocalyptic standstill. I spent the morning cleaning my apartment (still furnished with broken appliances and without roommates), but in the afternoon I went over to Asher's to go for a bike ride through deserted Tel Aviv.

As Daniel had noted, Tel Aviv on Yom Kippur was special and eerily beautiful, as though the whole world had gone to sleep in the middle of the day. Not a single car drove down the streets, and I didn't see one shop or restaurant open. The only people I spotted were a few parents who watched as their children rode scooters and bicycles in figure eights along the street. Other than that, Tel Aviv was at rest.

Asher and Mati wanted to bike across the Ayalon, the main highway that connects Tel Aviv with Jerusalem, so we swept through lower Tel Aviv, ignoring the flashing lights directing the nonexistent traffic. As we sped through a short tunnel and down the on-ramp to the highway, miles of black pavement and an expanse of blue sky greeted us. We stopped for a minute, photographing the rare sight of a highway with no cars. "It's really like being in a sci-fi movie," said Asher.

We rode at full speed, weaving in and out of the highway's lanes as if we owned the earth. I was a nervous biker given my poor skills, but the lack of cars and obstacles in the street calmed my nerves. Occasionally we passed the odd biker or inline skater, our greetings to them accompanied only by the sounds of the wind. We decided to bike up through Dizengoff Square, which marked the center of Tel Aviv, over to the beach, and finally down to the clock tower at the southern end of the city in Jaffa.

"Why did you decide to move to Tel Aviv?" I asked Asher as we whizzed along the boardwalk, a gentle ocean breeze caressing our faces.

"Well, I was coming here pretty regularly beginning in college, and then I kept coming back for school holidays and whatnot," he told me. "After I graduated from college, I moved back home, but rather than feeling like I was home, I felt like I was away from my true home of Tel Aviv. So I decided to move here and continued loving it. A year later I became a citizen, which was easy to do, obviously, being Jewish, and I've never looked back." Like so many of us, he was searching for that sense of self and place; unlike so many of us, he had found it.

We then rode back toward Kate and Asher's house, trying to make it home before the sun set. When you fast, your head becomes lighter and a little clearer, and you view the world with a new perspective. My hunger, along with the silence, allowed me to notice my surroundings more than usual: the sound of a child's foot hitting the pavement as he ran across the street; wet laundry flapping in the wind from a balcony's clothesline; the sound of my own breathing as I gazed at the cloudless cerulean sky. Mati and Asher rode next to me as the sinking sun cast shadows over the city. Everyone from the night before was returning to Kate and Asher's to reenergize with a break-the-fast meal.

Back together, we dug into Kate's mushroom-barley soup, an onion kugel, and a giant boureka pastry featuring a combination of spinach and cheese inside flaky dough. We feasted amid laughter and cheer, and sharing that meal, I decided at that moment, was even better than going hungry together.

Recipes for Fasting and Feasting

When breaking a fast, you want to eat foods that are high in calories to regain your strength. The following recipes provide both nourishment and fulfillment in addition to being great dishes to share with friends.

CARMELLA'S CHICKEN LIVER PÂTÉ

True, pâté isn't exactly what springs to mind when I think of Jewish holiday meals, but it does bear a resemblance to chopped liver, a staple of any good Jewish deli. Carmella serves it along-side a salad of arugula, pears, pretzel croutons, and red wine–poached onions, but I recommend serving it on small pieces of toast as hors d'oeuvres for any celebration.

SERVES 10 TO 12 AS AN HORS D'OEUVRE

> 2 tablespoons chicken fat or unsalted butter
> 1 medium yellow onion
> 1 pound chicken livers
> ¼ cup pistachios
> 1 teaspoon kosher salt
> ⅛ teaspoon freshly ground black pepper
> 1 teaspoon dried thyme
> 1 tablespoon port
> 1 tablespoon cognac
> 7 tablespoons unsalted butter, cut into a few pieces,
>   at room temperature

Preheat the oven to 350 degrees F. Heat 1 tablespoon chicken fat in a skillet over medium-high heat. Slice the onion into thin rings, then add to the skillet and sauté until caramelized and golden brown, about 10 minutes. Set aside to cool. Meanwhile, clean the livers by cutting off any sinew or yellow green parts.

Toast the pistachios in the oven for 6 minutes. Remove and let cool, then roughly chop them.

Melt the other tablespoon of chicken fat in a skillet over high heat. When it begins to smoke, add the livers and season with the salt, pepper, and thyme. Cook until nicely browned and firm to the touch, about 4 minutes per side. Remove the livers and set aside to cool completely. Add the port and cognac to the skillet and deglaze, scraping the bottom of the pan. Pour the liquid over the livers. Cool in the refrigerator for 1 hour.

In a food processor, combine the onion, the livers and their liquid, and the butter, and puree until smooth, about 1 minute. Transfer to a bowl and stir in the pistachios.

Line a loaf pan with plastic wrap in both directions so that no part of the interior is exposed. Pour the pâté into the pan and spread until evenly distributed. Knock the bottom of the pan against a flat surface to remove any air bubbles. Wrap the plastic over the pâté and then wrap the entire pan in plastic wrap. Refrigerate overnight until firm. To serve, cut into slices and serve on plates with a small salad, or spread onto bread or toasts.

CHEESE BOUREKAS WITH ZHUG

Bourekas are one of my favorite Israeli snacks. After all, how can you not like puff pastry filled with cheese? Bourekas are popular throughout the Balkans and the Middle East, eaten for breakfast or as snacks, frequently filled with a soft white cheese similar to feta, a mixture of spinach and cheese, or "pizza" filling, which combines cheese, tomato, olives, and spices. For our post-fast meal, Kate prepared a large spinach-and-cheese boureka, but I prefer to make single-portion bourekas filled with cheeses and served alongside zhug, a popular spicy Yemenite condiment. The zhug packs a punch, so feel free to alter the heat according to your taste.

SERVES 4

FOR THE BOUREKAS:
1 cup feta cheese, crumbled (preferably Bulgarian-style feta)
¼ cup grated Parmesan cheese
1 egg, separated
1 tablespoon flour
Pinch of kosher salt
1 (14-ounce) package frozen puff pastry, thawed according
    to directions on package
1 teaspoon sesame seeds

FOR THE ZHUG:
1 large bunch coriander (about 4 cups of leaves,
    with some stems)
2 teaspoons chopped green or yellow habanero peppers,
    seeds removed
½ teaspoon kosher salt
¼ teaspoon ground cumin
1 tablespoon olive oil
2 teaspoons water

Preheat the oven to 375 degrees F. In a mixing bowl, add the cheeses, egg yolk, flour, and salt, and stir until the mixture is smooth.

Cut the dough into four squares and use a rolling pin to roll out each square until it is about half its original thickness. Divide the cheese filling among the bottom halves of the four squares. Brush a thin line of egg white around the cheese filling, then fold the dough over the filling to form a rectangular-shaped pastry. Crimp the edges in place using the tines of a fork, then prick the tops of the bourekas all over with a fork. Place on a baking sheet lined with either parchment paper or silicone.

Evenly brush the top of each boureka lightly with the egg white and sprinkle with sesame seeds. Bake for 30 minutes, or until browned.

Meanwhile, prepare the zhug: Place all ingredients in a small food processor and pulse until a paste forms.

Remove the bourekas from the oven and let cool slightly. Serve with zhug on the side.

MASCARPONE "ICE CREAM" WITH HONEY AND PISTACHIOS

Kate taught me her instant ice cream technique when I helped her prep for the Yom Kippur dinner, and I was surprised that it set up so well in the freezer and didn't require an ice cream maker. Try this also with silan, which is a honeylike syrup made from dates that's popular in Israel. It should be available at Middle Eastern markets or specialty food stores.

SERVES 6

1⅓ cups mascarpone
⅔ cup sweetened condensed milk
¼ teaspoon kosher salt
⅓ cup unsalted, shelled pistachios
3 tablespoons honey (or silan)

Combine the mascarpone, milk, and salt in a mixing bowl, and whisk until smooth. Cover with plastic wrap and place in the freezer for 4 hours or until frozen.

Preheat the oven to 350 degrees F. Bake the pistachios for 5 to 7 minutes, or until light golden brown. Let them cool, then roughly chop them.

Spoon the "ice cream" into 6 serving bowls and drizzle with the honey. Top with the pistachios.

Chapter 11

EVEN THOUGH MY HEBREW barely advanced beyond the words for "sirloin," "beef," "grouper," "parsley," and "cilantro," working at Carmella was easy and fun. Sometimes the language barrier made me feel like a fish out of water, but I was able to devote my attention to my cooking. I was holding my own when it came to kitchen skills, even though most of the plates at Carmella were simple dishes that could be made at home by a skilled cook. I liked Daniel's market-driven philosophy behind the cuisine, and I appreciated several culinary gems sprinkled throughout. But as the days went by, I grasped that not everyone shared my view.

"What's your favorite dish on the menu?" I asked Brown-Eyed Shai as I began to plan for my mother's upcoming visit to Israel in a few weeks.

"Well, it's not really my type of food. When you've been here for two years, it's hard... The herb salad is good, though."

A few days later, I asked Hamoudi the same question.

"Nothing. Well, I don't know...," he said, raising an eyebrow.

"Oh," I said, perplexed. Since Daniel Zach wasn't in the kitchen every night demanding perfection, and these guys didn't live and breathe food the way the wd~50 guys did, maybe they were bored. Cooking the same food day in and day out becomes humdrum, and chefs get antsy, often leaving for new positions after a few months. As time passed, I became more attuned to the chefs' attitudes and sensed an apathy tainting the kitchen, and I wondered if the diners could taste it in the food.

⌒

ONE AFTERNOON as I was packing away boxes of squid I had just cleaned into the upstairs storage freezer, Daniel called out from his office, "Lauren! Can you come here and help me write an e-mail in English to one of my suppliers?"

I nodded and typed quickly as Daniel dictated. "Look good?" I asked when he'd finished.

He scanned the screen. "Yes. Wow, that would have taken me an hour to write," he said, amazed by both my typing speed and my proficiency in English.

"No problem, glad to help. If I ever need to write something in Hebrew, you can return the favor," I said.

"You should stay and learn Hebrew here. Do you think you are going to stay?"

"I do like it, but I'm not sure I'll stay." Tel Aviv hadn't called to me yet the way it had to Asher, Alex, and Sharon. While Vietnam had seemed like home after two weeks, I couldn't shed the feeling of being just a temporary visitor in Israel, even though I enjoyed working at Carmella and had made great friends, perhaps even closer ones than those in my Hanoi circle.

"Is it because of a job? If I offered you one, would you stay?" Daniel said.

I smiled, flattered. "That's very nice of you, but I'm not sure the timing is right," I replied. Although I had yet to find a job in

Paris, I had set my sights on going there after Tel Aviv to complete my culinary education. Especially after Carmella's casual culinary approach, I had become determined to immerse myself in the very top echelon of haute gastronomy to gain a full mastery of different cooking styles.

"If you change your mind, let me know. Your mother is coming to visit soon, right?"

"At the end of the month."

"Well, you must have dinner here, on me, of course."

"Yes, we were planning to come here. I've told her all about it. She'll be here from the twenty-seventh to the twenty-ninth, and then we're going to travel around Israel."

"Will you be driving?"

"No, we don't really drive." This was an understatement—the last time my mother drove a car had been when my parents took me to Chicago for my freshman year of college. My father tired of the driving somewhere in rural Pennsylvania, at which point my mom took over. After forty-five minutes of having her at the wheel, though, my father ousted her, since whenever anyone passed her on the left, she would veer right, into the shoulder of the highway. Like many born-and-bred New Yorkers, I have my driver's license, but I can count on my fingers the number of times I've driven a car, and the number of times I've driven alone in a car is a whopping zero. So no, we wouldn't be driving.

"How will you get around Israel?"

"Bus, I guess?"

"I want you to visit my other restaurant, Helena. But it's about forty-five minutes away. Maybe I will drive and we will all go together."

"Really? That would be great. Thanks," I said. I was definitely interested in learning more about Daniel and his other ventures.

⌒⌒

THE FOLLOWING WEEK, Hamoudi, the jovial Arab cook, and I were in the kitchen, waiting for the dinner rush to begin and for the orders to come through on the automated machine. To help me out, the waitstaff had kindly programmed English translations into the machine that emitted the appetizer tickets. Once a ticket appeared, I scanned it for any special instructions and then plated each dish, saving the salads for last so that the dressing wouldn't wilt the greens. Usually I handled the tickets alone, or if I happened to be working the shift with Mikhael, we divided up the dishes equally, and no dish took longer than a minute or two to plate.

I had gone through my prep list, crossing off all the daily tasks after checking the refrigerators to make sure we had enough prep work for the night. "You know, you are the best *stagiarim* I have ever worked with," said Hamoudi, seemingly out of the blue.

"Really?" I said.

"Yes, I see you making the gnocchi and you know how to think quickly and you have a feel for it. I know how to make gnocchi, but it took me a long time. In Arabic, we have a saying that if you want to be a cook, you have to have the heart for it. If you do not have the heart, then you shouldn't be a cook."

Ever since stepping foot into the professional restaurant kitchen, I had grappled with this concept. I wanted to cook because I was passionate about food. I love the sound of laughter over a dinner table and the personal satisfaction you get when someone devours your food and asks for seconds and then thirds—like the kind of cooking and eating I was doing at Kate and Asher's. But restaurant cooking is totally different. Certainly the rush that comes with cooking and plating several dishes in under five minutes is exhilarating, the sounds of clanking plates and hissing meats and the chopping of knives on a cutting board are all melodious in their frenzy, and a perverted camaraderie forms among cooks in a restaurant kitchen; but the basic pleasure of cooking for others is diminished, or at least it was beginning to for me. You begin to think less and less about making each plate perfect because you know you've got only two minutes to finish up five more. You curse silently at the rowdy party that comes in five minutes before the restaurant closes and orders seven different dishes because your back and feet are killing you, and all you want to do is wrap up the evening so you can go home and shower off all the oil and grime clogging your pores and collapse into bed. I had the heart for home cooking, but as I spent more and more time in the restaurant, I struggled with whether I truly felt the same way about professional cooking. I wondered if it were even possible to simultaneously have the heart for both.

⟨⟋⟍⟩

ELI AND I had become close friends, mostly because we ran the evening shift together, with me on appetizers and Eli on entrées, and we were the last two in the kitchen after the souschef left at around ten thirty. Eli topped me by only a couple of inches and was playful and impish in the kitchen. I welcomed his generous explanations of how the hot dishes were made. One evening, as he gathered ingredients for the final ticket of the night, he pointed to the steak sitting on his cutting board and asked, "Do you want to make it?"

"Yes." *Of course I wanted to make it.*

"Okay. Here," he said, handing me the meat.

"So I add it to the pan?"

"Wait until it starts smoking, then add salt and pepper, and flip it over." I scraped the flattop clean and added oil, which danced across it in a swirling shimmer. The beef slices sizzled and hissed as they hit the flat surface, their flesh searing to a brown crisp as I added salt and pepper.

"Okay, so flip the meat, and then put the pepper sauce in this pan. Then put the meat in and the spaetzle on top."

The heat flushed my cheeks and warmed my hand as I placed the pan back on the stove. It was exciting, touching the meat to ascertain when it was done cooking and hearing the sizzles and splatters.

"You got it. Perfect," Eli said as I presented him with the finished plate and a satisfied smile.

⌒

ABOUT THREE WEEKS before my *stage* ended, another female cook joined me at my station. She was slightly taller than me and also drowning in a black cotton uniform a few sizes too big, her curly black hair hidden under a pale yellow bandanna.

"Hi. I'm Lauren. Sorry, I don't speak any Hebrew," I said, regretting that I'd never made it to *ulpan*.

"Hi, I'm Inbal," she said in English. She kept her head down as she concentrated on chopping herbs, so I started setting up for the evening shift.

"Hey," said Mikhael, reaching for a few roasted red peppers and sliced radishes to garnish a plate of bread topped with ikra (a fish roe spread). "There isn't too much to do, but we'll go over the list. Grapes, no, red onion, no, cheeses, all okay. Herb salad I made earlier, but you might want to make an arugula salad. Roasted pepper, you need to do that, and eggplant you need to grill, too. Remember to pierce the eggplants before grilling them or they'll explode all over you. And count the number of carpaccios and then ask Shai if you need to make more. And fill up the pass all the way; today will be busy, so I want everything filled to the very top."

"Yeah, yeah, I know."

Later in the day, Shai said, "Lauren, will you show Inbal how to clean the squid?"

"Sure," I said, happy to have someone else clean the squid, a laborious and dirty process.

I took a squid and held it up. It was slippery, about five inches long, with a speckled skin the color of wet bricks and legs that dangled like wet stockings hanging on a shower rod. "Okay, so you take the squid, and you reach in with your fingertips and pull out the legs and guts, all this white stuff. Now you want to squeeze between the eyes and pull off the legs. See this little circle? That's the mouth, and you want to get rid of that, so just pop it out with your thumb."

She imitated my gesture but failed to separate the legs from the eyes.

"Yeah, it takes some practice. Pinch hard between the eyes. Now rinse the legs off in water. Then take the body and pull out the spine, which feels like a strip of plastic, and scrub the inside with your fingers."

"Ah, okay." She fiddled with it for a few more minutes. "Now okay?"

"Yeah, that looks good. If it's hard for you to scoop everything out, you can clean them in a bowl of water."

"So you are here for a short time?" she said.

"Yeah, just for two months."

"And it is good? You learn a lot? Right now I'm working in a small café, but I've been working in restaurants for fifteen years.

But I wanted to apprentice here because it's a top restaurant."
The faint wrinkles at the corner of her smile suggested she was
in her mid-thirties, which is pushing old in the kitchen.

I liked Inbal's enthusiasm and her calm demeanor. She was
slow at first, but she listened attentively and followed my directions, gaining speed. It was a slow night, so in between orders I
helped her clean the squid. We stood side by side, bending over
bowls of disemboweled squid and giggling when we were accidentally squirted by an exploding sac of finger-staining black
ink. And, as much as one can in a restaurant kitchen, we got in
some girl talk.

Another new face appeared in the kitchen a few days after
Inbal's arrival, this one belonging to a strapping, good-looking
guy in his early twenties. He approached me, saying something
in Hebrew.

"Oh, I'm sorry, I don't speak Hebrew," I said for the ump-
teenth time.

"Ah, okay. But you work here?" he said in English.

"Yes, I am Lauren."

"Moshe. Nice to meet you," he said as we shook hands.

Moshe's left forefinger was covered in a large bandage underneath a latex glove, which signaled a kitchen mishap. On my
first day of culinary school, we had practiced chopping vegetables into precise shapes and three students ended up with bleed-
ing fingers because they weren't used to working with sharp
knives for extended periods. So far in my kitchen career, I had
escaped serious injury, though I had some nicks and minor cuts.
As our instructors had told us throughout culinary school, the
sharper your knife, the less it will hurt when it cuts you. A dull
blade is far more dangerous than a sharp one. And my knives
were sharp.

Later in the afternoon, Moshe was given the task of making the herb salad, which requires you to make quick slicing motions (as opposed to haphazard chopping) through bunches of tied herbs to avoid bruising and discoloring the leaves. I watched him slice slowly—too slowly—and then taking pains to go through every leaf to make sure none was too big. Nervous hesitation marked his every action and chopping motion. I knew in that moment that he was a first-timer.

"Moshe will be working with you this evening, so you will show him what to do, okay?" said Brown-Eyed Shai after we had finished our family meal of homemade falafel, chopped salad, and tehina. Shai widened his eyes, implying I should keep an eye on Moshe.

"Yeah, no problem."

"Okay, how can I help?" Moshe said.

I looked at the latest ticket. "Okay, so we have an herb salad and a fish carpaccio. I will show you how to make the herb salad."

"Okay."

I opened the refrigerated drawer underneath our workstation that contained our salad leaves. "This is the herb salad. You're going to take two handfuls of salad, a handful of cashews, a pinch of salt, some lemon juice, and some olive oil. Then you mix it together in a metal bowl and put it in this serving bowl."

"This much?" he said, showing me a handful.

"Yes, maybe a little bit more."

He withdrew a small handful of the herbs from the drawer where we kept salad greens, paused, put a little bit back, and then changed his mind before taking a little more.

"That's fine. Okay, now mix it all up and place it in the bowl."

While he painstakingly mixed the herbs with the dressing, I felt a sudden kinship with Tom, my wd~50 nemesis. "Hurry up already!" I wanted to yell. I couldn't have been *this* slow when I started, could I?

Moshe plopped the salad into the bowl, managing to get parsley and cilantro leaves all over the rim.

"You want to make it more compact so it's like a ball in the middle. You don't want any touching the sides," I said.

He nodded and began wiping the plate with a paper towel and rearranging all the leaves into a sphere.

"It's fine for now. But next time make sure it looks good," I said.

I showed him how to make the remaining appetizers as the orders came in, and each time an order for the herb salad arrived, I gave it to him. The herb salad is easy to plate, since it's just heaped in a mound in the center of the plate, but Moshe struggled to finish one salad in the time it took me to finish three other dishes, constantly rearranging leaves and second-guessing the amounts of oil and lemon juice. My eyes were rolling in the back of my head. After the service ended, I showed Moshe how to break down the station for cleaning. "Can you clean the squeeze bottles for me? Just do a quick scrub and rinse under water."

He nodded and took the dressing-filled bottles to the sink. I watched as he spent three full minutes scrubbing a single bottle, going over every inch of plastic with the sponge four times. I was nearly done scrubbing the whole work surface in the time it took him to finish one bottle.

"You can do it quickly, like this," I said, sweeping the sponge over the bottle and rinsing briefly under the running water.

"Oh, okay."

"Have you worked anywhere before this?" I wanted to confirm my suspicions.

"No, I used to sell credit cards, and then I was in the army," he said, referring to Israel's compulsory military service, a stint that usually lasted for two to three years for all citizens, male and female, between the ages of eighteen and twenty. "But then I decided I want to be a cook, so here I am. And you, you went to school?"

"Yeah, I went to school for cooking, and then I've worked in some restaurants since then," I said.

I wanted to be kind and patient with Moshe, remembering that only a short time ago I, too, had been a novice. But I nearly lost it a few days later while we were working side by side; Moshe was putting away bunches of parsley and cilantro while I butchered sirloin.

"These are all the same?" he asked me, pointing to the herbs.

I glanced over. "No, you have both parsley and cilantro."

"Ah, okay," he said, and I returned to the ruby red flesh in front of me, deftly carving out the white threads of tendon and slicing off the inedible silver skin hidden beneath a wrinkled layer of creamy white fat.

A few minutes later, he held up a bunch of cilantro. "This, kusbara?"

"What?"

"Oh, um, not parsley?"

"Cilantro?"

"Yes."

I looked at it. "Yes, it's kusbara."

"And this, parsley?" he said, holding up another bunch.

"No, that's also kusbara. See the difference? See, look at the leaf. Parsley is pointed at the end and cilantro is rounded," I said as politely as I could muster. What I wanted to say was, "Are you fucking kidding me? Just taste it if you aren't sure, or smell it. You live in Israel, for God's sake! Parsley and cilantro are in practically every dish here; can't you see and smell the difference?"

As he finished wrapping up the herbs, pausing occasionally to examine the shape of the leaves, I thought about Four-Hour Parsley back at wd~50. Maybe I hadn't given him enough of a chance. Maybe I was swayed by the force of collective opinion and wanting to be part of the group more than wanting to be a nice person. I wondered what the rest of the kitchen staff thought of Moshe. It's possible they had discussed his incompetence in Hebrew, and I hadn't understood. Or maybe they didn't care that he was slow. Apathy, I had learned, ran rampant in this kitchen.

I often compared Carmella's staff with wd~50's—people who lived and breathed and died for food so much that it was scary to a neophyte. Sure, they were burned out and probably tired of the lifestyle that wd~50 afforded (or didn't afford) them, but they believed in Wylie and his food. At wd~50, we had embraced cleanliness and hygiene as second nature, changing *mise en place* containers several times throughout the evening and meticulously scrubbing every surface area. At Carmella, we simply wrapped up *mise en place* containers and called it a night after a decent scrub-down. Yet Carmella's laid-back kitchen allowed me to take charge and run with the ball; I cleaned fish and butchered meat and ran the appetizer station and worked the hot line. I was one of the chefs here—no longer just an apprentice. But you can go only so far with talent and skills. True, unbridled passion for restaurant cooking is what separates the good from the great.

⌒

MY LAST DAY at Carmella was low-key, and after completing the morning shift, I got dressed and casually said good-bye. "Bye," the cooks all said in succession, and that was that.

I expected to see them again in a few days, though, after my mother's arrival in Israel. She was taking a two-week vacation from teaching, while my father, too busy with work, as usual, stayed behind.

Daniel had invited us to dine at Carmella, and we went the day after she arrived, a warm and hazy late October evening. One of the managers had helped me preselect the nicest table, a two-seater next to a large mirror in the center of the main dining room with a good view of the other diners.

We scanned the menu while sipping Prosecco that Daniel had sent over. "How about the herb salad? It's one of the restaurant's specialties. Or you might like the pâté. Some of the entrées are a bit heavy, but you might like the herb-crusted fish with the eggplant mashed potatoes," I said.

"You're the chef, honey. Whatever you think. Although you know I'm not the biggest fan of eggplant."

"I don't think they are super-eggplanty. They're really good. And we can share our food, anyway. I think I'm going to get the herb salad and then the sirloin with the gnocchi."

"Chef Daniel says that if you don't want to get hurt, you must have more food than that," said Gilad, our waiter. "So we are going to send you another appetizer. How is a carpaccio? Do you like beef or fish?"

"Beef," said my mother, and I agreed.

"Okay, and then along with your entrées, we are going to send you a special. A seafood cannelloni. It's a little spicy, but with a tomato sauce and very nice, and new on the menu. I don't think you've seen it," he said to me.

"No, I haven't. That sounds great," I said.

"Lauren, this is delicious. I don't know why you said the food was only so-so," my mom said after our appetizers arrived. She had smeared a hearty chunk of pâté on a pretzel crouton and popped it into her mouth.

"Yeah, it's better than I thought it would be. I don't know why, but the same food doesn't taste as good when you're sampling it in the kitchen. Maybe it's the ambience or the fact that you're not working. But it's been like that everywhere I've worked," I said.

After our appetizers, Daniel appeared. "I'm Chef Daniel Zach. And you must be Lauren's sister, no?" he joked.

"No, I'm her mother, but thank you," said my mother, beaming.

"I can see the resemblance. I hope you've enjoyed the meal. I have to go home now, but we're on for tomorrow?"

"Yes. What time should we be here?" I said.

"Ten o'clock? Then we will drive up to Caesarea, and you can walk around and then have lunch." Daniel's other restaurant, Helena, was in Caesarea, an ancient port city a short drive up the coast. Daniel went there a few times a month to check on things and to pay the bills and had scheduled this month's trip around my mother's visit so we could dine there.

Over dinner, we caught up on the last five months, the longest we'd ever been away from each other. I recounted my cooking adventures and dinner parties with Kate, Asher, Mati, and Alex; my motorbike adventures around Hanoi's Old Quarter with Son and Thanh and my authentic eating adventures with Hung; how I had sipped cocktails with Belinda and Lucy while watching the sunset over Tay Ho Lake. I described the flaky, cheese-filled bourekas and finger-staining, fresh pomegranate juice I had fallen for at the Carmel Market. I told her the five months had seemed more like five weeks.

"You've found what you love, Lauren. That's why it seems like time is flying," she said.

"It's been hard recently, though, because I don't know if I want to make a career out of restaurant cooking. Not so much in Vietnam, but so many of the chefs I've met so far this year appear disillusioned with the profession, and I don't want that to happen to me," I said.

"You don't need to be a restaurant chef. We've never expected that of you. Of course we want you to be successful, but your father and I would rather see you happy. At least you can take comfort in knowing that the way to a man's heart is through his stomach. You'll now have the skills to find a husband," she joked.

"You mean you wouldn't be upset if after all this time and money I didn't become a professional cook?"

"Lauren, don't be silly. I think your father will honestly be relieved, and I will be proud of you no matter what you do."

"I don't want to let you down."

"Why would you be letting us down? You followed your passion and went around the world and made some amazing friends. I don't see any downside to that. Just don't worry."

I smiled. "Okay."

Our entrées followed, accompanied by the new cannelloni special sandwiched between our two plates. The dining room was now fairly full, with a few American and French tourists sprinkled among the secular Tel Avivians.

"Do you like the potatoes? They're good, aren't they? We have them a lot at family meal, too, because the batch made for the lunch service can't be reused for dinner."

"They aren't my favorite, but I don't love eggplant."

"When you're in Israel, you *have* to like eggplant. There is a saying here that a woman can't be married off until she knows how to make fifty different eggplant dishes."

"I hope you're at forty-nine, then," she said.

"Very funny."

After dinner, I introduced her to Mikhael, Moshe, and

Brown-Eyed Shai. "So this is where I worked," I said, pointing to my station.

"It's big," she said, and I could tell she was remembering the wd~50 kitchen.

"Yeah, there's a lot of space, which is nice."

"So you had a good meal?" asked Shai.

"Yeah, it was great. Even better than I expected," I said.

He turned to my mom. "You know, we said she should stay in Tel Aviv. And I've got lots of nice Jewish friends I could set her up with."

"Yeah, get on that and find me a husband," I said, and everyone laughed.

The next morning, we met Daniel at the restaurant and hopped into his car for the forty-five-minute ride to Caesarea. Daniel began zigzagging through Tel Aviv's traffic-clogged streets to reach the coastal highway heading north. From the passenger seat, I watched my mother's face in the rearview mirror as she absorbed the sights and sounds of the city.

"I wouldn't have recognized the city from how it looked thirty years ago when I was last here. Israel still had control of the Sinai Peninsula in Egypt then."

"Tel Aviv has changed a lot since those days, and not just in land size," said Daniel.

"I'm sure. Were you born here?" she asked Daniel.

"No, I came here when I was nine months old. I was born in Germany," he said.

"Oh, so you're not a real sabra," said my mom. A sabra, Hebrew for "cactus fruit," was the colloquial term for an Israeli-born Jew, although it was also often used to describe the Israeli temperament, which called to mind key qualities of the cactus fruit: sweet on the inside, prickly on the outside.

"No, I'm not," he replied, and told us about his childhood. His mother was Israeli but his father was German and not Jewish. "It was hard for my father. He was a window dresser for department stores, and there were no jobs in Israel for him then. Kids teased me because he was German, calling him a Nazi..."

"And so when did you open Carmella?" I asked, trying to change the subject sensing Daniel's discomfort at the memory.

"September eleventh, two thousand one. Well, not exactly that date, but that week. There were three restaurants, big restaurants—Carmella, Chloélys, and Daniel—that all opened that month, and we're all still here."

"Tough timing," I said.

Daniel shrugged. "There's the Dan Hotel. That's where I got my culinary training," he said, pointing to a 1970s-like structure whose exterior needed a face-lift, but which remained one of the nicest hotels in the city.

"But enough about me. Let's talk about Lauren. What do you think you're going to do when you go back to New York?" Daniel asked me as we left Tel Aviv's outskirts.

"I'm not quite sure. I'd like to keep cooking, but it's hard," I said.

"Yes, what I recommend for you is to open your own place as soon as possible. You can make your own work schedule, and be in charge. As a woman, especially, you don't want to work for others."

"We'll see what happens. There's a lot of risk in owning a restaurant, especially in a place like New York, where restaurants fail so frequently. You need financial backers and a really good concept that differentiates you from the thousands of other restaurants there."

"Have I told you about my new restaurant concept?" he said.

"No, I don't think so."

"No? Well, I was in the States and I went to a restaurant and really liked the concept. You know Houston's?"

"Yeah," I said. Houston's was a quasi-upscale steakhouse chain.

"So I want to make it like that, a steakhouse, but also make it Asian. There will be burgers and steak, but instead of cole-slaw, it will come with an Asian side dish. And you know about Monica Lewinsky?" he said.

"Sure," I said, bewildered.

"I just love her. So I'm going to call the restaurant Asia Monica."

"How interesting," I said. *What?* He wanted to name an Asian-American steakhouse after the hapless White House intern? I was perplexed, to say the least, but I gave Daniel points for originality.

When we reached Caesarea, Daniel dropped us off at the front gate so we could tour the ruins while he focused on business at Helena. My mother and I finally made our way to his airy seaside restaurant after ambling for an hour through the impressive ruins under the blazing sun. Daniel guided us to a table on the outdoor terrace perched literally over the Mediter-ranean, which was calm and sparkling.

Daniel leaned back in his chair, his dark sunglasses shield-ing his eyes. Ever the gracious host, he suggested that we order wine. We were the only ones on the vast terrace, but it was still early on this bright fall weekday.

"Cheers! *L'chaim!*" we said, clinking glasses together.

"What did you think about working at Carmella?" he asked me.

"I was given more responsibility at Carmella than any other place I've worked, so that was nice."

"You aren't *given* responsibility, Lauren. You create it for yourself," he said in a firm tone.

"I guess so."

"You know, everyone liked you. The other chefs, they said, 'Oh, keep Lauren, let's offer her a job.'"

"Thanks," I said. Maybe Daniel really wanted me to stay and eventually become the sous-chef at Asia Monica!

"What do you think?" he asked my mother.

"Well, I think it's Lauren's decision," she said diplomatically.

"Maybe another time," I said.

At that moment our appetizers arrived, and I was grateful to have the distraction. Daniel had ordered dishes for the table: grilled calamari with lemon and hyssop leaves in a sheep's-yogurt sauce, garden salad with olives and the local specialty cheese called hameiri, jackfish in creamy tahini sauce dotted with olive oil, and freshly baked herb focaccia. The food was lighter than Carmella's, taking its cue from the oceanscape.

"When you've got good people running the place, you don't need to go as much and manage," Daniel said, explaining that he visited Helena about twice a month, mostly to sign checks or approve invoices. The menu, which clearly evoked his culinary philosophy, was nevertheless created mostly by the sous-chef. Daniel's influence was more in name and in raking in the profits. But we happily dug into our Mediterranean–Middle Eastern medley of entrées that now graced the table: siniya, an Arabic fish stew with chard and tahini, a simple dish of fish and chips, and shrimp with pickled lemon and okra. We followed it with two desserts: a pale cream custard floating in a pool of electric pink sauce and a dish of beige-colored ice cream. Daniel pointed toward the ice cream. "This is halvah. You know it, I'm sure."

"Yes, the candy made from sesame seed paste," I said.

"I love halvah. Just love it. It is the best thing we stole from the Arabs," he said with an impish grin.

"This is halvah?" said my mother.

"Yes, in the ice cream, and on top."

"This is so good, but I normally hate halvah. At least in America, halvah is so thick and chalky. I never would have chosen this, but it's really delicious," she said, lapping up spoonfuls.

We sat overlooking the cascading waves and sipped espressos. I thought about the past eight months of my cooking career. Although both meals Daniel treated us to were delicious, they didn't match the level of wd~50's innovation or La Verticale's emphasis on unique flavors. However, Carmella had taught me that I didn't have anything to worry about in the kitchen. I still might not have had the fastest knife skills, but I worked cleanly and efficiently. I could prepare and organize food for service, and I had common sense when it came to running a kitchen. I was even in charge of the appetizer station! Who cared about titles; I wasn't a bona fide hot line cook yet, sweating over a flaming stove, but even handling the cold line, I was a cook. And I was good.

"Ready to go?" asked Daniel.

I hesitated for a second. "Yes, I am."

Recipes from and Inspired by Carmella Bistro

In each of the following recipes, I've taken bits and pieces from what I learned at Carmella (the gnocchi dough and the roasted eggplant mashed potatoes), or from what I learned or ate in Israel, and added my own spin.

GNOCCHI WITH TOMATO-EGGPLANT SAUCE

Making gnocchi isn't a weeknight dinner project, but rather one for a lazy Sunday afternoon. It was one of my favorite tasks at Carmella, because it let me channel my inner Mediterranean grandmother. Take care not to overwork the dough when kneading and rolling it out or the gnocchi will become tough. I've used both russet and Yukon gold potatoes when making this, and both turned out well, although I slightly prefer Yukon golds.

SERVES 4 AS AN ENTRÉE

FOR THE GNOCCHI:
1½ pounds potatoes
Scant 2 cups flour, plus extra for dusting
½ cup grated Parmesan cheese
3 egg yolks
2 teaspoons kosher salt

FOR THE SAUCE:
1 medium eggplant
¼ cup olive oil
3 cloves garlic, thinly sliced
1 (14-ounce) can chopped plum tomatoes
Pinch of cinnamon
½ teaspoon kosher salt, or slightly more, as desired

Prick the potatoes with a fork, then place in a steamer basket over boiling water and steam until done, about 30 minutes (if you stick a knife into the potato and it drops off the knife, it's done). Refrigerate until cold, about 4 hours. Peel the potatoes. Using a box grater, grate the potatoes into a large mixing bowl. Add the flour, cheese, egg yolks, and salt, and rub your hands together through the dough until the texture is crumbly and sandy. Then knead the dough until it is a homogeneous mass.

Take a small amount of dough and roll it into a log ½ to 1 inch in diameter; repeat until all the dough has been rolled into logs. Then, using a bench scraper or knife, cut the logs into 1-inch pieces (this will go faster if you do four to five logs at a time). Dust the pieces with a little flour and place them on a waxed paper–lined baking sheet. Let sit in the refrigerator for half an hour or until ready to use.

Meanwhile, prepare the sauce. Preheat the broiler to high. Pierce the eggplant all over with a fork or a knife and cook until all sides are charred and the flesh is soft, about 20 to 25 minutes. When the eggplant is cool enough to touch, cut off the top and make a vertical slit down the base. Using a spoon, scrape out the flesh and place in a colander to remove some of the excess liquid. Meanwhile, pour the olive oil into a saucepan over medium heat and add the garlic. Sauté the garlic until softened but not browned, then add the tomatoes and cinnamon. Bring to a boil, then lower heat to a simmer. After 15 minutes, add the eggplant pulp and continue cooking for another 15 minutes, breaking up the tomatoes and eggplant chunks with a wooden spoon. Add the salt and stir, then keep warm until ready to use.

Bring a large pot of salted water to a boil. Add the gnocchi and cook for about 3 minutes, or until they float to the surface. Drain and return to the pot. Add the tomato sauce.

Toss the gnocchi with the tomato sauce and serve in bowls.

CHICKEN SCHNITZEL WITH ROASTED EGGPLANT MASHED POTATOES

It may seem odd, but chicken schnitzel and mashed potatoes are some of the most ubiquitous foods in Tel Aviv and made for a popular family meal at Carmella as well. Everyone likes mashed potatoes, but they can get a little boring. That's why roasted eggplant mashed potatoes are great: They are lightly smoky in taste and possess a depth not usually associated with the starchy spuds. Three pounds of potatoes serves four to six diners, so if you have any leftovers, you can use the cold mashed potatoes to make potato croquettes.

SERVES 4

1 small to medium eggplant
3 pounds yellow-fleshed potatoes (like Yukon gold)
4 chicken cutlets (boneless, skinless chicken breasts)
¼ cup flour
2 eggs
2 cups panko or bread crumbs
2 teaspoons minced fresh thyme
2 teaspoons minced fresh rosemary
3½ teaspoons kosher salt
¼ teaspoon freshly ground pepper
8 tablespoons unsalted butter
1 cup whole milk
Pinch of freshly grated nutmeg
4 tablespoons olive oil

Preheat a grill or broiler to high. Pierce the eggplant all over with a fork or a knife, then grill on all sides until the skin has blackened and charred completely, about 20 minutes. Set aside to cool slightly. While it is still warm, cut off the top and make a vertical slit down the base of the eggplant. Using a spoon, scoop out the flesh into a bowl and mash with a fork. Set aside.

Peel the potatoes and cut into quarters. Place in a large pot, cover completely with cold water, and bring to a boil. Lower the heat to a simmer and cook until the potatoes are tender, about 20 minutes or so. The potatoes will be done when you pierce them with a knife and they fall off the blade.

Meanwhile, place the chicken breasts on waxed paper or a cutting board and pound them with a mallet until they are about ¼ inch thick. Place the flour on a plate. Beat the eggs and place in a shallow bowl or plate. Combine the panko, herbs, 2 teaspoons salt, and pepper in a bowl, and place on a plate. Dredge the chicken breasts in the flour, then dip them in the egg, and then the panko mixture, until fully covered.

Heat the butter, milk, remaining 1½ teaspoons salt, and nutmeg in a saucepan over medium heat until the milk is steaming and the butter has melted completely. When the potatoes are done, drain them. Then, using a ricer or food mill, puree the potatoes back into the pot you cooked them in and stir in the milk and butter mixture and the eggplant pulp and stir gently until combined. Keep warm.

Heat 2 tablespoons olive oil in a skillet over medium-high heat. Add two of the chicken cutlets and cook fully until golden brown, about 5 minutes per side (you may add a little more oil to the pan if all is absorbed). Add the remaining 2 tablespoons olive oil to the pan, and repeat with the remaining two cutlets.

Place a large spoonful of mashed potatoes on the center of each plate, and top with the chicken cutlet.

DRIED MEDITERRANEAN FRUIT MEDLEY

Fruits steeped in sugar syrup are popular in Israel, and this version is great for dessert or breakfast. It's rather sweet, so I like to serve it with plain yogurt or as a topping for pound cake, but it's equally delicious eaten plain. Depending on the size of your fruits, you may want to cut them in half before serving.

SERVES 4

> 1 cup sugar
> 1 cup water
> ½ vanilla pod
> ¼ cup white wine
> 1 cinnamon stick
> Zest of 1 lemon, peeled in large strips with a vegetable peeler
> ½ cup dried figs
> ½ cup dried apricots
> 1 cup dates, seeds removed
> ½ cup red grapes

Place the sugar, water, vanilla pod, white wine, cinnamon stick, and lemon zest in a pot, and bring to a boil. Turn off the heat and let sit for 15 minutes.

Place the figs, apricots, dates, and grapes in a bowl. Strain the syrup using a fine-meshed sieve and pour over the fruit. Cover and refrigerate at least overnight and for up to a week. Serve the fruit with a few spoonfuls of syrup.

HALVAH ICE CREAM

My mother became a halvah convert after eating the sesame-flavored ice cream at Helena. Hopefully you will, too, after trying my version. This ice cream, thick, rich, and silky, will be a welcome change from chocolate and vanilla. It's best to cool the batter in the refrigerator overnight; don't worry if it thickens considerably.

SERVES 4

> 1 cup whole milk
> 1½ cups heavy cream

(continued)

Pinch of kosher salt
1 cup sugar
3 egg yolks
2 teaspoons vanilla
¼ cup tahini

Combine the milk, cream, salt, and ½ cup of sugar in a sauce-pan over high heat, and bring to a boil. In a small bowl, beat the egg yolks and remaining sugar. Add about ½ cup of the milk mixture to the eggs to temper them, then pour the eggs back into the pot of milk.

Add the vanilla and tahini and cook over medium heat, stirring constantly, until the mixture thickens and coats the back of a wooden spoon, about 7 minutes. Strain the mixture into a bowl using a mesh sieve, and refrigerate, covered, until cold. The mixture will be quite thick, but do not force it through the sieve; instead, swirl the mixture with a spoon and it will eventually strain. Transfer to an ice cream maker and follow the manufacturer's directions for freezing.

Senderens

9, PLACE DE LA MADELEINE

PARIS, FRANCE

Chapter 12

THERE ARE TWO TYPES OF PEOPLE in the world: diehard Francophiles who simply *adore* Paris and everything French, and those who don't. I used to be in the former camp, believing that I'd end up living happily ever after in a lovely Left Bank apartment in Paris, madly in love with a Frenchman named Jean-François or something equally stereotypical and doing my daily shopping at the local *marché* after sipping a café au lait and reading *Le Monde* at the nearest café. Then I actually went to France to study during my junior year of college and learned the truth: Paris, while unquestionably beautiful, is gray and gloomy for most of the year and is populated by Parisians, a clan of snobbish people about as open and friendly to outsiders as, oh, Germany's National Socialist Party in the 1940s. Okay, so maybe they weren't that bad, but the experience had left a bad taste in my mouth, and my love of Paris quickly dissipated.

But it's really hard—if not downright impossible—to be in the food industry and not appreciate the culinary mastery that's come out of the French gastronomic tradition. So even though I still had some latent dislike for Parisians, my culinary ambition shone brighter than my personal sentiments. Paris was where I'd find the culinary Holy Grail. And I needed to be specifically at one of Paris's grand restaurants, the type of place with three

Michelin stars reserved for diners with expense accounts (or really, really rich husbands), steeped in elegance and tradition. This would be the last stop on my cooking adventure, so I reasoned that I'd better go big or go home.

But finding a Parisian restaurant willing to take me on proved more difficult than I'd anticipated, despite my fluency in French and new restaurant stripes. Clearly, Parisians still had it in for me. After no success with three-star restaurants, I zapped off e-mails to a majority of the two-star restaurants and finally received one response, this one bearing good news. I translated: "Miss Shockey, we have received your letter of interest and are happy to inform you that Senderens will be happy to take you as a *stagiaire*, under the conditions that you understand that this is an unpaid position and that you must have insurance in case of an accident." I immediately accepted their offer and told them I would call them to confirm exact dates once I was in Paris. I found an apartment to rent through a friend of a friend (and confirmed this time around that it was in good condition!), booked my plane ticket, and said shalom to Tel Aviv and bonjour to Paris.

⌒⌒

AFTER THE LAID-BACK vibe at Carmella, I had expected a change of pace at Senderens, but the second I crossed the threshold on my first day of work, I knew I was about to experience a whole new ball game.

The kitchen was the largest one I'd worked in, with a huge rectangular stove in the middle separating everyone's workstations. A floor-to-ceiling shelf next to where I stood was weighted down with stacks of copper pots and saucepans engraved with the restaurant's name, while white china plates, bowls, and saucers were hidden underneath the workstation in front of me. Everything was well organized and immaculate.

I was five minutes early for my appointed nine a.m. start time, but the entire kitchen staff—about thirty cooks, give or take—was already hard at work, their faces blotchy and sweaty from steaming pots and their aprons spotted with sauce and animal blood. The mood was tense and hurried, with baby-faced line cooks rushing from station to station. I caught a whiff of chicken stock simmering in an enormous pot at the back of the room, and for a fleeting moment its rich aroma enveloped me like a security blanket. Although I had brushed up on some French kitchen vocabulary—words like "peel" and "wash" and "mince"—my brain went blank as I scanned the room. What was the word for "scale"? "Strainer"? "Whisk"? "Cutting board"?

I approached the head chef, Jérôme, whom I had met a few days before to confirm the dates of my *stage*. He was huddled like a coach with another chef. He and Jérôme resembled each other, both in their late thirties. His blindingly white, spotless chef's jacket read "Arnaud Jeunet" in cursive across the left breast. All the chefs wore different types of jackets, but each had his name embroidered in the same place. The only people who weren't dressed in white were the two dishwashers, who were sectioned off in their own area.

Jérôme and Arnaud greeted me. "Get her a toque," said Jérôme to Hélène, one of only two female cooks in the testosterone-heavy room. At least I'd now bring the tally of women to three.

The white cotton baker's cap I was wearing, which had served me well at all the other restaurants, didn't cut the mustard here. The cooks all wore tall white paper toques that shot up into the air authoritatively, looking at once impractical, uncomfortable, and ridiculously French. Hélène handed me a toque, and I removed the tape and fitted it to my head.

"You'll be with Etienne at the fish station," said Jérôme, indicating a cook at the other end of the kitchen. Etienne looked young but focused, and he waved me over.

"*Salut,*" I said.

"You can put your knives in the oven," he said.

"The oven?" Was this a joke they pulled on new *stagiaires*?

"Yeah, the oven. This one is for storage; we do most of the cooking on top of the stove here, and when we need an oven we use the large one in the corner." He opened the oven, revealing several plastic containers and another knife roll, with a little room left for mine.

After I got organized, Etienne told me to remove the hard outer shells from three trays of langoustines in front of him. "Hold the langoustine with two hands and, using your thumbs, press the underbelly until the shell cracks. And gloves are over there." He pointed to a cardboard box of gloves marked "Large" in English.

"Are there any small gloves?" I asked.

"No." *Go figure.* I thought wistfully of the extra box of gloves that I had left behind in Vietnam.

I slipped on the loose gloves and began cracking the langoustines' shells, which was much harder than Etienne had made it look. He worked next to me, slicing tomatoes into quarters at a frenetic pace. After struggling for ten minutes, I succeeded in shelling five langoustines, while he had whizzed through half the tomatoes. A skinny Japanese chef peered over my shoulder, then turned to Etienne and said authoritatively in accented French, "No, Etienne, you do the langoustines and she can do the tomatoes." I quickly gathered he was the *chef de partie,* or station chef.

I looked at Etienne sheepishly. "Don't worry. Here, take the tomatoes," he said.

"So I cut them into four pieces? Like this?" I asked, demonstrating. Having to communicate in French was also harder than I expected. Kitchen French wasn't the same as the formal French I had learned in school, and these cooks talked a mile a minute and peppered their speech with slang that was unfamiliar to me.

"Yeah, like that is fine," said Etienne. "It's just for tomato confit, so it doesn't matter as much how it looks since it cooks down in the oven."

I managed to cut and seed the tomatoes properly and placed them on a baking sheet with oil, a sprig of thyme, and a bay leaf. Etienne explained that we had to bake them in the oven at a low temperature for a long period of time so that the water would evaporate and the flavor would become deeply concentrated.

"Now you can wash and pick the chervil, and afterward this lovage," said Etienne, handing me two different bunches of bright green herbs wrapped in paper towels. "Put the chervil in this container filled with water so it won't wilt and will be nice looking for service. But we're going to fry the lovage leaves, so just put those on a plate."

I grabbed a bowl and began filling it up with cold water. Because many herbs, particularly chervil, are delicate, it's best to fill a bowl with water and submerge the picked leaves in it. Eventually, any dirt or sand will sink to the bottom and you can scoop out the leaves and set them to dry on paper towels. If you just rinse the herbs under water, you might miss some of the grit, and the water pressure from the faucet will be too strong for the fragile leaves. The same goes for washing lettuce or other leafy greens, though they can usually withstand a bit more jostling (for instance, putting them in a salad spinner instead of air-drying them on paper towels is perfectly fine).

"Do you want to keep the lovage stems?" I asked, handing him the plate of leaves.

"No. Only parsley stems are saved to flavor stocks. The rest is thrown away. So where are you from?"

"America," I said, dismayed that my accent had already betrayed me as a foreigner.

"And how long are you here for?"

"Two months. How long have you worked here?"

"Not long, maybe a month and a half. So I'm new, too," he said, winking. I was glad to be working with Etienne, since he wasn't mean or bossy. Maybe it was his rank—*commis*, or junior cook—or his age; I figured he couldn't be older than twenty. Or perhaps it was that he wasn't Parisian!

After I had finished with the herbs, he brought over a small container of lemon zest strips and a smaller container of the zest minced as fine as desert sand. "Can you do this?" he asked.

I nodded and began thinly slicing the zest into hairlike strips, which I then gathered into a stack and minced as I had been taught to do at wd~50.

"Oh, look at that," he said in approval as I exhaled in relief. Maybe things would be okay here after all.

When I finished, Etienne announced, "Okay, we eat. Take off your apron and toque and get a plate of food. We eat downstairs in the refectory."

I walked to the pass, where a massive pot of mushy, army fatigue–colored green beans and a tray of broiled beef accompanied by a small pot of an oniony sauce awaited us. It was a far cry from the family meals at wd~50 or Carmella, but I filled my plate and followed my new colleagues downstairs to the basement's storage area, where four dining tables with benches were crammed together. The room was cold, dark, and cavernous, and everyone gobbled their meal in mere minutes. I instantly longed for the leisurely meals we had had at Carmella, where everyone from the lowest apprentice to the executive chef all sat at the same large table, taking food from the communal serving plates. My broiled beef and green beans tasted better than they looked, but not by much, and I chuckled to myself that the worst family meal I'd eaten was at the ritziest of all the restaurants I'd worked.

Etienne and I then began setting up for the restaurant's lunch shift. Lunch tends to be the most important meal of the day in France, and the restaurant was busy, with about eighty people dining over the course of two hours. Etienne was a *commis* for the fish station, helping to assemble components for the fish cooks, although he was also solely responsible for making and plating the langoustine appetizer, which he said we could do together.

For a mere 35 euros (a little more than $45), the diner received three langoustines that had been dredged in a mixture of slivered almonds and tiny squares cut from sheets of brik, a supple North African pastry similar to phyllo dough. We served the langoustines along with a small cup of buttery sauce flavored with slivers of lovage leaves and a spicy Thai-style condiment of bell peppers, chiles, ginger, and soy sauce. We then garnished the langoustines with half of a baby bok choy cabbage that we topped with a small mound of foam. Etienne showed me how to make the foam by pureeing the buttery sauce in a deep, narrow container with a hand blender and using a flat spoon to scoop off the foam from the top. All in all, the dish wasn't too complicated to remember, especially with two people working together. Etienne even let me fry the langoustines and plate the dish all on my own under his supervision as the lunch service got under way. Success! I was working the line at a two-star restaurant!

Still, service was intimidating: The kitchen clattered with

whisks clanking against pots, and Jérôme's booming voice cried out every other minute, calling out new orders and demanding those that needed to be brought to the pass. *"Deux langoustines, à suivre un cochon, un lièvre!"* he yelled, meaning two langoustine appetizers were to be followed by the pork and hare as entrées. *"Quatre menus bar!"* signaled that four prix fixe menus had just been ordered at the bar, which served less expensive versions of the food in the main dining room. And two seconds later he screamed, *"Au pass, un saumon, un langoustine, un foie gras,"* demanding the finished plates for the salmon, langoustine, and foie gras appetizers. Rather than cooking on the line, Jérôme, as executive chef, maintained the kitchen flow, calling out orders to each station rather than forcing each station to rely on a digital ticketing system. After Jérôme's command, the cooks responsible for each dish cried out in return, *"Oui, Chef!"* or simply, *"Chef!"* and the vocal assault jarred my ears like a rocket blitz.

Although *garde manger* had its own station at the front of the kitchen, the fish station was responsible for making all the appetizers that contained fish or shellfish. Thus, communication among all stations was essential, and before bringing up a fish appetizer to the pass, we had to yell, *"Au pass?"* to the *garde manger* chefs to confirm that everyone was good to go. It was the same when we were bringing up entrées—only then we had to shout across the kitchen to the meat station. If for some reason we hadn't communicated and a plate sat in the pass waiting for its companion plates for too long, Jérôme set off in a screaming frenzy. We were also required to shout, *"Chaud! Chaud devant!"* to signal that we were bringing food to the pass from our stations and you'd better not get in our way. Needless to say, there was a lot of yelling during service.

"You have to shout louder," Etienne told me when I trotted

back to our station after bringing up two plates of langoustines to Jérôme.

"Okay," I acknowledged. But the noise was so intimidating, and I was also worried about sounding stupid yelling in French or not being able to make myself understood.

"Don't be afraid. You have to yell!" he said, and darted off to simultaneously steam lobster meat and blend the accompanying vanilla cream sauce.

The cacophony finally subsided at around two thirty, signaling the end of the lunch service.

"You, go downstairs with Etienne and start cleaning the walk-ins," said Julien, one of the *garde manger* cooks. He, too, looked young, but his gruff attitude, broad shoulders, and stocky build gave him an air of authority.

"After every service, we clean here. Organize the shelves and wash the floor," said Etienne when we reached the walk-in refrigerator in the basement and began organizing crates of lemons, radishes, and arugula. "When we're done here, then we go upstairs and help clean up there," he said. Finally, at three fifteen, the Senderens kitchen sparkled anew, and we cooks were allotted a forty-five-minute break. Most of the cooks threw off their aprons and headed straight for the door, pack of cigarettes already in hand, and Etienne signaled for me to follow suit. I went with them outside to the arcade that opened onto the place de la Madeleine, one of the most expensive addresses in Paris, where the inhabitants were always dressed to the nines. Everyone began smoking cigarettes and making phone calls while leaning against the damp stone walls. Some of the cooks used this break to run quick errands, but mostly it was a time for socializing. The cooks didn't go out of their way to include me in their conversations, but they didn't ignore me, either, and I stood next to Etienne and a few of his friends under a cloud of tobacco smoke. I asked Etienne how their schedule worked, and he replied that the cooks worked from seven thirty in the morning to eleven thirty at night.

"Sixteen-hour days?" I said in shock. *Was that even legal?*

"Yeah, but there are two different groups of cooks. We work three days on, three days off, three days on, three days off. But, yeah, that last day is hard. But it'll be easier for you since you'll be working the *stagiaire* schedule, only nine to seven, but it is five days a week. This week, though, you're working both the lunch and dinner shifts, so you can see what it's like. Prepare to be tired by the end of the week," he said.

We all returned to a serene kitchen, since Jérôme and the sous-chefs were still on break, and the mood was genial.

"You can peel the potatoes and then take the parsley leaves that you picked earlier. You know how this works?" said Etienne, who was assembling a small green-and-white machine that peeled vegetables into long, thick, noodlelike strips.

I nodded. At wd~50 we had used it to make long, thin strips of sweet potato, which were then pickled to accompany fried sweetbreads.

"And get eight sheet trays. The heavy ones. And get a *cul-de-poule*," he said.

"A *cul-de-poule?*" Translated literally, that meant a hen's butt.

"Yes, a *cul-de-poule*," he said, pointing at his butt and then making a flapping chicken motion.

"What is that?"

"The large metal bowls that are flat on the bottom, you know." *Yes, of course, a metal mixing bowl is called a hen's butt. What idiot didn't know that?* When I asked Etienne why it was called that, he shrugged. I later attempted to research the etymology and came up empty-handed.

After I peeled the potatoes, Etienne began slicing them on

the machine and then used a small plastic rectangle to cut out squares. "These are chips for the brandade. You know brandade? It's a puree of potatoes with salt cod," he explained.

Etienne showed me how to line up the potato squares on a tray lined with buttered parchment paper and instructed me to brush the potatoes with melted butter. Once the potatoes were buttered, a single parsley leaf was placed in the center and dabbed with butter to hold it in place before another parchment sheet and another baking sheet were placed on top, so the chips would bake flat and the parsley wouldn't fall off. The chips were then baked for an hour at a low temperature. When they emerged from the oven, golden brown, translucent, and fragile to the touch, they looked like sheets in those old-fashioned books meant for drying and pressing flowers, only edible.

"Try one," Etienne said, handing me a chip after we had baked them off. It was buttery and light and shattered into tiny shards as I bit into it.

"Mmm, it's good," I said, and he handed me another.

We worked side by side until the early evening family meal, an uninspiring dish of bland rice with pink, baked salmon slices and wedges of lemon, and then Etienne and I began setting up the station for the dinner rush, which he said lasted from about eight to eleven.

"So, do you remember how to do everything? I won't be here for the dinner service, so it's just you."

I panicked. Just me? I was pretty sure that I had mastered the langoustine dish, and I had taken notes on how the other fish dishes were plated. But I knew I would be in trouble when it came to responding to the incoming orders, and I'd end up "in the weeds"—kitchen slang for royally fucked. Then I noticed Etienne's grin. A jokester disguised as a chef.

"Did I just scare you?" he said.

"Yeah, a little," I said.

"So what do Americans think of the French?" he asked. I liked that even though this was a really serious kitchen, we could talk, and Etienne was very friendly, not like some of the cooks working the meat station, who appeared unapproachable. They were probably Parisian.

"I don't know, that they're chic and fashionable? What do French people think of Americans?"

"That they're all fat and you'll get killed if you leave your house." Funny—this was what Son and the other cooks in Hanoi had thought.

"Well, a lot of Americans are really overweight," I conceded.

"They like McDo. I'd like to go to America so I could get a supersize at McDo. We don't have that here in France."

"I don't think we have it anymore either after the movie *Super Size Me.*"

"But people still eat at McDonald's after seeing that movie?"

"Yes," I said, shrugging. To me it seemed that in general Americans preferred quantity, while the French opted for quality. That was why so many French people still shopped daily at the butcher, cheese shop, vegetable market, and pastry shop instead of going weekly to the supermarket: They wanted the best, even if it took longer and could be more expensive. Of course, things were evolving, but in France, much more so than in America, the act of sharing a meal together was still highly valued. Eating was about much more than the food itself; it was about sustaining relationships with the community by patronizing different shops and about knowing who was making your food.

"Okay, so you're ready for the dinner service?" asked Etienne, who by now had organized everything we'd need for the next several hours. I nodded.

Etienne and I worked in tandem throughout the dinner service, which essentially replicated the lunch service, only this time we were serving one hundred customers spread over two seatings. I made most of the langoustines while Etienne helped out with the other fish dishes. The language barrier was becoming less intimidating as the day wore on, and Etienne helped me out by repeating instructions for each order.

At ten thirty, Jérôme called out from the pass, "Lauren, go home."

I nodded, gathered my knives, and said good-bye to everyone, although they were still preoccupied with the dinner shift. Jérôme shook my hand, and I thanked him for a good first day. And then I headed for the Metro, homeward bound to my cozy sublet in the Fifth Arrondissement, just off Place Monge. Once home, I immediately crawled into bed, exhausted to the bone.

AFTER WORKING five fourteen-hour days in a row, I was beyond ready for the weekend. I had spent the week at the fish station, the first three days with Etienne, and then the last two with Nico, who was the *commis* for the second group of fish cooks and who also looked barely old enough to shave.

While Nico and I had been setting up for service, Arnaud approached me and asked, "Would you rather do prep or service?"

"Whatever is best for you."

"No, you decide."

"Service." I was able to keep up with the pace and had been sending out nice-looking plates. Why would anyone want to do prep work when they could be working the line?

"Good choice," said Nico. "So, why are you here? How old are you?"

"Twenty-five," I said, knowing that I was an old maid in this kitchen. The regimented French educational system forced you to decide (or decided for you) in the eighth grade if you would attend an academically oriented high school or a vocational one, and nearly all the French cooks at Senderens had taken pre-professional high school courses and essentially begun their careers at the age of fourteen. So Nico, who told me that he was eighteen, already had four years of professional experience under his belt, even though he was only a *commis*.

"When some people are young, they say they want to be firefighters or something, but me, I always wanted to be a chef," he said as we minced pickled ginger.

"Was your father a chef?"

"No, he's a police officer. My sister, too. But I had an uncle who had a restaurant, and I started out there."

"How long have you been here?"

"A month or so. I'd like to stay one year, two years."

"And do you live in Paris?"

"Right now I'm living in a hotel. I'd like to find an apartment, but it's hard. But the hotel is on Place de Clichy, do you know it? It's only ten minutes away by bike, so it's not bad," he said, shrugging.

Place de Clichy is a shady area of Paris, similar to Times Square before it got cleaned up, and let's just say that the types of hotels there aren't in the Ritz family. Renting a room in a cheap hotel would be cheaper than renting an apartment, but I pitied Nico. He looked so, so young, and he kept to himself during family meal. That lifestyle sounded so depressing: working, hoping to stick it out for two years, shuttling back and forth in the big city between work and a drab hotel room until his résumé was good enough for him to go somewhere else.

"Oh. How do you like living there?" I asked.

"It was good when I first came because I had a friend here, so he showed me around Paris," he said. Tellingly, I thought, he didn't mention anything about how things were now.

⌣⌢

AFTER MY FIRST WEEK OF WORK, my British friends Carole and Andrew invited me out for Sunday lunch. They were family friends from our expat days in Budapest in the early 1990s. They had two sons close to my age, and we had all remained in touch over the years as we returned to our respective native lands. However, Andrew was currently living in Paris for work, and Carole, based in London, visited once a month while Andrew commuted to see her on the other weekends. I hadn't met anyone in Paris outside of work, so I was especially happy to see them. I walked along the banks of the Seine to Andrew's apartment on the Île de la Cité, in the heart of Paris.

"We want to hear all about your kitchen slaving over lunch, Lauren. We were thinking we'd go to Chez Paul next door—it overlooks the river. It's good, very French, you know," Carole said as she poured us mimosas.

As Carole promised, Chez Paul was a quintessential French restaurant. Its menu offered the predictable favorites like steak tartare and lamb chops, while specials that probably never changed were written in script on the mirrors that lined the walls.

"It's great how the French go out for Sunday lunch. It's just what's done. They don't get dressed up or anything," said Andrew, attired casually in slacks and a button-down shirt.

"They do get dressed up. Look around," said Carole. Several tables of families were leisurely sipping wine, while an elderly couple in their Sunday best sat behind us.

"Oh, I suppose so," Andrew conceded.

"That's the other thing that I like about going out to eat in Paris. I don't feel like I'm automatically the oldest person in the restaurant. In London, we always feel so old. Where do they put all the old people in London? In homes for the soon to be departed, I reckon," Carole joked. Indeed, with the exception of cheaper, quick-service brasseries and sandwich shops populated by younger people, most restaurants in Paris had a diverse clientele agewise. In London as well as in New York, the restaurant scene is dominated by the newest, trendiest places to see and be seen. But in Paris, a city that embraces tradition and is slower to change, restaurants are still places to eat and enjoy food, not acquire cultural capital.

"The problem with the French, though, is that they can't stray beyond their own food. It's always just *so French*," said Andrew, perusing the menu.

For the most part, he was right. At "typical" French bistros and brasseries, you'll find the exact same menu. It never changes and features the classics: eggs with mayonnaise, leeks vinaigrette, frisée salad with lardons, roast chicken, steak with béarnaise sauce, and steak with peppercorn sauce. The slogan for French cuisine could be "Why change it when we got it right the first time?"

I felt compelled to defend my employer, though. "You know, at Senderens they actually do a good job of incorporating some international ingredients. In the veal tartare, there's a little wasabi along with the mayonnaise and capers and cornichons, and in the lobster ravioli we use a bit of pickled ginger. Also, in the langoustines that I make, there's dried soy and coriander in the sauce, and the squid is sort of Spanish influenced with its chickpeas and chorizo. But it's true, even when it's somewhat international, it's still very much French, with all of its stocks and sauces and butter and cream."

"And how is your job?" asked Carole.

"It's good. I've mostly been doing prep work for other people, though I've been doing a little cooking. I had much more responsibility in Tel Aviv, though, so it's been a bit of a downgrade."

"It must be so unglamorous inside the kitchen," she said wryly.

"But the people are friendlier than I expected, and the food seems really good, from the bits and pieces I've sampled, although it should be delicious at the prices they're charging."

"Yes, we went to the restaurant's website and looked at the menu and nearly died at how expensive it was," said Carole.

"I know. I can't even afford to eat where I'm working."

Carole smiled. "At least you're in Paris and can console yourself with all the marvelous and inexpensive pastries at the corner bakery."

"Yes, pastries and wine and cheese and bread. I'll embrace the French paradox of eating lots of fattening foods without gaining weight. And to that, cheers," I said, raising my glass of red wine. Then I ate a forkful of my foie gras salad, which, as I could have guessed, was more foie gras than salad, but delicious, even if predictably so.

⌒

"LAUREN, GET THE BAR," said Arnaud on Monday morning, after I had spent an hour washing sand off hundreds of scallops and arranging them neatly on a sheet to dry. I looked at him, bewildered.

"*Le bar.*"

"*Le bar?*" I repeated. What was I supposed to get at the bar? I looked at him blankly, which unfortunately was my usual reaction to orders that I didn't fully understand.

"Sea bass," he said in English with a heavy accent.

"Oh, okay," I said.

"And come here," he said. Sweeping his hands across my waist, he pulled the apron strings together and retied it tightly around me. "You must be proud of your profession! Now you look so sexy," he said, smacking his lips together and winking.

After I returned with the fish and we gutted and cleaned them into pristine filets, Arnaud announced that he and I and Stéphane, a sous-chef, would go upstairs and begin preparations for Alain Senderens's birthday celebration.

I hadn't even glimpsed the great Alain Senderens yet, although I had met his wife, who occasionally dropped by the restaurant office, located next to the prep kitchen. Although Senderens emblazoned his name on both the marquee and the menu, Jérôme ran his kitchen. Now in his seventies, and having worked a lifetime in kitchens, Senderens had taken a step back from the wheel. But he was still the boss, and no expense was spared for his birthday. Stéphane followed Arnaud into the kitchen and began attacking hundreds of dollars' worth of truffles for the celery root gratin. I was given the menial task of peeling the celery root, but they let me help with the layering of the gratins.

But the fun was short-lived; after the gratins were in the oven, it was back to chopping. And although I had worked the line at the fish station during my first two weeks, this past week I hadn't helped out with service at all but had been relegated to prep work in the upstairs kitchen, either alone or occasionally with Henri, the other long-term *stagiaire*, who was a seventeen-year-old culinary school student from Paris. I had thought the first two weeks had gone well, and I couldn't recall having made any serious mistakes, but maybe I was wrong. My working hours were now divided between destemming case after case of arugula and using a pastry tip to punch out hundreds of circles of thinly sliced pickled ginger.

Henri and Sébastien, the meat *commis*, had been sent upstairs with a massive bowl of roasted red peppers that the three of us were supposed to mince together by hand. The task would have been much easier if we had been allowed to partially chop the peppers in a food processor, but oh, no. *Pas possible!* So for three hours, we chopped. And chopped. And chopped. After the first two hours, Henri told me to guard the door, and he grabbed a huge handful of the peppers and threw them in the garbage, hiding them under a mound of paper towels. "What they don't know won't hurt them," he said, grinning. I was nervous that one of the chefs would find the discarded peppers, but the thought of spending another two hours chopping was even worse. So we all smiled at one another, guarding the secret.

⌁

LATER THAT WEEK, I forced myself to stand with the other cooks during the smoking break that occurred at the end of family meal. As it was, family meal lasted about twenty minutes, with about five to ten minutes devoted to eating and the rest to smoking outside in the arcade. As I wasn't a smoker, I often stood in the gloomy arcade feeling like an outcast on the school playground. But Henri and Erez, one of the fish cooks, had been friendly to me in recent days, so I joined them.

"Hey. So, things are going well?" asked Erez, who hailed from Israel and was tall and thin, with delicate features and long eyelashes—I would have developed a serious crush on him if he hadn't been married and a father.

"Things are good," I said.

"You're lucky that the chefs like you. They don't like all the *stagiaires*. And Henri, too, they like him."

I thought about that. A *stagiaire* named Fabien had started with me on the same day, but the cooks didn't take to him and he "disappeared" after one week, presumably fired.

"Yeah, they have been really nice to me, which is good."

"Well, you're nice and you work hard," said Erez.

"Thanks." I was relieved to hear his words of reassurance because I had been second-guessing myself a lot. But maybe I was just being my own worst critic; it was something my mother had often spoken to me about.

"Lauren, you come and do the crab," said Arnaud when I returned to the kitchen after the break. He handed me a gargantuan pot filled with the giant stone crabs the French call tourteaux. The restaurant had just unveiled a new appetizer, a black radish rémoulade mixed with flecks of crab and topped with large crab chunks, paper-thin slices of mushrooms, and a garnish of exactly twelve micro herb leaves. Since cleaning and shelling crabs is a long, tedious task, it was the perfect job for me, the lowest person on the totem pole.

"I have a trick for this. I have a blacklight so you can see the shell. I will bring it upstairs," said Arnaud. He reappeared later, holding a box containing the blacklight, a single fluorescent tube. We switched off the lights and placed the blacklight on top of two upside-down bowls to shine over the tray holding the crab. It illuminated the tiny pieces of cartilage, indistinguishable to the naked eye, hiding amid the meat. It took about an hour to sift through all of the crabmeat, and although I could find a certain *CSI*-like glamour in the situation, I was disappointed that I was whiling away my time sifting through crabmeat and not cooking.

With the Christmas season approaching, I had become relegated to a daily exile of washing and organizing hundreds of scallops before tackling the crabs, whose smell lingered on my skin even after multiple washings. I worked in the empty upstairs prep kitchen, where there was lots of room and it didn't matter if I made a mess whacking the crabs with my giant knife. But with only dead crabs for company, the conversation was limited.

"And Lauren, after you're done with the crab, let me know so we can get naked and sunbathe in front of the blacklight," said Arnaud.

What? I looked at him like a deer in headlights. I didn't know how to react. So I kept quiet and took it like a man.

(Almost) Michelin-Starred Meals

As you might expect at a restaurant with two Michelin stars, most of Senderens's recipes are complex. The following recipes are almost identical to those served at the restaurant, but some steps or ingredients have been adapted or modified to make them easier for the home cook—not that your guests will be able to tell the difference.

LOBSTER "RAVIOLI" WITH VANILLA CHAMPAGNE SAUCE

The lobster ravioli at Senderens was one of my favorite dishes. It evokes all the decadence and luxury that one should expect from a top Parisian restaurant. The original version comes covered in a mountain of foam made from the remaining sauce, but that's an unnecessary step for the home cook (the dish is time-consuming enough as it is!), and the following recipe is my adaptation. Look for square dumpling wrappers made out of wheat dough, although thin sheets of flat pasta would also work. This will serve four as an entrée, although it's on the light side, so you might want to add an appetizer and dessert—and, of course, lots of bread to soak up the delicious sauce.

SERVES 4

1 cup spinach leaves

3 tablespoons sliced, pickled ginger (available at Asian specialty stores)

4 tablespoons unsalted butter

2 medium shallots, sliced (about 1 cup's worth)

1 vanilla bean

½ cup champagne or other dry, sparkling white wine

1 cup heavy cream

Heaping ¼ teaspoon kosher salt

2 (2-pound) live lobsters

½ teaspoon minced lemon zest (if you have a Microplane, use it to grate the lemon, and then mince the zest until it resembles sand)

4 dumpling wrappers (available at Asian specialty stores)

Slice the spinach leaves into ¼-inch-thick ribbons. This can be done quickly by stacking several leaves together and slicing several at one time. Set aside. Mince the pickled ginger as finely as possible; then, using a paper towel, squeeze out all of the water it contains until it feels relatively dry.

Prepare the sauce: Melt 2 tablespoons of the butter in a medium-sized saucepan over medium-high heat. Add the shallots and cook until soft, about 4 minutes. Slice the vanilla bean in half and scrape out the seeds. Add the seeds, bean, and champagne to the shallots, and cook until reduced by half, about 5 minutes. Add the cream and simmer over medium-low heat for about 10 minutes. Strain and discard the solids, then return the sauce to the saucepan. Whisk in the remaining butter and season with salt. Keep warm.

Place the lobsters in a steamer basket set over boiling water and cook until done, about 10 minutes. The lobster should be bright red and the meat inside opaque and white. Deshell the lobster. If there's any white gunk on the lobsters, rinse it off, and devein the lobsters. Cut each of the tails and half of the claws into large pieces, about 1 inch. Chop the knuckles and remaining claws into smaller pieces, about ¼ to ½ inch.

In a small saucepan over high heat, combine the ginger with the lobster, lemon zest, and half the sauce. Cook until the mixture is hot, about 3 minutes.

Bring a small pot of water to a boil. Blanch the spinach by submerging it in the water and immediately removing it with a slotted spoon. Set aside. Using the remaining water, add the dumpling wrappers and cook until done, about 30 seconds.

Spoon the lobster-vanilla sauce mixture into four bowls. Place the spinach atop the lobster, then drape one dumpling wrapper over the spinach. Top with the remaining sauce. Serve immediately.

CRISPY SHRIMP

While working the fish station, I helped prepare and plate this dish, which is made with langoustines for the downstairs restaurant and with shrimp for the bar. Langoustines are prohibitively expensive—not to mention hard to find—in America, so I opt for shrimp at home. Brik are thin sheets of North African pastry dough, available online or at a specialty store. At the restaurant, we garnished this dish with a soy-butter sauce, but I think it goes especially well with homemade tartar sauce.

SERVES 4 AS AN APPETIZER

> ½ cup slivered almonds
> 12 jumbo shrimp
> 1¼ cups flour
> 1 cup beer
> 1 teaspoon baking powder
> 10 sheets brik dough (may be called feuilles de brick)
> Vegetable oil for frying, about 4 cups
> Kosher salt

Preheat the oven to 350 degrees F. Bake the almonds for 5 minutes. They should not brown but should have just a wisp of color.

Shell the shrimp, leaving the tail intact and attached. If desired, remove the shrimp's vein by inserting a paring knife into the body near the tail, lifting out the brown intestinal tract with your knife, and pulling it out with your fingers. You do not want to devein by slicing down the whole shrimp, as you want it to keep its shape.

Combine the flour, beer, and baking powder in a small bowl. Stack the sheets of brik and cut into ¼-inch squares (they don't need to be perfect squares, as this isn't Senderens). Combine with the almonds and spread half across the bottom of a plate or flat, shallow bowl. (If your brik sheets are stuck together, you can break them apart by rubbing a handful between the palms of your hands.)

Holding a shrimp by the tail, dip it into the batter, shake off any excess, then place on the brik-almond mixture. Cover and pat with the remaining brik-almond mixture, then toss gently from hand to hand to shake off any excess dredging. Repeat until all the shrimp are breaded.

Pour the vegetable oil into a small pot over high heat. To test if the oil is hot enough, drop in a small square of the brik; if it bubbles and rises to the surface immediately, add 3 to 4 shrimp to the pot. Fry until the shrimp are golden brown, about 3 minutes, turning them over if necessary. Remove with a slotted spoon and dry on paper towels. Sprinkle lightly with salt. Keep warm. Repeat with the remaining shrimp. Serve immediately.

VEAL TARTARE, SENDERENS STYLE

Veal tartare is one of the classic dishes at Senderens, served both at the bar and in the main restaurant. I am not the biggest fan of steak tartare because I find that it can often have a strong flinty taste, but raw veal is much more delicate. Because the veal is eaten raw, make sure to buy the highest quality available.

SERVES 4 AS AN APPETIZER

½ pound veal cutlets
1 egg yolk
1 teaspoon Dijon mustard
¼ cup plus 2 tablespoons vegetable oil
1 teaspoon wasabi paste
Pinch each of kosher salt and freshly ground black pepper
2 teaspoons minced cornichons
2 teaspoons minced chives
1 teaspoon minced capers
½ teaspoon lemon zest, grated with a Microplane

Trim any remaining fat off the veal, then cut into small cubes, about ¼ inch on all sides, and place into a large mixing bowl. In a separate bowl, prepare a mayonnaise: Combine the egg and mustard and whisk together for about 30 seconds. Slowly whisk in the oil a few droplets at a time. Whisk in the wasabi and the salt and pepper. Add the mayonnaise to the veal and combine well.

Stir in the cornichons, chives, capers, and lemon zest. Adjust seasoning, if needed, and serve immediately.

Chapter 13

"OH, LAUREN, there is no crab for you to do this week. Isn't that good news?" Arnaud said, shaking my hand firmly as he did every morning upon my arrival.

It had taken me a few weeks to grasp the French custom of circulating and greeting every member of the kitchen staff personally with a "Bonjour" and a firm handshake. I initially felt awkward walking around the vast kitchen and saying "Bonjour" thirty times, but I ultimately appreciated how it helped build camaraderie and a sense that even the most inexperienced cook was an essential part of Team Senderens. And this occurred not once, but twice a day. My shift at Senderens ended only after I shook Jérôme's hand good-bye and tossed off a round of "Au revoirs."

"Great," I said, relieved not to have to spend another week in perdition. The previous week, I had devoted thirty hours to shelling crab in the upstairs prep kitchen and I was ready for a change.

"He's just kidding. There are fifty kilos upstairs," said Jérôme, who was standing next to Arnaud and chopping thousands of dollars' worth of pungent black truffles. The holiday season was now in full swing, and truffles were showered on dishes like confetti at midnight on Times Square. An earthy, primal scent invaded the kitchen every morning when the truffles were brought out from a special refrigerator kept under Jérôme's lock and key.

"Yes, Chef," I said, crestfallen but putting on a brave face.

"No, I'm joking. There's no crab this week," said Jérôme. Like Arnaud, he enjoyed poking fun, and particularly at me, the foreigner. The other women on staff weren't treated this way.

"Oh, okay. Right," I said, still not entirely sure who was kidding. It's difficult to discern irony and get jokes in a foreign language, and I viewed myself as the most gullible person ever to walk into the Senderens kitchen because I assumed every word spoken to be the truth. In any case, I approached the meat station instead to assist them with their *mise en place*.

"*Salut*, Lauren. Can you dry these cabbage leaves?" asked Allesia, one of the other female cooks.

The cabbage leaves were blanched in a deep pan and then filled with a creamy, buttery mixture of minced cabbage, bacon, and onions and baked until it formed a dense cake. After I separated the leaves and wrung out the water, I layered them on paper towels and enclosed the sheet in plastic wrap so that Allesia's *mise en place* would be primed for the following day.

The meat station had run out of its plastic wrap, so I went to the pastry kitchen for more. While I was waiting for Hliza, one of the pastry cooks, to finish using the plastic wrap, an unfamiliar guy approached me, pointed to a pot of custard, and asked, "*Qu'est-ce que c'est?*"

"I don't know what it is. Are you American?" I said in French, detecting a foreign accent in his speech.

He nodded. "From Canada, actually."

"Great. I'm from New York." I was happy to have a new friend in the kitchen. After all, nothing brings two people together quicker than being outsiders with an imperfect grasp of the language in a foreign country.

I shouldn't have been surprised by his arrival. The professional kitchen isn't like other workplaces, where when someone leaves, he or she sends out a mass e-mail good-bye or gets a low-key party with cake. Here, people came and went in a steady stream, with new faces replacing old ones, no explanations or introductions given. But while any professional kitchen engenders a high turnover, there seemed to be a permanently revolving door at Senderens.

I later learned that the new cook's name was Seth and that he had just moved to Paris to be the new *commis* for the fish station (replacing Nico, who was moving to the *garde manger* station). During his first two weeks, Seth struggled as I had: I noticed the vacant look that comes from searching for the ladles because no one gave you a proper kitchen tour or not knowing that the words for metal mixing bowl and ladle are *cul-de-poule* and *louche* because you hadn't had occasion to learn them.

A few days later, Seth and I were cleaning the walk-in refrigerator after the lunch service, working in an assembly line to remove the overloaded crates of eggplant, lemons, peppers, and radishes so we could mop the floor. While I began filling up a bucket with soapy water, Stéphane, now finished with running the lunch service, stalked over to Seth. Frowning deeply and shaking his fist, he scolded Seth, "You can't stand around doing nothing during service. You have to work."

"But the plates were different with this group of chefs," said Seth in broken, awkward French. I had spent all of the lunch service in the prep kitchen mincing lemon confit, but from their conversation, I gathered that Seth hadn't done well helping Allesia at the meat station.

"Don't make excuses. I work with both teams, and the plates aren't that different. You've really got to step up the pace or else. This isn't just any restaurant. We've got two Michelin stars here. You know, if you work hard here for a while and keep up with the pace, then you'll be able to get a job at any restaurant in the world," said Stéphane.

"Yes. It's good for the résumé," Seth said sheepishly. I continued to organize the vegetable crates at my feet while eavesdropping on their conversation. I sympathized with Seth—I knew he was trying, and being called out by one of the head chefs is humiliating.

"Do you understand me?" Stéphane snarled, and Seth nodded. Although the commanding chefs were amiable and joked with me, moments like these made me worry about my job performance. Since starting at Senderens, I woke up at least twice nightly, anxious about the next day, and I had developed a stress-related eye twitch, something I hadn't had since my days working at the PR firm. Ridiculous, yes, but working (even unpaid) in a restaurant of Senderens's level was flat-out humbling.

But I gained a little confidence a few days later while trimming red endive into heart-shaped slivers for the scallop dish. "You know, every day you get better," said Erez, who was working next to me, cutting spinach into thin strips. Erez was one of my favorite people in the kitchen, calm and thoughtful but not overly serious, and an all-around nice guy.

"Thanks. It's hard at first, thinking in a foreign language and not knowing the different words for kitchen tools or not fully understanding instructions," I said.

"Of course. I see Seth and I know it's hard for him, too." Erez understood the lifestyle adjustments required when living abroad and being unable to express everything exactly the way you want. Three years before, he had followed his French girlfriend, whom he'd met in Israel, to Paris. Now he was fluent in French and married with a baby daughter, but he still didn't feel totally at home in France.

"Did you light the candles for Hanukkah?" asked Erez. The eight-day holiday was already under way, and Erez knew I was Jewish from a prior conversation.

"No, I didn't, and... I don't know..." I was ashamed that I'd been too lazy to buy even an inexpensive menorah and unwilling to admit that I didn't want to celebrate alone. Hanukkah was one of the few Jewish holidays that we celebrated together as a family, lighting the rows of blue candles and feasting on crispy, fried potato pancakes with sour cream and applesauce.

"Well, would you like to come to my house to celebrate?"

"Are you sure? I don't want to impose."

"It's not imposing. Come over to my house on Friday. I'll cook something for us all."

His invitation touched me. I had a real friend in the kitchen and, now, outside the kitchen, too.

⌒

IT TOOK AN HOUR and a half on the RER, the regional train system, to reach Nogent-sur-Marne, the Parisian suburb where Erez and his family lived. It was the last night of Hanukkah and I didn't arrive until way after sundown, but no one minded pushing back the ritual candlelighting by a few hours.

"How was the rest of your week?" asked Erez once we were inside the warm and cheerful apartment.

"Good. Pretty much the same as every week. I shelled lots of crab," I said.

He shook his head and said to his wife, "Every day we boil kilos and kilos' worth of crab and then we give them to Lauren to shell upstairs. It takes hours." He turned back to me. "But at least you'll get really good at it so if you work somewhere with crab on the menu, you'll know what to do."

"All the *stagiaires* do work like that?" asked Erez's wife.

"They aren't really in the main kitchen much," Erez told her. At least Erez appreciated that shelling crabs was arduous. Simply put, menial prep work is the apprentice's way of life at a two-star Michelin restaurant.

"So I've made a small something, more Israeli than French. Do you know of bourekas?" Erez asked me after he had said the prayers, the nine flickering candles illuminating a green-and-blue mosaic menorah.

I definitely remembered the flaky pastries I had savored so often in Tel Aviv. Sitting around Erez's simple wooden coffee table, we ate the bourekas and several other dishes he had whipped up, including hummus, eggplant spread, and tomato-and-mozzarella salad, which made me nostalgic for my friends in Tel Aviv and the meals we had shared together.

"Have you seen this?" Erez asked, bringing over a prepackaged meal of veal blanquette with girolle mushrooms and rice from the refrigerator. He pointed to the picture of an old man in glasses. The one and only Alain Senderens. My boss, technically, whom I still hadn't met.

Scrutinizing the box, I shook my head. Dominating the upper-right-hand corner was a large white logo for Carrefour, the supermarket conglomerate, while the box itself displayed inviting veal chunks in cream sauce with wild mushrooms on a plate next to a glass of wine. Regal and rather formal, this box was the Rolls-Royce of TV dinners. Although in France they would never have called this a TV dinner; eating in front of the television was a faux pas. This was a "Carrefour Selection meal," marked with an expiration date only two weeks away.

"There are lots of different ones," said Erez, pulling out more boxes from the refrigerator. I saw guinea hen with chanterelles, Mediterranean vegetable tart, penne with arrabbiata sauce.

"Oh, is that why the Carrefour people were having a function at the restaurant the other day?" I guessed that Erez had received these meals for free.

"They come in a lot. It's good for Senderens. He gets a lot of money from it."

"I bet. It's so funny to think that he makes frozen dinners, though." Carrefour is the largest retailer in Europe and the second largest retailer in the world, selling everything from food to DVDs to clothing to furniture. Millions of people probably now recognized Senderens not for his herculean achievements in haute cuisine, but for his face in the freezer aisle.

"Yeah, but money is money," said Erez.

⟡

"YOU'RE IN PARIS for a year?" I asked Seth as we shivered in the covered arcade during our brief break following lunch.

"Yeah. It's a good experience so far at Senderens, but I'd also like to work at a three-star restaurant. Do you think it's that different?" he asked Erez, who had joined us. I, too, had been wondering what differentiated a two-star restaurant from a three-star one. Certainly the price and prestige would be greater, but given how intense the Senderens kitchen was, I couldn't imagine it being much more serious elsewhere.

"At a three-star place, they are only doing sixty plates per service, so they have more time to focus on each plate."

"So it's less pressure?" asked Seth.

"Not less pressure, but a different kind of pressure. Those plates have to be absolutely perfect, with twenty different components on each plate. Here, we're doing ninety, a hundred covers, and it's more rushed, so there isn't quite the same attention to details."

Funnily enough, though, in its former life Senderens *was* a three-star restaurant. Before it became Senderens, 9, place de la Madeleine housed the restaurant Lucas Carton, a hallowed temple of haute French gastronomy, which Alain Senderens took over from its previous owners in 1985. Back in the 1970s, Alain Senderens was credited with introducing a "nouvelle cuisine" that swept away the heavy butter- and cream-laden dishes of the past. Lucas Carton snared three Michelin stars—the pinnacle of gastronomic success.

After running its kitchen for twenty-eight years, he finally bought the restaurant in 2005 and made the shocking decision to return his stars to Michelin, claiming he no longer wanted to appeal to their standards by charging exorbitant prices while obsessing over details like how napkins were folded or the exact words waiters had to use to greet guests. So he closed Lucas Carton and launched Senderens, a "bistro de luxe," with less fussy food, prices that were 40 percent lower, some new personnel, and a simpler decor (the belle époque dining room gave way to questionable space age, color-changing mood lighting along with a shaglike carpet covering the upstairs floor). Senderens fared just fine without the stars—profits apparently skyrocketed. And Michelin awarded him two stars anyway, which he decided to keep.

Now balding and wearing unfashionable bottle-thick glasses, Senderens would roam the restaurant's hallways, but I never saw him cooking in the kitchen, and we hadn't ever been introduced. He breezed through about once every two weeks, checking on paperwork in the office and speaking only to Jérôme, while we cooks looked on with equal parts fear and admiration.

In many respects, converting Lucas Carton to a bistro was clever, and not only for Senderens's bank account. Despite being called a "bistro," Senderens is not a place for a quick bite, nor is it cheap. Appetizers run up to $50, while entrées hit $60. Add dessert and wine, and you're looking at about $200 per person. It is not the type of restaurant you patronize on a whim or on a regular basis (unless you're a titan of industry or a celebrity), but it's a popular choice to celebrate a special event or a Christmas bonus. And it is the new face of haute cuisine.

While molecular gastronomy may intimidate the diner who doesn't know what to expect, the haute cuisine of decades past prepared the diner for pomp and circumstance, heavy food, and an empty wallet. Vestiges of haute cuisine can still be found in France, but old-guard restaurants like Taillevent and Tour d'Argent have lost their cachet (and Michelin stars) in recent years. Senderens, meanwhile, was keeping up with the times and showing me the importance of continually adapting a cuisine. To be a successful restaurant, I was learning, you had to give the people what they wanted and you had to figure out what the people wanted before they even knew it themselves. And Alain Senderens had figured this out not once, but twice.

AS THE DRAB gray dusks of a Parisian winter turned into black nights, I kept busy and warm by cooking up a storm for myself after I got home from work. Even though my Parisian kitchen was small—minuscule, really—it didn't stop me from whipping up creamy squash soup, seared steaks with homemade béarnaise sauce, quiche Lorraine, and mixed herb omelets, washed down with glasses of crisp wine and decadent pastries from the corner bakery. But in late December, people suddenly surrounded me. Max, a good friend from New York, was apprenticing for a month at Fromagerie Trotté, a tiny cheese shop in the Marais (apparently, getting a PhD in French literature wasn't enough to keep him busy), and my parents popped over for a short Christmas visit. I worked during the day while they roamed the city's slush-covered boulevards, enjoying Paris's wealth of museums, monuments, and cafés. We dined together at restaurants I couldn't afford or had been too intimidated to try on my own.

"Should we eat at Senderens?" Mom asked when we were debating Christmas Eve dinner.

"Of course we will," said my father.

"I'm not sure. It's okay for you guys to come, but I'm afraid to ask for any special treatment. I think the restaurant will invite me to eat there when I'm done with my *stage*, so I don't want to make things awkward now by asking," I said.

"I'm sure it won't be awkward," said my mom. "You remember how nice Wylie was to us at wd~50? And Daniel at Carmella? He drove us to that other restaurant forty-five minutes away, for goodness' sake, and treated us twice."

"Mom, you don't understand. This place isn't like the others."

"Fine, we don't have to go. I thought you'd want us to see where you're working."

"I do, but... well, maybe you can go without me on a different night."

"Don't be ridiculous. We're not eating dinner in Paris without you. Anyway, I'm fine with not going. I don't need fancy food; I'm a simple southern girl at heart. Maybe your father can have lunch there after I go back to New York. He can even use an alias so no one will know you're related," she said.

In truth, I find holiday meals at a restaurant depressing, as if the diners don't have an inviting home or friends. I'm sure the Christmas meal at Senderens would knock my parents' socks off—at several hundred dollars, *it should*—but to me, the holidays are about comforting foods hinting at luxury, not luxury foods hinting at comfort. I wanted to prepare a meal for my parents to show them firsthand how I was growing as a cook. I'd pull the stops out on Christmas Day, but since I'd be working until seven on Christmas Eve, I decided to serve an easy buffet of smoked salmon, salad, and cured meats. When Max confessed he was planning to spend Christmas Eve alone at his Parisian residence hall, I immediately invited him, and he promised to bring cheeses from his shop. On the Saturday before Christmas, I took my parents and we stood on line for twenty minutes along with many chic Parisians to place an order for a bûche de Noël, the traditional chocolate Yule log for Christmas Eve, at the legendary pastry shop Pierre Hermé.

For Christmas Day, I planned a traditional French festive meal for my parents, but with a few surprises. Having enjoyed pickled chanterelle mushrooms served with aperitifs, I wanted to replicate that, although I'd be winging it without a recipe. When I told Arnaud I would be spending Christmas Eve with my family, he promised to give me a log of Senderens's foie gras, and I decided that green beans in vinaigrette would be the perfect counterpart to its rich, buttery goodness. I wanted something classic and hearty for the entrée, and without missing a beat, I chose beef Bourguignon. And for dessert, I opted for simple vanilla pots de crème—a fancy term for baked custard— with a warm salted caramel sauce, which I pictured runny and hot before it cooled slowly into a chewy confection, the custard only an excuse to eat the caramel.

As I composed the menu in my head, and then later on paper, I was confident that it would work. And on Christmas Day, rich aromas from the burgundy-and-port-flavored beef stew and simmering caramel enveloped my little apartment. We feasted, and at midnight all three of us declared, *"Fini,"* happy and full.

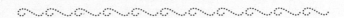

French Fare for Holiday Celebrations

What you serve when you entertain others should be easy to make, but with a hint of the luxurious and unexpected. Ideally, much of it should be prepared ahead of time, because what fun is entertaining if you're in the kitchen the whole time your guests are over? The following recipes are what I prepared for my family. Hopefully you'll enjoy them as much as they did, whether it's a special occasion or not.

NEARLY PICKLED MUSHROOMS

This is the type of simple hors d'oeuvre that's different yet elegant and can be prepared hours in advance. It works best as a small bite along with cocktails, perhaps accompanied by French breakfast radishes and salted almonds.

SERVES 4 TO 6 AS AN ACCOMPANIMENT TO DRINKS

>   1 tablespoon unsalted butter
>   1 tablespoon olive oil
>   ½ pound oyster mushrooms, trimmed of the large central core,
>   individual mushrooms cut in half if exceptionally large
>   Large pinch of kosher salt
>   Small pinch of freshly ground black pepper
>   2 tablespoons sherry vinegar

Melt the butter and olive oil in a large skillet over high heat. When the butter starts to foam, add the mushrooms and cook until golden brown, about 5 minutes. Make sure not to overcrowd the pan or to stir too frequently. Add the salt and pepper and stir. Remove from the heat and add the sherry vinegar, making sure to coat all of the mushrooms. Remove the mushrooms from the pan and let cool completely, uncovered, in the refrigerator. Serve slightly cold or at room temperature.

FOIE GRAS AND GREEN BEAN SALAD

Foie gras and green beans make an exceptional pair; the crisp freshness of the green beans and the acid from the vinaigrette help cut the richness of the foie gras. Foie gras doesn't come cheap, but this is a holiday dish. The green beans on their own or topped with cherry tomatoes or even slices of cured ham would make for a nice, less decadent starter.

SERVES 4

> 1 pound haricots verts (French-style green beans)
> 1 tablespoon Dijon mustard
> 1 teaspoon balsamic vinegar
> Pinch each of kosher salt and freshly ground pepper
> 3 tablespoons olive oil
> 2 ounces cooked foie gras (look for foie gras that is labeled
>   "torchon" or "mi-cuit")

Trim off the tops and tails of the haricots verts. Meanwhile, bring a large pot of lightly salted water to a boil. Add the beans and cook over high heat until they are done but slightly crunchy, about 5 minutes. Drain into a colander and run under cold water until beans are cool to halt the cooking process. Spread them out on a paper towel to dry.

In a small bowl, whisk together the mustard and vinegar along with a pinch each of salt and pepper. Slowly whisk in the olive oil until fully combined. One hour before serving, toss the beans with the dressing and let sit at room temperature.

Slice the foie gras into thin slivers. Divide the beans evenly among four plates and top with the foie gras.

BEEF BOURGUIGNON

Beef Bourguignon is arguably the most French of French dishes, a stew so timeless because it is so perfect. I like a sauce that's rich with a strong beefy taste, so I usually add a little Bovril, which is a meat extract paste. Unfortunately you can't get Bovril in America anymore, but a strong beef demiglace will work. Letting the stew refrigerate overnight really helps the flavors develop; just reheat it in the stove the next day.

SERVES 4

> 4 tablespoons unsalted butter
> 2½ pounds boneless beef chuck, cut into 1½-inch cubes
>   and trimmed of fat
> 2 tablespoons brandy
> ½ pound white pearl onions, peeled
> ½ pound small button mushrooms (you may halve or quarter
>   them if they are large)
> 2½ tablespoons flour
> 2½ tablespoons meat extract paste (like Bovril) or beef
>   demiglace
> 2 tablespoons tomato paste
> 1½ cups Burgundy or other red wine
> ¼ cup dry sherry
> ¾ cup port
> 1⅓ cups beef stock
> ⅛ teaspoon pepper

1 bay leaf
Kosher salt, as desired

Preheat the oven to 350 degrees F. In a Dutch oven or other oven-safe, heavy-bottomed pot, melt the butter over medium-high heat on the stovetop. Brown the beef cubes, making sure not to crowd the pan. If necessary, do this in two to three batches. Remove the beef and set aside.

In a small saucepan, heat the brandy over medium-high heat until you see a vapor rising. Light a match (ideally a long one) and carefully tip the lighted end into the pan so that a large flame ignites. Let cook until the flame eventually dies, then pour the liquid over the beef.

Return the Dutch oven to the stovetop. There should be about 2 tablespoons' worth of butter/fat remaining. Heat the pan to medium-high, then add the onions and cook, stirring occasionally, until they turn golden brown. Add the mushrooms and continue cooking for another 3 minutes.

In a small bowl, combine the flour, meat extract paste, and tomato paste until blended. Add to the Dutch oven and stir. Add the wine, sherry, port, and beef stock, and bring to a boil. Add the reserved beef cubes with their juice, the pepper, and the bay leaf, and stir until coated.

Cover the Dutch oven and bake in the oven, stirring occasionally, for at least 2½ hours, or until the beef is fork-tender. Let cool, then refrigerate overnight.

The next day: Preheat the oven to 300 degrees F. Remove the pot from the refrigerator and scrape off any congealed fat that may have risen to the top. Place the pot in the oven and cook for an additional 45 minutes or so, or until piping hot and thick. Add salt to taste (about ½ teaspoon), and serve with crusty bread.

VANILLA POTS DE CRÈME WITH SALTED CARAMEL SAUCE

Salted caramel is hands down my favorite flavor when it comes to dessert. If there's salted caramel anything on a menu, I'll order it. I'd eat this sauce straight out of the pot with a spoon, but when I have guests, I serve it with baked vanilla custard.

SERVES 6, OR 4 IF YOU USE LARGER RAMEKINS

FOR THE CUSTARD:

2 cups half-and-half (or 1 cup cream and 1 cup whole milk)
1 vanilla bean, sliced in half and seeds scraped out
5 large egg yolks
½ cup sugar
Pinch of kosher salt

FOR THE SAUCE:

1 cup sugar
½ teaspoon lemon juice
¼ cup water
1 teaspoon kosher salt
4 tablespoons cold unsalted butter
3 tablespoons heavy cream or whole milk

Preheat the oven to 300 degrees F. Bring the half-and-half and the vanilla bean and seeds to a boil, then remove from the heat and set aside, covered, for 15 minutes. Discard the vanilla bean.

Place the egg yolks, sugar, and salt in a bowl, and whisk until pale yellow, about 2 minutes. Slowly whisk in the cream mixture until fully combined, then strain using a fine-meshed sieve. Pour the strained custard base into 6 ramekins or other small baking dishes, leaving about a ½-inch space from the rim.

Place ramekins in a baking dish, then add enough hot or boiling water to the baking dish to come halfway up the sides of ramekins. Cover the baking dish tightly with foil and bake until the custard is set but slightly jiggly in the center, about 20 to 25 minutes.

Transfer individual ramekins to a rack to cool completely, uncovered, about 1 hour. Chill in the refrigerator, covered, until cold, at least 3 hours. About half an hour before serving, prepare the caramel sauce. In a heavy-bottomed pot, combine the sugar, lemon juice, water, and salt, and bring to a boil. Continue cooking at a boil until the sugar is a dark amber color, about 6 minutes, but do not stir the mixture. (You can swirl the pot occasionally once the mixture turns dark amber.) Remove from the heat and add the butter and cream, stirring until thoroughly combined and the butter has melted (the mixture will bubble and steam vigorously). Let cool slightly.

Pour a few tablespoons of the warm caramel sauce into the ramekins so that the sauce covers the custard. Serve immediately.

Chapter 14

"*ÇA VA, CHÉRIE?* What are you looking for?" asked Arnaud when I dashed into the downstairs kitchen to retrieve a pair of latex gloves. Six Styrofoam boxes filled with pricey Madagascar shrimp for the following day's New Year's Eve family meal awaited me, and I didn't want to wind up with fishy-smelling, red-stained hands.

"Gloves."

"Gloves? I don't want to wear a glove when I make love to you!" he said. I ignored him, annoyed that so many of our conversations took a sexual turn.

Although the family meals at Senderens never really improved beyond canned beans, except for the one time we had merguez sausages with ratatouille, the kitchen *did* go all out on Christmas Eve and New Year's Eve. Although I had opted to spend Christmas Eve with my family, Arnaud insisted that I take part in the New Year's Eve family meal, even though I wouldn't be working the evening's dinner shift. The chefs planned the menu nearly two weeks in advance, sparing no expense, and my fellow cooks and I were busy with all the prep work needed for this feast: shelling the superb, succulent shrimp; slicing whole smoked salmon filets; poaching delicate quail eggs and making a mayonnaise for dipping; slicing brioche into triangles for the marbleized pink wedges of foie gras; and combining minced shallots and red wine vinegar for a mignonette sauce to accompany the briny, raw Brittany oysters. The previous evening, I had even been entrusted with making the gratin dauphinois.

Just before six p.m. on New Year's Eve, the fish station began frying a whole tray of the langoustines, while the pastry kitchen added the final touches to two large bûches de Nöel, one pistachio with lemon and the other chocolate studded with hazelnuts.

"Lauren, are you eating with us?" Allesia asked.

I nodded and took off my apron and paper toque.

"Come on," said Erez, beckoning me upstairs to the bar, which was covered with heaping platters of edible delights. Rose petals were scattered on shelves and window ledges, more for the amusement of paying customers than ours, but the ambience was inviting.

"You should stay with us and work tonight," Allesia said after we had piled our plates with food and sat down.

"I'm going to a party," I replied. I was a little embarrassed to be leaving after dinner while everyone else had to stay and work, but I wasn't about to offer to stay.

"No, go have fun tonight," said Erez, smiling.

"You guys will be off by around midnight, right?" I said.

"Yeah, or a little after. But it's a set menu, so there's not that much to cook," said Allesia.

Instead of the usual twenty minutes, we luxuriated in the full hour we had to eat and relax, and wine-filled glasses replaced our standard plastic cups of water. It wasn't an over-the-top affair, as Alain Senderens and Jérôme had already left for their own celebrations, but the mood was jovial. We slurped down our oysters, cold and salty and slippery on the tongue, before digging into the creamy veal with oyster mushrooms.

We indulged in seconds of smoked salmon and pâté before hitting the dessert table. For once, family meal didn't feel like refueling with fellow soldiers in the barracks.

After dinner, I rushed to meet Max at his residence hall. It was a glorified dorm for international students, and Max had become fast friends with the other residents. They had decided to host a New Year's Eve dinner and asked everyone to prepare a dish from his or her home country. Max's contribution was a selection of cheeses from the store, including a delicious, creamy Vacherin Mont d'Or and a tangy Valençay, and I brought the remaining foie gras that Arnaud had given me. With food that good, no one minded that we represented our host country more than our native home. The Tunisian students prepared tuna-and-caper-filled triangular pastries made with the same brik pastry dough we used for the fried langoustine appetizer at Senderens, while the Portuguese students made pão de queijo, small rolls similar to gougères, a type of French savory pastry made with Gruyère. The Mexicans whipped up fajitas, which didn't quite go with the smoked salmon toasts presented by the Scandinavians, and our dining room was a fluorescent-lit common area with Formica tables that matched the Formica floor, but who cared? We toasted with champagne to a room of friends, new and old, in a multitude of French accents and then dug in.

⌒

MY NEW YEAR'S HOLIDAY didn't last long, though, and on Monday morning I was back in the proverbial salt mines. After greeting everyone in the kitchen, I faced a huge bowl of sandy scallops to clean, scrubbing off the grit with my thumbs, followed by the thankless job of removing all the bones from a pan's worth of poached pig trotters to make a terrine. If you've never had to debone a pig's foot, you're lucky—a single trotter has tons of tiny bones wedged amid skin and gelatin. But nothing could compare with the case of giant stone crabs I faced. The tourteaux were still warm and menacing-looking, as though they could foresee their future.

I was now the bona fide crab expert at Senderens. At first, I hated shelling crabs because it took so long, but this was mainly because no one had shown me the proper way to do it. But after the fifth round of crabs, I nailed it. Now a whole case of about fifteen (yes, fifteen) crabs took only about four hours from start to finish—two hours off my initial time. First I pulled off the steamed crab's claws and legs; then I wedged a knife into its body just above the abdomen to dislodge the carapace, or outer shell, from the fleshy part. I then washed the crabs under cold running water to remove any sand and pulled off any inedible hairy bits. After the crab had been cleaned, I whacked at the claws repeatedly with full force, using the back of a heavy knife, while crab juice and bits of shell ricocheted onto the white-tiled wall. Then I repeated the process with the smaller legs, though with less force so that the shell wouldn't shatter all over the meat and into the crab. I cut the body of the crab in half down the middle, and then each half again, though horizontally this time to maximize the number of flesh-containing pockets. After about two hours, I had finished all the legs, claws, and knuckles and was left only with the bodies. They were the most arduous part of the job since they don't yield much meat to begin with, and I needed a small, narrow pick to scrape the flesh out of the carcasses' nooks and crannies. Then, after a short lunch break, I climbed the kitchen stairs again, this time with my blacklight in tow. I set up my faux forensics lab and turned off all the lights to sift through the crabmeat, which was always littered with specks of shell no matter how meticulous I had been. Handful by handful, I placed the meat onto a lined baking sheet and poked around it repeatedly until the tiny shards of shell were gone. Then I repeated this process because one go-around wasn't enough. After all, if a patron bit into a stray crab shell—*quelle horreur!*—I was clearly the one to blame. I finally finished around one thirty, the fifteen-pound case of crabs transformed into a pricey two pounds of meat packed neatly into small jars and vacuum-packed bags. So much work, so little reward.

After cleaning up, I returned to the main kitchen, where the lunch service was beginning to wind down. If it was busy, I helped the *garde manger* chefs plate their last remaining dishes or assisted them in breaking down their stations, but after about ten minutes, I'd hear, "Lauren!" and be directed to clean the walk-in refrigerators along with the others toiling at the bottom of the culinary pyramid. Usually this was Seth, Etienne, or Benjamin, whom I liked because they often joked around. Once they played an improvised version of *pétanque*—the French version of the game bocce—in the hallway, using the restaurant's supply of clementines instead of the traditional metal balls. Of course, this was only when they were certain Jérôme, Arnaud, and Stéphane were sure to be far, far away.

We usually cleaned the vegetable walk-in first, followed by the meat walk-in, and then we put anything on the floor outside the room so that we could scrub, wash, and dry the floor. While Etienne was organizing containers of onions and potatoes in the dry storage area one room over, I dried the vegetable walk-in's floor with an apron affixed to the bottom of a large squeegee.

One afternoon, Arnaud came downstairs to inspect our handiwork. "How's it going?" he asked.

"Good, I've just finished in here," I said.

"So the meat refrigerator is next?"

"Yes," I said as we both headed there.

Arnaud grabbed a clementine from a cardboard box, and we entered the cold walk-in refrigerator, sandwiched between vats of stock and a phalanx of dead quails hanging upside down, their necks floppy and dripping blood.

"Konki, if we're not out in ten minutes, you can come in," Arnaud yelled out to the Japanese cook, who spent his entire day in this downstairs prep room, butchering all of the meat for the restaurant. Konki's French wasn't very good, but he smiled. I hoped this was due to his good nature and not because he'd fully understood Arnaud's words. At least for my sake I hoped he hadn't.

When I recounted this incident to Max over kirs in my apartment later that evening, Max said, "You should totally get with him. I mean, it seems like he's into you, right?"

"But that's the thing. I don't think he actually likes me. Not in that way. I think it's just like a big game to make me feel awkward. Like the time he said he wanted to spread mayonnaise on my naked body."

"But he isn't making comments to anyone else, right?"

"No. I guess theoretically he could like me, but I think it's more likely that I'm someone he can get away with making comments to. And now because he knows he can, there's no turning back. At this point, there's really nothing I can do," I said, shrugging.

⁘⸴

IN ANY EVENT, my time at Senderens would be ending soon, so I e-mailed Henri, my *stagiaire* compatriot, to see if he'd like to get a good-bye drink. He had finished his six-week *stage* at

Senderens right before the Christmas holiday, but since he lived in Paris we had stayed in touch via e-mail and I had kept him abreast of what was happening in the Senderens kitchen. I had told him about how Seth had unfortunately vanished, presumably fired, as had my other friend Sébastien, who was the meat station *commis*. And of the Brazilian *stagiaire* named Carlos who didn't last even two days; after arriving unshaven and without a proper uniform on day one, he got the ax, even though he told me that he had moved to Paris specifically to apprentice at Senderens for three months. And I had related the story of Marianne, a seventeen-year-old French *stagiaire* who was personally fired by Jérôme after her first week when she sauntered in for work half an hour late without an apology, listening to her iPod as though it were no big deal.

"Sounds like things are busy at Senderens," he wrote back. "Yes, let's have a drink. There's a cool bar in the 20th arrondissement that we can go to next week."

A few days later, though, he wrote again suggesting that we cook something at my apartment instead. I hesitated but then agreed, figuring that it would be fun to cook together outside of a restaurant setting. "Let's make something very French," I wrote.

"Perfect!!!! We can make mushroom risotto; it's very 'Frenchy,'" he replied. "I'll come over on Friday night."

I didn't see how risotto—an Italian specialty—was very French, but I knew how to make it and snagged some great-looking chanterelle and oyster mushrooms at the market the day before.

At eight on the dot, Henri rang my doorbell. Dressed in slacks and a button-down shirt, he looked so different from the Henri in bulky chef whites I was used to. But he still looked young.

"*Salut, chérie,*" he said, kissing me on each cheek.

"Hi," I replied.

"Very nice," he said as he looked around my apartment.

"Shall we get started on the risotto?"

"Yes, I can start the rice if you want to do the mushrooms."

I handed Henri the rice and began wiping the dirt off the mushrooms with a wet paper towel, since I didn't want them to get waterlogged. Henri chopped an onion, added it to the pot along with the rice, and began sautéing it. "Do you want to cook the mushrooms in this?" he asked, pointing to a frying pan.

"Sure. So are we going to add them on top afterward?" I thought this sounded like a bizarre way to make risotto, but Henri nodded authoritatively.

Two main schools govern risotto cooking: the "add a lot of water and then beat in the butter vigorously at the end" and the "stir constantly as you go." We opted for the latter method, even though it meant that every five to ten minutes we had to jump up to check its progress.

"Do you want some wine?" I asked, and Henri nodded. I opened a bottle of chilled Chablis and poured us each a glass.

"Thanks," said Henri. Then he looked at me intensely. "You really have the most beautiful eyes. Has anyone ever told you that? They are just gorgeous and catlike."

Oh crap. Did he think this was a date?

"Um, thanks. Yeah, I get told that a lot," I said, trying to deflect the compliment. "Should we check the rice again?"

"Yes." He extended his hand so I could get up from the sofa. "Oh, your hands are so lovely and soft."

Our risotto still had twenty minutes left, and I was on a date with jailbait.

"So why is this risotto 'Frenchy'?" I asked.

"The rice is Italian, but the mushrooms are French," Henri said matter-of-factly. "It is like French kissing. Not really French, but it's named French, you know. Do you like French kissing?"

I gave him points for trying. "Henri, we are not going to be French kissing tonight," I said.

"But why not?"

"Well, for one, you are seventeen and I am twenty-five. I think I'm a bit too old for you."

"No, in France we think it is good to have an older woman."

"Well, not in America."

"But we are in France."

"I don't need to complicate my life with a man right now."

"So you'd rather be with a woman?" he asked with a devilish grin.

"No, I'm just saying that we're not going to be kissing, Henri. I'm leaving Paris soon anyway," I said, trying to let him down gently.

"That's perfect. I will be visiting America soon and you can come stay with me. I will rent us an apartment near Central Park," he said.

"Um, let's check the risotto again; it should be ready by now." I got up to go to the kitchen.

Clearly crestfallen, Henri complied, and we portioned out our risotto into bowls and topped them with the mushrooms. We ate quickly, accompanied by an awkward silence.

"Do you want more?" I asked Henri when he'd finished his bowl.

"No, I'm not very hungry," he said. "I should probably go now, anyway. I'm supposed to meet a friend soon."

"Sure, no problem. Thanks for coming over for dinner. Maybe we can do it again sometime," I said, knowing we would not be having dinner again in the near future.

Henri nodded, but I could tell his teenage ego had been crushed. I walked him to the door and bade him farewell. We hugged. We didn't kiss. Then I went back to the kitchen and made myself another bowl of risotto. Unlike the earlier version, this one was perfect.

⟶

"THAT'S SO TYPICALLY FRENCH. You know, the French-men...," said my friend Paule when I told her about Arnaud's comments and Henri's advances.

Paule was a petite, vivacious Frenchwoman who taught cooking classes and led market tours for tourists. When I was a college student in Paris five years earlier, I had worked part-time as Paule's assistant, helping prep for her classes and assisting with cleanup. Paule looked exactly the same, although her kitchen had gotten a professional makeover. She now lived in a spacious apartment in the northern part of the Marais in central Paris, and her red-walled kitchen, filled with bookshelves of cookbooks and a large marble island, also functioned as a classroom. She had graciously invited me to join one of her classes, and I looked forward to the lavish lunch that would conclude the class, featuring all the dishes prepared during the lesson. Three others joined us: Robin and James, a California couple in their sixties on vacation in Paris, and Brett, an American expat who was a regular fixture in Paule's classes.

"Where did you learn to cook, Paule? Did you cook in restaurants?" asked James as he separated eggs for the cheese soufflés we were making for that day's culminating meal.

"Oh, no," Paule replied. "I love to entertain, and you can't see people enjoying your food when you work in a restaurant. I learned to cook from my grandaunt Léo, who would now be one hundred and ten years old. She went to the Cordon Bleu in the 1930s to train to be a *cuisinière en maison bourgeoise*, which is the equivalent of a private chef today, cooking for well-to-do families in their homes. She learned the very complicated style of cuisine that was practiced then. Anyway, in the early seventies she taught me a number of recipes to cook for my husband and friends, all classics and fairly simple . . . lapin à la moutarde, petit salé aux lentilles, gnocci à la parisienne, tarte aux pommes, riz au lait—"

While listening to Paule reel off her list of classic French dishes, I had begun to prepare the cilantro for the fish stew. When she glanced in my direction and saw me meticulously picking over each leaf and twig, she broke off and walked over, frowning. "No! Lauren, look at how you are doing that. You should put it all in the salad spinner. This isn't Senderens here!"

"Well, I wanted to do it properly," I said.

"It will taste just as good if you do it my way, and it will be a lot quicker," instructed Paule. No argument there.

"Oh, and then I did a course in patisserie to add to my repertoire," Paule continued as she flitted about the kitchen, procuring bowls and plates.

"At the Cordon Bleu?" said James, who had finished the prep work for the soufflés.

"*Mais non!* Today the Cordon Bleu is just for Americans! And so expensive. No, I went to the local state school, and of course, it was free," Paule said with a hint of French superiority.

"Really?" said James.

"But it is from my *tante* Léo that I learned to make the famous Caillat family crust that you might have heard about. Now, Lauren knows the secret to this tart, but she better not spoil it," she said, gathering the butter, flour, and a pinch of sugar while we observed and took notes.

"I won't," I said.

"Okay. Now, you don't know where I'm going, and you can't imagine," said Paule, addressing the other students.

Having seen her demonstrate the recipe before, I knew its secret, but I was as mesmerized as the first time. Traditionally, tart crusts are made by working cold butter into flour, letting the dough rest, and then rolling it out and placing it in a tart shell. Paule's crust couldn't be more different. First, she combined butter, vegetable oil, salt, and sugar in a bowl and heated it in the oven until it boiled and the milk solids that floated to the top turned light brown. Then she scooped out some flour and dumped it in one go into the boiling butter. The other students stood rooted to the spot.

"How much flour do you use?" asked Robin.

"I'm not sure. A cup or so," Paule replied.

"You mean you don't measure it out?"

"No, I just stop when it feels right, and then I press it directly into the pan," Paule said, nudging the sand-colored dough into a flat disk in the shell.

"You don't even have to roll out the dough! I'm definitely going to make this at home," said Robin, impressed.

"Yes, yes, and I have students who write me back and say that it works perfectly in America even though the flour and butter are different. But use a high-fat butter if you can, like Plugrá." Paule seemed pleased that her tart dough was infiltrating kitchens worldwide.

She then instructed Robin to mix the hot caramel we had cooked with a combination of melted chocolate and butter, which hissed vigorously as a volcano of steam erupted. "This is another thing that shouldn't work, because you'd think either the chocolate would seize or the caramel would crystallize and harden, but they don't at all," Paule said with a self-satisfied expression.

Once the tart was filled with the chocolate caramel and sprinkled with a dusting of sea salt, we set the table and refilled the wineglasses, and then we reaped the fruits of our labor. The soufflés were airy and creamy, pale golden in color, flecked with chives. We collectively oohed and aahed as we passed around the main course, a French-Moroccan tagine of monkfish with potatoes, and the aromas of cilantro and preserved lemon engulfed Paule's airy dining room. We ate our lunch, lingering at the table until there was no more food left; when I glanced at my watch, I saw that it was nearly dinnertime.

〜

ON MY LAST DAY OF WORK, Jérôme presented me with a cookbook written by Alain Senderens (whom I still hadn't met), in which Jérôme had inscribed in French, "Good luck in the future. Thanks for your work and kindness."

"Thank you for the experience of working here. I'm now a crab expert," I joked.

"Now that you're gone, we're going to have to take the crab dish off the menu," said Jérôme, grinning. *Very funny.*

"I'd also like to invite you to dinner at the bar if you'd like. You can bring one friend," he added.

"Yes, thanks," I said, thinking that was a little tightfisted. The bar? Two months shelling the entire crab population of the northeast Atlantic and I didn't get to eat in the main dining room? But it was a thoughtful gesture nonetheless.

On the appointed evening, I brought along John, a college friend whom I'd just discovered was living in Paris and working as an English teacher.

Arnaud greeted us after we'd settled into the comfy, cream-colored leather lounge chairs at a small round table across from the bar. "Hello, *chérie*. This is your friend? How nice to meet you. I'm Arnaud, one of the chefs here. Don't worry about looking at the menu; we will send you lots of things. You'll be well taken care of tonight," he said.

And we were. John and I began with two small cups filled with soy butter, each topped with a fried langoustine, followed by a game meat–studded terrine. Our next course featured three delicate gnocchi swimming in a truffle crème and capped with fat slices of black truffle. Three perfectly destemmed, uniformly sized arugula leaves wove between the gnocchi, a hint of health amid decadence. Waiters poured fresh wines with each new dish, and we were then served rich lobster ravioli under a mountain of snow white vanilla foam. Next came two plates, each consisting of a single scallop flanked by a few leaves of arugula and red endive. A touch of horseradish lent the dish a quick spicy note, while buckwheat added crunch. The dish was perfect, with clean flavors melding together. Suckling pig came next: three tiny rectangles of pinkish white flesh with a single ravioli filled with pork and pequillo peppers perched next to it. And we ended our seven-course feast with two dessert choices served simultaneously: a coulant de Samana (a fancy-sounding description for a warm circle of melted dark chocolate) and a Sichuan pepper dacquoise, a meringuelike cake flavored with lemon confit and ginger ice cream.

To my utter surprise, at the end of our meal, instead of an "Au revoir!" I was presented with a bill for 90 euros, or about $140, for the two of us. Yes, it was absolutely discounted from what would have been a sticker price of about $500, but I had automatically assumed that by "invitation," Jérôme had meant a comped meal. Did I actually have to pay for my postgrad culinary education in French haute cuisine? And although the food was delicious, I was left with a somewhat bitter taste in my mouth; I had ultimately found the food at Senderens too precious and too fussy.

After spending countless hours over the course of a year mincing herbs and destemming greens and cutting vegetables into perfect little squares, I was now jaded by the over-the-top preciousness of fine dining. As John and I had consumed our three-hour dinner, we had spoken only in hushed tones, aware of the deep-pocketed diners around us and their expectations of decorum. I missed the conviviality of Paule's cooking class meal. Her food wasn't as refined, but it had heart, and her space was homey and welcoming. At Paule's, I had left not only stuffed, but sated. I couldn't say the same for Senderens.

French Recipes for When You Realize You're So Over Haute Cuisine

An haute cuisine meal is made to impress. Restaurants like Senderens do pamper the guest, offering edible luxury at every turn. While truffles and oysters and lobster and caviar rarely disappoint, one hardly ever chooses them to be comforted. Truth be told, they aren't really the foods we want to cook ourselves. The recipes that follow *are* those foods: easy comfort for when we need it most.

CREAM OF CHESTNUT SOUP

SERVES 6

> 2 tablespoons unsalted butter
> 1 carrot

1 leek
1 stalk celery
1 onion
3 cups chicken stock
2 cups water
2 (15-ounce) cans chestnut puree
½ cup heavy cream
Kosher salt and freshly ground black pepper, as desired

In a large, heavy-bottomed pot, melt the butter over medium-high heat. Roughly chop the vegetables and add them to the pot. Sauté until the onion turns translucent, about 5 minutes. Add the stock and the water, and bring to a boil. Lower the heat and simmer at a lazy boil, uncovered, for 30 minutes.

Strain the stock and discard the solids. Return the stock to the pot and whisk in the chestnut puree. If your chestnut puree is clumpy, you can use an immersion blender to smooth out any lumps. Bring back to a boil and cook at high heat for 10 minutes. Skim off any foam that may have risen to the surface. Add the cream and stir until incorporated. Cook an additional 5 minutes at high heat, then season with salt and pepper to taste (about 1 tablespoon salt and a pinch of pepper). Serve with croutons, if desired.

ROAST CHICKEN WITH TARRAGON

I hate to be a person who touts the supremacy of French products, but French chickens do taste significantly better than their American counterparts. If possible, purchase a chicken that is both free-range and organic; in addition to being healthier for you, it will be tastier and better approximate a French chicken's flavor. I prefer the two-step method of searing and then roasting, as it helps render some of the fat for a crispy, golden brown skin and slightly lowers the overall cooking time.

SERVES 4

1 (4-pound) chicken
1 bunch tarragon
2 garlic cloves
1 teaspoon kosher salt
⅛ teaspoon freshly ground black pepper
2 tablespoons vegetable oil

Preheat the oven to 425 degrees F. Rinse the chicken under cold water and remove any viscera from the cavity. Pat dry with paper towels. Mince 1 tablespoon's worth of the tarragon and insert it under the chicken's skin above the thigh and breast meat. Place the remaining tarragon in the cavity, along with the garlic cloves. Truss the chicken—either completely with a trussing needle or simply by tying the legs together with twine, then going across the thighs, and tying the twine under the wings on the bottom of the bird. Pull the chicken breast above the string crossing the legs, and if necessary, tie together the flap of open skin.

Season the chicken all over with the salt and pepper.

Heat the oil in a pot large enough to hold the chicken. When the oil starts to smoke, place the chicken, skin side down, in the pot and cook until the skin is browned, about 4 to 5 minutes per side. Turn and cook until the skin is brown on all sides.

Place the chicken on a rack in a roasting pan and roast for 20 minutes. Then lower the heat to 350 degrees F and continue cooking for 1 hour, or until the juices run clear when pierced with a knife. Remove from the oven and let sit for 10 minutes before carving.

ROAST LAMB WITH PROVENÇAL HERBS

Roast leg of lamb always reminds me of the holidays and getting together with friends and family. This is a fairly simple recipe, so the dish is dependent on the quality of lamb used, meaning you'll want to find a reliable butcher. Make sure the lamb is at room temperature before putting it in the oven.

SERVES 6 TO 8

> 1 boneless leg of lamb, about 6 pounds, tied (ask your butcher
>   to do this)
> 3 tablespoons olive oil
> 1 tablespoon kosher salt
> ¼ teaspoon freshly ground black pepper
> ¼ cup herbes de Provence

Preheat the oven to 400 degrees F. Cover the lamb with the olive oil and season generously with salt and pepper. Cover the lamb with herbes de Provence (you may want to place the herbes de Provence on a plate and roll the lamb in it, or you can pour the herb mixture into your hand and press it into the lamb). Place on a rack in a roasting pan and roast for about 1½ to 2 hours for medium, turning the meat over every half hour. Lamb that is medium will have an internal temperature of about 140 degrees F. Remove from the oven and let sit for 15 minutes, covered in foil, so that the juices redistribute. Using a meat slicer or large knife, carve into slices and serve.

BUTTER-BRAISED ENDIVES

Soft and buttery, these endives are the perfect counterpart to any roast chicken. The bitterness of endive lessens when it is cooked.

SERVES 4

> 3 tablespoons unsalted butter
> 1 pound endives, trimmed and sliced in half
> ¼ cup water
> ½ teaspoon kosher salt
> 1 teaspoon lemon juice

In a skillet or pan large enough to hold the endives in one layer, melt 2 tablespoons butter over high heat. Once the butter begins to foam, place the endives facedown and cook until they begin to brown and caramelize. Add the remaining butter, water, salt, and lemon juice, and cover. Turn the heat to medium-low and cook for 15 minutes. Remove the lid, turn over the endives, and continue to cook, uncovered, for another 10 minutes or until done.

THE BEST POTATO GRATIN

On a cold winter day, there's nothing I want to eat more than a creamy potato gratin, all bubbly and gooey with melted cheese and cream. Although you can't really go wrong with any combination of cream, cheese, and potatoes, this version has added depth from the addition of garlic, bay leaf, and thyme. Comté and Gruyère are essentially the same cheese, although Comté is from France while Gruyère is Swiss. Comté may be more authentic for this recipe, but it's easier to find Gruyère in America.

SERVES 4 TO 6

> ½ cup whole milk
> ½ cup heavy cream
> 1 teaspoon kosher salt

⅛ *teaspoon freshly ground black pepper*
⅛ *teaspoon freshly grated nutmeg*
2 *cloves garlic, lightly crushed*
½ *bay leaf*
4 *large russet potatoes*
Unsalted butter for greasing
1 *cup grated Comté or Gruyère cheese*
1 *teaspoon minced fresh thyme leaves*

Preheat the oven to 375 degrees F. Add the milk, cream, salt, pepper, nutmeg, garlic, and bay leaf to a saucepan, and bring to a boil. Let sit for 10 minutes, then discard the garlic and bay leaf.

Peel the potatoes and thinly slice them on a mandolin into ¹⁄₁₆-inch slices. Butter a 9 × 12-inch ovenproof baking dish and place a layer of potatoes on the bottom of the dish, overlapping the potatoes slightly. Cover lightly with a little of the cream mixture, then a little cheese, and a pinch of thyme. Cover with a new layer of potatoes, pressing down slightly with your hands to distribute the cream evenly. Repeat process until there are no potatoes left and all the cream, cheese, and thyme have been used up (depending on the size of your potatoes, you may have some cream left over). Bake, uncovered, for 1 hour. Cool ever so slightly before serving.

CHOCOLATE CAKE WITH A HINT OF PIMENT D'ESPELETTE

Piment d'Espelette is a chile pepper that comes from Espelette, a Basque enclave near the Spanish border, but is popular throughout France. If you can't find piment d'Espelette, cayenne pepper is a great alternative. Don't worry if the center of the cake is still molten after baking; that's how it's supposed to be. Vanilla ice cream is a delicious accompaniment to the cake and helps offset its spiciness.

SERVES 8 TO 10

10 tablespoons unsalted butter, plus extra for greasing
  the cake pan
8 ounces dark chocolate (I particularly like Valrhona
  Le Noir Gastronomie 61% cacao)
2 teaspoons piment d'Espelette
6 eggs
1 cup sugar
Pinch of kosher salt

Preheat the oven to 350 degrees F. Bring a saucepan of water to a boil, then lower to a simmer. Cut the butter and chocolate into small pieces and place with the piment d'Espelette in a metal bowl large enough to sit on top of the saucepan. When the butter and chocolate have melted completely, set aside and stir until well combined. Let cool slightly.

Meanwhile, separate the egg yolks from the whites. Whisk the egg yolks together with the sugar, then add the chocolate mixture.

Using a mixer, beat the egg whites and salt until stiff peaks form. Fold half of the egg whites into the chocolate batter, then fold in the remaining egg whites. Let sit in the refrigerator for 1 hour.

Grease a cake pan with butter, then pour the chocolate batter into the pan. Bake for about 20 to 25 minutes or until cracks start to form on the top of the cake. Serve hot.

ALMOND TART WITH MIRABELLE CREAM

This tart uses Paule Caillat's famous crust, which goes against all the rules of tart making: You use boiling hot butter instead of chilled butter, you don't let it rest, and you simply press it into the pan instead of rolling it out. Yet you end up with a flaky, buttery crust, proving that in this case, at least, the ends justify the means. I like to flavor the whipped cream with Mirabelle, but feel free to use any other flavored brandy or liqueur like kirsch or Calvados.

SERVES ABOUT 8

FOR THE DOUGH:
6 tablespoons unsalted butter
1 tablespoon vegetable oil
3 tablespoons water
1 tablespoon sugar
Large pinch of kosher salt
1 cup flour

FOR THE FILLING:
½ cup unsalted butter
½ cup sugar
¾ cup almond flour
Pinch of kosher salt
2 whole eggs plus 1 yolk
1 teaspoon vanilla

FOR THE WHIPPED CREAM:
1 cup heavy cream
¼ cup confectioner's sugar
Pinch of kosher salt
1 tablespoon Mirabelle or other plum brandy

Preheat the oven to 400 degrees F. In a medium-size oven-proof bowl or 4-cup Pyrex measuring cup, combine the butter, oil, water, sugar, and salt. Place the bowl in the oven for about 15 minutes, until the mixture is bubbling and the butter is just beginning to brown on the edges. Remove the bowl from the oven (carefully, as the bowl will be hot), and add the flour all at once. Stir quickly, until it comes together and forms a ball that pulls away from the sides of the bowl.

Transfer the dough to a 9-inch tart mold with a removable bottom. Once the dough is cool enough to handle, pat it into the shell with your palm and use your fingers to press it up the sides of the tart mold. Prick the dough all over with the tines of a fork, and press the tines up against the rim of the tart shell. Bake for 10 minutes.

Meanwhile, prepare the filling: Using an electric mixer, cream the butter and sugar until light and fluffy. Then add the almond flour and beat until well combined. Then beat in the remaining ingredients.

Once the tart shell has been removed from the oven, lower the heat to 350 degrees F. Fill the tart shell with the almond filling, then return the filled tart to the oven and bake for 30 minutes.

While the tart is baking, prepare the cream: In a large mixing bowl, combine the heavy cream, sugar, and salt, and beat with an electric mixer or whisk until soft peaks form. Stir in the Mirabelle.

Remove the tart from the oven and let cool. Serve at room temperature with a large dollop of the whipped cream.

Epilogue

I RETURNED HOME TO New York City shortly after my *stage* at Senderens ended, my culinary odyssey and year of training at the stove over. I could now chop, slice, and dice with the best of them, and I had proved that I could make it in the restaurant world. I wore my kitchen war wounds—the scars, burns, and cuts—with pride. The professional kitchen no longer intimidated me. Which was why friends were surprised when they asked me where I'd be working back in New York and I replied, "My own kitchen."

Perhaps the greatest kitchen lesson I absorbed, one far more important than mastering the fine art of shelling crabs or perfecting a *brunoise*, was that while I liked restaurant cooking, at the end of the day I *loved* home cooking. If you're working in a restaurant, you never get to do it. Like Paule, I came to realize that although restaurant chefs might be in the business of hospitality, they don't often get to see people enjoying the food they've prepared. They don't get to linger over a pot of simmering stew, glass of wine in hand. Unless you work in an open kitchen and inexplicably find yourself with free time in the middle of service (which is not a good sign), you never get to appreciate people savoring your food or even take a bite yourself. You can never sit down with your guests and enjoy the meal with them.

Although restaurant cooking is great for learning how to perfect dishes and to maximize speed and efficiency, the repetition of professional cooking can be, well, repetitive. What I loved about cooking was discovering new ingredients and combining flavors. Home cooking brings spontaneity and whimsy and the freedom to cook according to your own desires. No tarragon in the fridge? Use thyme instead and experience the element of surprise. Never cooked with lemon leaves before? Buy some and experiment! If it tastes bad, you'll know for next time and you're no worse off.

On a physical level, being in a professional kitchen is generally harder for a woman. But it's not impossible. Although I will never be as tall or as strong as the men I cooked with, I held my own for the most part. Instead, it was the emotional aspect of working in a restaurant that I found more difficult. The professional kitchen is loud and brash and can be tough if you're not part of the boys' club. I learned to assert myself more and to take pride in what I could do. The only way you become weak in the kitchen is if you let others make you weak. The hardest part of being a woman in the professional kitchen is that there aren't many other women in there with you. And although I was always aware of being one of only a few women in a male-run, male-dominated kitchen, it wasn't until I got to Paris and became the brunt of sexual jokes that I truly saw how gender factors into the equation.

Whatever your gender, though, working the line at a restaurant is grueling: It's exhausting being on your feet all day, the hours are long, and you don't get paid much. This is why cooking in restaurants is a profession for the young. In the four kitchens where I cooked, my co-workers were almost always in their late teens or twenties, with the sous-chefs and head chefs in their thirties to forties. With the exception of Wylie, the executive chef at each one never (or very rarely) worked on the line. When you reach your late forties, your priorities and stamina change. Most of the celebrity chefs out there aren't working in restaurants anymore (again, Wylie is an exception), and they'll all probably tell you it's more important to have a camera-ready personality than top-notch knife skills. While I'm still relatively far off from having my own family, I don't want a life where I see my husband and children for only a couple of hours each morning. Of course, this happens in many professions, but it's particularly telling that in high-level restaurants like wd~50 and Senderens, the majority of people in relationships are with other people in the restaurant industry. I'm not saying that these are bad things about restaurant cooking. On the contrary, I have tremendous admiration for the men and especially the women who get out there every day and cook their asses off in restaurants, whether at the corner diner or at the city's finest eatery. No matter how much you cook at home, you will never know just how intense cooking can be until you step behind the restaurant burner.

So was this one big time-consuming and cost-inefficient lesson? I certainly think that anyone who has decided to be a chef and wants to go to culinary school should spend time in a professional kitchen *before* shelling out money for culinary school. Believe me, restaurants are more than happy to take on free labor, even if you don't have any experience. It might seem like an expensive way to spend a few months, but if you end up deciding that restaurant cooking isn't for you, you've saved yourself $40,000 (and you'll get some free meals out of it); if you can't commit full-time, my guess is you can still probably *stage* once a week on Saturday nights.

And to be totally honest, working in restaurants is the best way to learn how to work in restaurants. Even if culinary school teaches you a million different ways to chop carrots, it's not going to matter unless you're chopping the carrots exactly how the restaurant wants their carrots chopped. You learned to sear and season steaks perfectly in school? Great, but you're probably not going to be running the meat station at your first job out of school, especially if you choose to work at a highly prestigious restaurant. Culinary school is a lot of fun and can give you a good overview of food and cooking, but it's also a great way to get into debt—not exactly what you're looking for when you're making $30,000 that first (and second and third) year of work.

I have no regrets about my year of professional cooking. Books and schools may teach you about cooking and about various cuisines, but you can never truly know a cuisine without experiencing it firsthand: by going to markets and learning about products, by dining out in both upscale eateries and hole-in-the-wall joints and with local home cooks. I ate banh bot loc, che, and even thit cho (aka my beloved dog meat)—dishes that I've never seen in Vietnamese cookbooks or in restaurants in America. Living in Tel Aviv, I shopped like a local in the Carmel Market and played around with newly discovered ingredients like zaatar and silan in my kitchen. And even though I spent an inordinate amount of time shelling crabs and doing prep work, Paris gave me a deep appreciation for the tradition and influence of haute cuisine and what it takes to succeed in that world. Cooking in restaurants will teach you speed, precision, discipline, and hard work. It's like the army: It can be tough while you're doing it, but you come out of it that much stronger, with a band of brothers. Hopefully a few sisters, too.

So what if it took going around the world to realize I wanted to end up at home, in my own kitchen? I discovered what I loved: cooking for my friends and family and sharing the bounty of the table together. And the friends I made along the way taught me that home can be anywhere, and so can your home kitchen. It's those you share it with who really matter.

So when I returned to New York, I wanted to have a dinner party to catch up with my friends. I invited Rebecca and Max to dinner, and I also invited Nell and Joe, two friends I met shortly after coming home. I didn't know them well, but I figured that almost everyone enjoys a dinner party, and if I'd been able to make new friends all over the world, why shouldn't I be making some in New York?

Our dinner party took place on a balmy spring evening. I was living at my parents' apartment temporarily while getting my life in order and finally finishing graduate school and cooking dinner for them nearly every night. They were the perfect guinea pigs for testing out all my new recipes and culinary techniques; everything I made was pronounced delicious, though maybe they were slightly biased. Or maybe not.

"Can I help with anything?" Joe asked as I washed the cucumber and tomatoes for the salsa.

"Sure, do you want to cut the shallot? Just cut it into small pieces. You can get uniformly sized pieces if you crosshatch it. Just make vertical and horizontal cuts into the shallot, and then you cut it on the remaining side, but if you don't want to do that, just cut it into small pieces," I said.

"I won't get fired from kitchen duty if they look ugly?"

"No, this is my kitchen . . . well, technically my parents', but I make the rules here. And as long as the end result tastes good, I don't really care how things are chopped. I chopped enough vegetables perfectly over the last year to last me a lifetime."

"Is there more wine?" Max called from the living room.

"Yeah, come and get it. Pour us all a round while you're at it. And we've got another bottle in the fridge, so don't be stingy," I said as I handed him my empty glass.

"So, Lauren, is it true that chefs drink all the time? Did you drink on the line?" asked Rebecca.

"Do you know how chaotic it is behind the stove, trying to fill as many orders as you can in a short amount of time? No; no booze during shifts. But after, yeah. But I also think the hard-partying reputation among chefs is a cultural thing. I drank more whiskey while working at wd~50 than I had in my life up until then, but that sort of work-hard/play-hard culture didn't exist in Vietnam or Israel, especially because the chefs went straight home at the end of their shifts. It was more of a job for them, and more of a lifestyle here," I said.

"Well, I for one am glad that you decided not to be a restaurant chef, because that means that I can enjoy your cooking more often," said Max. He dipped a spoon into the bowl of chopped cucumber, tomato, and onion. "Mmmm, delish."

"Don't nibble too much or we won't have anything to serve," I said, and handed him the bowl. "Here, be useful and spoon some out onto each plate while I take the steaks out and finish them."

"This beef is going to be the most exciting part of the meal, since it uses the pretend *sous-vide* technique my old supervisor Jared taught me at wd~50. It's faux *sous-vide* because you put the meat and any flavorings into a ziplock bag and cook it in a pot of water on the stove."

"How is it done normally?" asked Rebecca.

"You need an immersion circulator to control the water temperature, and you use special vacuum-sealed bags."

"And these bags work the same way?"

"Sort of. You have to submerge the bags in the pot until you reach the zipper part, then carefully seal the bag shut. The water pressure forces all of the air out of the bag, so it's close to being vacuum-sealed."

"Awesome."

"Yeah, it's a great trick, but it'll be a bit of a pain, because we'll have to constantly be checking the temperature of the water in the pot we're going to cook them in. But hopefully we'll be fine," I said, peering into the pot.

"Do you have to do anything else to the steaks?" Rebecca asked after I lifted out the bags with a pair of tongs.

"You can serve the steaks straight out of the bag if you want, but you won't have that nice sear that comes with cooking meats on the stovetop. Most restaurants will sear meaty proteins like beef or lamb quickly on the stovetop to get a nice charred crust," I explained.

"This is some four-star dining treatment we're getting here," she said.

"Here, I think they're done now anyway." I took the meat out of the bags and placed them into the skillet; it was beginning to brim with smoke from the oil I'd added, a visual cue that it was hot enough for the meat. The steaks hissed loudly as oil spattered onto the stove.

"I wanna see," said Nell, coming into the kitchen.

"You want to cook them for a quick second. Just until they sear. You don't want to spoil your *sous-vide* by cooking them too much on the stove," I said as my friends watched eagerly behind me. "Max, can you hand me the plates? Rebecca, do you want to add a dollop of crab to each one?"

We assembled the finishing touches together, and finally our dinner plates were heaped high. We brought them to the table while Max uncorked another bottle of wine. "To Lauren, the chef!" he said, raising his glass in a toast.

"And to my sous-chefs. Cheers to you all," I said, and we all clinked glasses.

"I still can't believe this is *sous-vide* beef. I'm so far away from being able to make *sous-vide* beef at home," said Rebecca. "Okay, who are we kidding? I'm actually pretty far away from making any kind of beef at home. But I'm definitely going to make this salsa this summer."

"Me too. And you know what would be nice in it, too? Avocado. You can never go wrong with avocado," Nell added.

I smiled as I sipped my wine. In this meal, I had incorporated bits and pieces of technique and kitchen wisdom from the four restaurants where I had worked to create an international surf and turf and a jewel-toned fruit salad, wholly original recipes that embodied what I loved about each experience. But recipes are not static; they are fluid and always evolving. So these recipes weren't just mine, they were now part of my friends' culinary repertoires, springboards from which they, too, could find their places in the kitchen.

Two Recipes Inspired by Four Kitchens

Figuring out what to make for my homecoming dinner party was tricky, because I didn't want to make four separate dishes, each representing a place where I'd worked. While there were elements of wd~50's cooking techniques at Senderens or of La Verticale's market-driven philosophy at Carmella, the four countries and restaurants where I had worked each exhibited a unique culinary point of view. Instead, I wanted to create individual dishes that melded my year of travel, and the following recipes were what I came up with. Serve both dishes together on a warm evening to a group of friends, along with lots of wine and merriment.

FOUR KITCHENS SURF AND TURF

This fake *sous-vide* technique is not perfect and requires much more supervision than traditional *sous-vide* cooking, but it's as close as the home cook can get. For the beef's garnishes, I was drawn immediately to crab (already shelled, though!) and was inspired by the traditional Israeli salad of cucumber, tomato, and onion. But I swapped in shallots instead, plus a little lime juice, fish sauce, and chile for a hint of Vietnam. If you prefer, try this with other cuts of beef.

SERVES 4

FOR THE STEAKS:
1 hanger steak, about 1 pound
Kosher salt and freshly ground black pepper
2 tablespoons olive oil
½ clove garlic, minced

FOR THE VEGETABLE SALSA:
½ English or regular cucumber, seeds scooped out
3 tomatoes, cored and seeded
1 large shallot
¼ teaspoon minced Thai chile, if desired
1 tablespoon fish sauce
2 teaspoons lime juice
1 teaspoon sugar

(continued)

FOR THE CRAB:
½ pound lump crabmeat
1 teaspoon mayonnaise
2 teaspoons minced chives
½ teaspoon finely minced or grated lemon zest
Pinch of kosher salt

Cut the steak into four pieces, season generously with salt, pepper, 1 tablespoon olive oil, and garlic, then place each piece in its own quart-sized ziplock bag. In the sink, fill a large pot with water. Zip the bags closed halfway, then carefully begin to submerge the bag into the pot of water, making sure not to get any water inside the bag. When the top of the bag is almost at the water's surface, press out any remaining air and zip the bag closed. There should now be very little air inside the ziplock bag, and it should almost look as if it is vacuum-sealed.

Heat a large pot of water on the stove over medium heat. When the water is 130 degrees F, add the ziplock bags. Cook for 3 hours, making sure that the water remains at a steady 130 degrees. (You'll need an accurate thermometer for this, and you may need to add more water to control the temperature.)

Meanwhile, prepare the vegetable salsa: Dice the cucumber, tomatoes, and shallot into pieces about ½ inch, then place in a bowl along with all the remaining ingredients. Refrigerate until ready to use.

Prepare the crab: Combine all ingredients in a small bowl and mix well. Set aside in the refrigerator.

Heat the remaining tablespoon of olive oil in a large skillet until smoking. Add the steaks and cook just until seared, about 30 seconds on each side. Transfer the steaks to plates.

To serve, add a dollop of crab next to each steak, along with several spoonfuls of vegetable salsa.

FOUR KITCHENS FRUIT SALAD

It was hard for me to think of a dessert that combined elements of four different countries (especially Vietnam, which doesn't have much of a dessert culture), yet one of the things that struck me most living and cooking outside of America was the freshness and variety of produce available and the strong food market culture in each region. So what better dessert than a fruit salad that incorporates some of my favorite fruits from each place? This fruit salad has a pomegranate for Tel Aviv, plums for Paris, lychees for Hanoi, and an apple to represent my hometown, the Big Apple.

SERVES 4

> 1 (2-inch) piece of fresh ginger, peeled and smashed with the
> back of a knife
> ¼ cup sugar
> ¼ cup water
> 1 pomegranate
> 2 plums, pits removed and cut into thin wedges
> ½ pound (approximately 10) lychees, seeds removed and cut into
> thin strips
> 1 red apple, peeled and cored and cut into small chunks

In a small saucepan, combine the ginger, sugar, and water over high heat. Once the mixture reaches a boil and all the sugar has dissolved, turn off the heat and let steep for half an hour. Discard the ginger.

Seed the pomegranate into a large mixing bowl, as directed on page 210. Add the plums, lychees, apple, and ginger syrup, and coat well. Let sit for 15 minutes before serving.

About the Author

Lauren Shockey is a food writer whose articles have appeared in many print and online publications including *The Village Voice, The New York Times, The Wall Street Journal, Slate,* and *The Atlantic Food Channel,* among others. A graduate of the University of Chicago, Lauren also holds a diploma in classic culinary arts from the French Culinary Institute and a Master of Arts in food studies from New York University.